WHO HELPS THE HELPLINE, WHEN THE HELPLINE NEEDS HELP

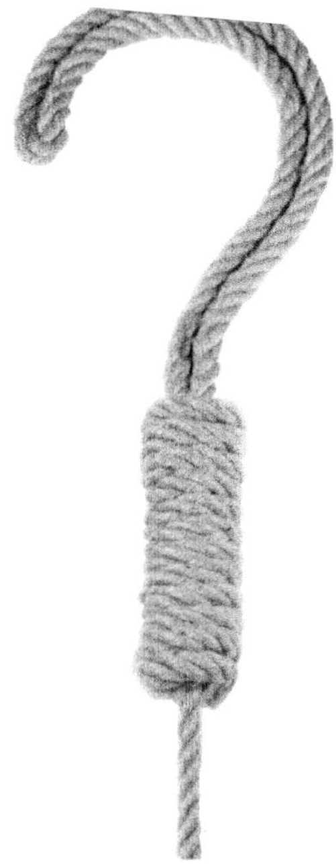

BY

KEVIN BENNETT

First published in Great Britain in 2023 by Kevin Bennett.

The information in this book is for general guidance and educational purposes only.

This book is not a financial, mental health, well-being, or legal advice source. It is for educational purposes ONLY. Any adjustments to your strategy or plan in reading this book should be undertaken only after consulting with a professional.

In addition, neither KBenaire nor the Author (Kevin Bennett) offers counselor or therapist advice, as a professional should undertake all mental health and well-being advice. Therefore, you should seek independent mental health or well-being advice before making decisions from reading this book. KBenaire and the Author do not guarantee positive results by using the methods illustrated in this book.

Cover photo credit: Oliver Morris.

Published by Kevin Bennett, KBenaire "Who Helps the Helpline, When the Helpline Needs Help?" is a registered trademark of Kevin Bennett.

A catalogue record for this book is available from the British Library.

ISBN: 978-1-8382077-3-1 (Paperback)

ISBN: 978-1-8382077-4-8 (Hardback)

ISBN: 978-1-8382077-5-5 (eBook)

Take pictures with your book and share your adventure with our community

#Whohelpsthehelpline

Scan me

DEDICATION

I dedicate this book to several people for a number of different reasons. I first want to dedicate this book to my mother and father. My mother is the first helpline I have ever experienced. Her first experience arriving from Clarendon, Jamaica, to England in October 1961 was seeing signs saying, "No blacks, no dogs, and no Irish". My parents experienced one door after another being slammed in their faces, from job opportunities to places to live. Imagine not being able to enter an establishment like a restaurant because of your skin color? At age 21, all my dear mother knew was the harmony of the Caribbean, not the cold brutality of the UK streets.

My mother and father are the only people I know who genuinely love unconditionally.

My parents carry the blood and soul of people who care and love. But at the same time, my parents will fight the resistance the way our Jamaican national heroes did, such as; Samuel Sharpe, Paul Bogle, and Nanny of the Maroons. Throughout my mother's career, she was the helpline to many people. In 1962, she was a mental health auxiliary nurse at Maudsley Hospital. She then worked in several hospitals, including Great Ormond Street Hospital where she was the helpline to thousands of sick children.

My mother raised six children on her own. Can you imagine what raising four boys and two girls in the seventies and eighties in London would have been like? It was challenging; however, she did so with great love. In later years, when she was just getting ready to retire, my amazing mother went on to adopt and raise four of her grandchildren due to my sister's struggles with her mental health. Her life has been one of struggle and adversity - having to bury three of her own children and losing her closest siblings in recent years.

The more she has served, the more pain has come her way. As a child observing my mother, I always wondered, Who Helps The Helpline, When The Helpline Needs Help? This question stayed with me up until this current day.

My father is the one role model who consistently maintains his integrity, regalness, and masculinity. He is a Godly man, a man's man; he is gentle, kind, wise, and powerful.

I also want to dedicate this book to my dear son Tristan and my granddaughter Ze'nayah. You are both the reasons why I push for excellence and the 'impossible'. One day, your children and grandchildren will read this book and be proud of us all. I am sure they will discover their confidence in our achievements. Ze'nayah, the new world order will try to move you away from God and your ancestors, use this book to stay closer to the teachings of your father, and I. Whenever you are feeling down, lost, or hurting, this book will guide you back on the path to your purpose, happiness, and fulfillment. And never forget the power of prayer. Stay close to God in all that you do.

Finally, to my siblings who have passed from this realm to another—Andrew Balfour (Andy), Michael Balfour, and Jackie Balfour. You may be gone, but your legacies live on. And to my dearest sister, Michelle: you are the epitome of a beautiful queen.

ACKNOWLEDGMENTS

My Community Is My Circle of Confidence

No one can do this thing called "life" alone. We all need a community— a circle of confidence.

I want to pay homage to my community, my circle of confidence, my friends, my family, and my loved ones. Here are your flowers.

A big thank you to Richmond Oduku (entrepreneur), Diana Wilson (cognitive behavioral coach and consultant), Oliver Morris (international art director), Kubi Springer (Global personal and business branding specialist), Michael Pusey, MBE (entrepreneur and founder of Peckham BMX Club), Aderito N'singi (personal trainer), Antonio Oladuti (software engineer), Stephen Bennett (software programmer), Samantha Williams (Marketing specialize), Jonathan Bennett (software programmer), Rhianne Elleston Pascall (improvement and transformation lead program manager), Ms. Gail Brooks (Christian Spiritual Mentor), Zena Josiah (entrepreneur), Josiah Elleston-Burrell (entrepreneur), Kerry Graham (Lawyer), Siontai Myrie-Mullings (Mind Mastery Strategist), Anna Brocklebank (Doctor, lawyer, and socialite), Ivan Yordanov (Business owner and tech entrepreneur), Mark Ussher, Michael Watson, Medina Christian, Damien Hanson, Hickey, Clifton Hayles, Leroy Bell, Gary Elliot, Kevin Sinclair, Leon, and Paul Ewart. You are my rocks, my mastermind group, and my family.

I want to say a special thank you to Dr. Alando Watkis. Without your teachings, mentoring, and guidance, I wouldn't be here today. You are my gift from God. You helped me through my traumas, trials, and tribulations. What you have taught me lives within the pages of this book. Your legacy continues through me.

To My Circle of Confidence.

Thank you all.

Kevin Bennett

CONTENTS

PROLOGUE

Being loved and nurtured is one of the most important processes during our infant and adolescent years. We often take for granted the most important people in our lives, such as our guardians and family. They are the cornerstones of our developmental necessities, emotional needs, psychological states, physical strength, and growth. But there are others who play an integral part in our lives. We confide in them like parents in times of trauma and tragedy. We see them as guardians in times of doubt, hopelessness, and worry. We depend on them for hope, comfort, self-understanding, and security. In times of ill health and sickness, they serve; we listen; we receive; we get better!

Their jobs are arduous and stressful, yet they guide and care for us with the same intensity as a child that needs to be fed and burped. We seem only to remember their importance in times of tragedies and trauma, yet we almost forget they exist when we are happy, winning, and healthy. They fight for our survival and way of life, and we criticize them in times of anger or frustration. We tell them, "You are not good enough; you are hopeless, stupid, and deserve to be sacked!" We publicly shame them, film them, and write blogs and reviews about how worthless they are, when we are not happy. They can't always fix the pains and problems we may have started, yet we want them to be God even when God wants otherwise. We point the finger whilst they suffer the effects of secondary trauma and compassion fatigue. No financial compensation can be traded for the depression and burnout they sometimes encounter while serving us, the people.

I know they can be better, but I am also mindful that we can do better as well. Day to day, I wonder, do we genuinely care for our doctors, paramedics, firefighters, dentists, nurses, social workers, and police officers with the same level of love and care they do for us? Who comes to mind when I say, "Who helps the helpline, when the helpline needs help?" Do *you* help the helpline, when the helpline is depressed, burned out, or suicidal?

Do we have a two-way relationship? Or are they really on their own when they need help? It's high time we thought about the people who tirelessly help us and what they must go through daily. So here's a question for you, how much do they give up for us? Our traumatic experiences become their internal emotional and psychological trauma.

We are constantly exchanging energies; we feel negative, ill, and hopeless, and they make us feel positive, well, and optimistic. We give them a bit of us, and they give us a bit of themselves until they have nothing left to give. The sacrifices of the first, second, and third aiders are taken for granted by us. So, let's reflect on that all-important question, who helps the helpline, when the helpline needs Help? Let's discover this adventure together.

INTRODUCTION

Traumatic events tend to enigmatically visit everyone at some point in their lives. Some of us see trauma as something that happens, part of life's journey, whilst others become engrossed with their traumas and start to investigate them fervently. I am one of those people.

So, why did I write this book?

I learned the hard way by pretending that most of my traumas and the events that caused them just never existed. This went on to cause me psychological pain in my later life. I silently hoped that my physical and emotional traumas would just somehow disappear. This turned out to be even more unrealistic and arduous than just seeking therapy in the first place. Not dealing with my previous traumas allowed my current traumas to attach themselves in a kind of romantic outlandish foreplay.

What stresses the mind sickens the body. It became normal for me to have shoulders and back pains, a stiff neck, and headaches. Yearly broken relationships and heartaches all stemmed from me running away from any loving relationship that made me feel even a hint of vulnerability. These were the prices I paid for not dealing with my traumas.

My masseuse Kate, whom I call my 'Jesus hands,' asked me to describe my body's pain and stress level from zero to ten—zero being no pain at all and ten being excruciating muscle pain. She then laid a hot towel on my lumbar area, attempting to soften my rock-hard muscles as she prepared to give me my weekly deep tissue massage.

"It's like a 500lb silverback gorilla climbing up my back, clamping onto my head and shoulders, and weighing me down, almost to the point where I cannot function anymore," I replied.

"Kevin, what stresses the mind, sickens the body," Kate responded. "What has been sickening your body?" She asked.

"The lack of trust," I replied.

"Please tell me more," Kate said, pushing her thumbs deep into my lower back.

Compared to life now, the '90s were like the wonder years for my friends and I. Even though life in London wasn't easy—in fact, it was pretty hard, but we didn't know any different back then. Being a young person living in Brixton meant you had to prove your hierarchical dominance almost by the hour, but definitely by the day.

Fights, shootings, and stabbings were daily occurrences, and we were desensitized to them. Living on a notorious council estate meant you had no escape from your abuser, attacker, or tormentor. Living above and beside aggressive and emotionally traumatized people meant you had to fight or flee. But if you were to run, where would you go? And for how long?

Stockwell Park Estate was less than four miles from Buckingham Palace, on the south side of London and a stone's throw away from the then-Brixton Academy (currently called the O2 Academy Brixton). It had 1,500 flats sectioned into 15 blocks, each block housing up to 200 small one to four-bedroom apartments. The landings were mainly narrow, and the stairwells were dark with the putrid stench of urine. Often, to get from the ground floor to the first floor, you had to pass drug addicts blocking the stairs. And forget about the elevators—they hadn't worked in well over 15 years. At night, you had to walk through poorly lit passageways and spider webs and through rodents to get to your home on the first, second, or third floor.

The feeling of an imminent ambush by either junkies, opportunists, or the police crossed our minds daily and at night. Young girls and women feared being mugged or raped, and the elderly hid their valuables just in case. Even as late as May 2023, it was reported that a woman was stabbed to death in broad daylight for her valuables in that same area. The apartment blocks in Stockwell Park Estate were so close to each other that you could look into almost anyone's home and see what they were reading, watching on TV, or cooking for dinner.

Tensions were still high from the race riots in 1985 due to the police shooting of Cherry Groce and then the death of Wayne Douglas, who died in Brixton Police Station whilst in custody ten years later. Working with or even talking to the police within our culture and community would get you ousted at best, or a death sentence at worst. It was simple; the police were the enemy. We kept our traumas and troubles to ourselves and pretended they never even existed when the police came to investigate crimes or abuse.

In the 1990s and early 2000s, under-18s had parties in the daytime during the summer holidays. Hundreds, and sometimes even thousands, of excited teens, who jointly shared their trials, tribulations, and traumas from the various south London estates flooded halls, parks, and streets to party and just let loose. We danced, sang, performed, and expressed ourselves to release our own developmental traumas. Some danced harder than others, and some sang loudly with such graceful voices—it was as though we were all releasing our subconscious depressions. But, now and then, our internal traumas progressed into external aggression.

The boys from our apartment block had many rules about leaving to go to a party or socialize away from home. We weren't a gang or some elaborate cartel, but we were friends solely because of our parents' placement when they immigrated to the UK. We were children who grew up together in a close-knit community. Now looking back with experienced eyes, our community was formed from the constituents of other communities that were themselves the results of transgenerational trauma.

We grew up quickly and learned the harsh realities of life that we needed to know in order to survive the outer rim of our apartment block fortress. We had rules, and they were to be obeyed at all costs.

Rule 1: Never leave your friends alone when partying or clubbing, not even to go to the restroom. If one went, we all went!

Rule 2: Never leave your friends facing any form of conflict. NO MATTER HOW DEADLY THE SITUATION!

Rule 3: If you leave home with a friend, you come home with that friend.

It's simple right? These rules were our mantra.

We discovered at a very young age that most killings and violent attacks occurred when a person was alone. From around the age of ten, we quickly realized that we couldn't afford to be vulnerable. Later in life, I discovered that rules one to three didn't just come from our vulnerability on the streets. Those rules were effective because many of my friends were vulnerable in their homes. Sisters stayed close to sisters; brothers did the same. Friends went to visit friends, then strategically overstayed their welcome. Many were violently and even sometimes sexually abused in their homes by their parents, parents' partners, or guardians. For most children, being left alone was a traumatic event within itself. Although we didn't know it back then, we were all in our own way, suffering from some type of trauma. The Black and Asian communities, up until this current day, are extremely apprehensive about addressing domestic abuse and sexual crimes within the home—not just regarding young boys and girls, but adults too.

The consequences of my environment visited me on a fateful day in 1991. At the age of 14 years old, I died. They pumped away at my chest and checked my vital signs frantically. I was told after being resuscitated "We lost you for a minute Mr. Bennett... you died!" The location, King's College Hospital.

In all honesty, I don't remember the year it happened. I was either 14 or 15. I cannot remember. I can't remember the journey to the hospital, the healing process after the surgery, or most things connected to that traumatic evening. The fact that I address it as *that* instead of *my* traumatic evening is a clear sign of me dissociating myself from ~~that,~~ my traumatic event. Not remembering is a sign of dissociation.

I spent so many years trying to block out the physical and psychological pain that I have somehow compartmentalized the good, and bad memories in my life. In the writing of this introduction, I have just realized that I couldn't remember, or perhaps I didn't want to remember some of my pains and traumas. But let me share what I do remember, with help from my friends and family; let's give it a go!

So, what do I remember from that evening?

I remember it was summertime. We called daytime parties "All-Dayers," and all-dayers mostly occurred from June to August but sometimes started in May. I remember it was dark. All-dayers began at noon and finished no later than midnight, so I approximate the time to have been around 9 to 10 p.m. I remember dark shadows surrounding me, and I couldn't quite make out the faces; they became my *Nightmare on Elm Street* that evening.

One of the most desired all-dayers of the summer finally arrived in a small community hall on the corner of Vassall Road, on the outskirts of Brixton. The hall legally held a maximum of 100 people, but who knows how many were there that evening? It felt more like 200. A cramped environment, coupled with drugs and alcohol will always be a recipe for disaster. A tapering walkway led to the main hall and the main exit door. Pushing and shoving in the narrow walkway caused shouting, screaming, and periodic threats among the young intoxicated partygoers.

There were two of us there that evening—me and my friend, whom I'll call "Mark". We were best friends, and our mothers were like sisters. Mark was one year older than I, and we lived 25 doors away from each other in Bedwell House. Mark prided himself on being a young man who could take care of himself in conflicts. He had a grandiose personality. He was always well-dressed, and he accessorized his outfits with a mischievous giggle. He had a thin build, weighing no more than 126 pounds, but with a personality that was twice his size.

As we left the main hall to exit the venue, the crowd's pushing and shoving intensified as more partygoers tried to enter the already packed venue. It was like a tsunami lifted us off our feet, sweeping us back into the wrong direction—back into the main hall, we were trying to leave.

A man twice our age and twice our size, clearly drunk and even more grandiose than Mark, pushed the crowd back. Young girls were losing their heels, and the boys were losing their balance. Mark was at the front of the crowd and wouldn't tolerate another push from him. I was about 20 partygoers behind Mark, which felt more like 1,000 because of the narrow hallway. Mark shouted, "What the flip are you doing man?" The man responded, "Who are you talking to?" Mark replied, "You, you dickhead!" I couldn't hear the man's reply, but it wasn't good. What I picked up from his body language was that something terrible was about to happen. Mark taunted the man, saying, "Come outside and say that again!" The man responded, "Ok!"

What I saw that Mark couldn't see was that this man was not alone; there were five, or maybe even ten of them together. One of the skills, or perhaps gifts, you pick up coming from the street life (if you are not drunk or on drugs, and I did neither) is an enhanced level of awareness and hypervigilance you obtain. Growing up around so much aggression taught me how to detect whether someone carried weapons or if their micro-expressions showed signs of anger or ill will.

I could also tell whether men or women in plain clothes were undercover police officers. We had an astute ability to know if we were being followed home or were under surveillance. We spoke in codes and languages no one else could understand. This situation was usually easy for us to read. But, at that time, Mark was too emotional to read it. Or maybe Mark didn't have what I thought was a natural aptitude for detecting danger.

You cannot teach or articulate spiritual awareness; you either have it or you don't! Every human being has some level of awareness, whether spiritual, environmental, or self-awareness. It was our awareness and hypervigilance that were unique to us. We relied on our rules and awareness to survive in Brixton. It was our CIA, our MI5, and our Mossad that kept us out of prison and safe from evil intent; however, alcohol, drugs, and emotions had the potential to blunt those abilities. I did not smoke, drink alcohol, or take drugs for these reasons. Mark's emotions diminished the aptitude that would have usually kept him out of harm's way. In situations like that, it doesn't matter who's right or wrong. What matters is who survives and goes home to their loved ones.

I called to Mark, "Let's go," as I pushed toward him using my extended arms and shoulders to make a path through the crowd. After a few minutes, which felt like an eternity, I reached the opposing parties. To buy time, I used my back to separate Mark from the group while firmly fixing my eyes on all the possible threats. As I eased Mark back to create precious time and space to escape, the opposing group prepared themselves for war. I wanted to flee; Mark wanted to fight.

We stumbled outside, "Mark, let's go!" I calmly but firmly said as I pulled on Mark's skinny arm. "No!" Mark shouted, pulling his arm back and clenching his fist. "Bro, there's a lot of them," I said as I tried to get Mark to see logic and reason. Mark only saw red and war.

What Mark said after was inaudible, as the crowds and the noise of the party broke the temporal communication between us. Groups of people spilled out in front of the community hall. I sensed imminent danger but couldn't tell friends from foes. Too many people at once blurred my prey-versus-predator instinct, and being surrounded didn't help.

Mark fixed his eagle eyes on his 'prey,' not caring or realizing that *we were* the actual prey and they were the predators. They were like hyenas ready to pounce, and we were deer pretending to be lions.

Mark threw a punch; it bounced off the man's chin like he had thrown a balloon at him. "Shit," I thought, remembering our rules. Rule 1: Never leave your friends alone, not even to go to the restroom. Rule 2: Never leave your friends in any form of conflict. NO MATTER HOW DEADLY THE SITUATION! Rule 3: If you leave home with a friend, you come home with that friend.

Now even more confident, the man threw his first punch, and Mark's head jerked back. Then a second punch and Mark's knees buckled. Mark replied with his flurry of tickling punches, which were effective but not enough to break the man's spirit. Mark backed up while the man advanced—one, two, three steps. Mark couldn't step back any farther, and the man threw a punch from the heavens. Well, it felt like the heavens to me, or maybe hell. This man was drunk but bloody strong. The punch hit Mark on the nose and destroyed his feeling of superiority.

Mark backed off as the man went in to finish him with a powerful blow—a haymaker. I instinctively jumped in front of Mark and took a punch on my left cheek. I would love to tell you that it was my grand moment of heroism, but it wasn't. It was just instinct. Would I have reacted differently if I thought about my actions first? Who knows. I was only 14 or 15. "Mark, watch my back," I said, knowing Mark was in no mood to fight anymore. I looked into Mark's eyes. He was emotionally depleted. "MARK, WATCH MY BACK!" I shouted, hoping for a miracle to intervene and save us.

I knew I had to take this man on, but I didn't want to. And I didn't want to provoke his hyena posse either. I didn't want to be vulnerable. I hated feeling powerless. Should I try to win and excite his goons? Or should I do enough for everyone to save face and go home undamaged? I have seen way too many unhinged situations where the innocent, weak, and vulnerable were beaten for the sake of it, and it never ended well. Ok, my decision was made.

Very consciously aware of what was about to happen, my body went into a new gear of fight mode. I was still summing this up as I measured the punching distance between me and this beast of a man, who was almost twice my age and size. Was this the same stressful situation a hunter-gatherer experienced 2.8 million years ago, or the same feeling a gazelle gets when being hunted by a pack of hyenas?

Am I going to be a victim of carnivores? It's funny how you can have a lengthy conversation with yourself in only a few seconds when your world and life could change forever. My childhood trauma was forming into adult trauma, and I was one experience away from adult issues.

My heart, blood pressure, and respiration rate increased; my glucose levels rose. My pupils dilated, and my muscles tensed up, so I had to shake my arms out to help them relax. I threw my first punch—smack! He backed up. My second punch—whack! The man stumbled. Why was I getting the results that Mark couldn't? I thought to myself, I have play fought with Mark many times before and he was much stronger than I. I knew it was my cortisol stress hormones that was giving me the strength I needed to survive against this bloody Hulk Hogan. But didn't Mark experience the same level of fight or flight I did? NO!

First, Mark's grandiose behavior dulled his ability to recognize that we were in grave danger. He had no genuine reason to defend himself until it was too late. And when it was too late, his responses moved from fight to freeze, then to flee. His initial focus was to prove a point, not protect us from harm. I hated the fact that Mark put us in such an unconscionable situation. And what about the mammoth man? His overblown confidence made him drop his arms and smirk when he broke Mark's spirit and potentially his nose. His haymaker dazed me, and he knew it. My first, second, and soon to be third blow would surely stop him. It had to, I prayed. But just before I threw my third blow to neutralize our threat, I felt a cold, sharp punch in my back. Mark's helpline needed Mark's help!

The world around me stopped and then progressed in slow motion. I looked down at my belly to discover it was sticking out like a tumor was protruding from it. I felt a second jolt in my back. I then realized a Rambo knife was being pulled out of my teenage flesh. I turned around in shock, holding my belly but knowing the entry wound was in my back.

I whispered, “Mark!” now finding it hard to breathe. “MARK?” Efforts to shout Mark’s name came out as only whimpers blowing aimlessly into the night wind. “Help Mark!” Where was Mark? There was no Mark. There was NO FLIPPING MARK. So, who helps the helpline when the helpline needs help? Not Mark. Over the shoulder of my attacker, who was holding the Rambo knife and waiting for orders to stab again, I saw Mark about 22 yards down the road, fleeing toward home and away from me.

Death is lonely. I felt lonely, brokenhearted, and dying. The only thing I could think about were the three rules. Then, my whole world faded to black.

Why is it that I remember the pushing and shoving in the hallway? The arguments? My self-talk throughout the entire ordeal? Why do I so vividly remember the punches and being stabbed? Why did the reenactment of this traumatic event repeatedly play in my head in 4K until Mark ran away? After that, like a Wi-Fi signal, my memory just drops. That’s it. I know.

It was Mark running away that was my real trauma. I was stabbed 4 inches away from my heart, and I accepted that. But Mark running away is what really broke my heart, and I couldn’t accept that part.

For my 14-year-old mind to cope with what happened that night, I had to block out Mark running away for more than 25 years; it wasn’t just our friendship that was in jeopardy. It was my adolescent belief system that was also at risk. It was our rules, bond, and journey; even my street mentors and elders' teachings were on the line. Although the stabbing was a traumatic event for me, Mark deserting me was a trauma that took 25 years for me to acknowledge.

It was 25 years of untreated trust issues, 25 years of trying to develop eyes in the back of my head, looking in any reflective object to see who was behind me, 25 years keeping my back to the wall in nightclubs, restaurants, and bars. 25 years of hypervigilant paranoia.

"We lost you for a minute, Mr Bennett... You died!"

"Where am I?" I asked, feeling woozy and bewildered.

The doctor responded, "You are in Kings College Hospital young man. You have a chance at life again. Don't waste it!"

So how did I make it to the hospital? Well, the same belief system and rules that broke my heart at that moment due to the desertion actually turned out to be my savior.

Two of the older boys from Stockwell Park Estate, Gary, and Sinclair, were randomly driving past the hall when they saw the commotion. They didn't know what or who was in the conflict, but their curiosity made them witness my final moments before unconsciousness.

I was later told that Gary and Sinclair picked up garbage cans, bottles, and anything else they could find to hurl at my attackers. Eventually backing them up, they pulled my lifeless, bloodied body into their car and drove me to the hospital. Rule 2: Never leave your friends in any conflict, NO MATTER HOW DEADLY THE SITUATION! Thanks guys!

Writing this introduction as a mature adult, I have now forgiven Mark. I have also forgiven my attackers. Forgiveness frees you from a depressed mind, a sickened body, and an imprisoned spirit.

Mark and I were way too young and naive to have such grown-up rules back then. My attackers could also have committed to their own rules that evening because of their own traumas. Perhaps they are themselves now therapeutically fixing their lives because of their practices and lifestyles. Misery loves company, and frequencies attract like frequencies.

We were all in an electron-broken place back then.

As you may remember from your school days, the constituents of an atom are made up of protons, electrons, and neutrons. The protons are positively charged elements, the electrons are negatively charged elements, and the neutrons are elements that stabilize both the protons and the electrons. When we are in a proton state, we are governed by the positive polarity of a proton. Proton's positive energy opens the spiritual and emotional consciousness of LOVE.

Once we are in that proton state and expression of LOVE, we start to experience positive emotions and feelings for ourselves and others. You can’t be in a place of blissful happiness without first being in a proton, positive, open spiritual consciousness of LOVE.

Then you have the electron spiritual entity of FEAR. This negative energy of electrons closes awareness and consciousness. We are in an electron state when we experience fear, depression, anger, worry, pessimism, doubt, and other negative feelings governed by the low vibrational frequency of FEAR.

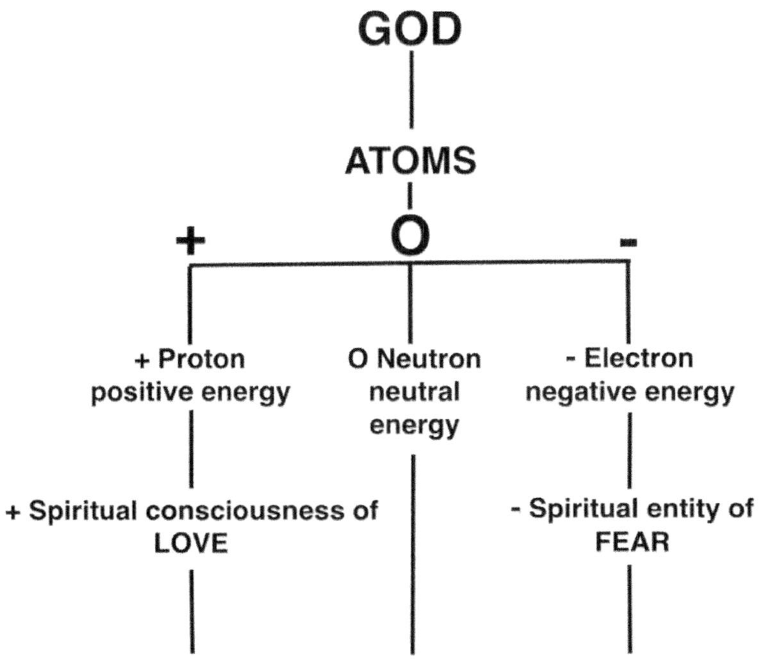

+ Proton positive Emotions & Feelings

+ Love
+ Happiness
+ Passion
+ Joy
+ Positive
+ Content
+ Gratitude
+ Fulfilled
+ Enthusiastic

O Neutron neutral Emotions & Feelings

O Optimistic
O Hopeful
O Confused

- Electron negative Emotions & Feelings

- Pessimistic
- Boredom
- Frustration
- Disappointment
- Doubt
- Worried
- Disheartened
- Anger
- Jealousy (enviousness)
- Sadness/ Unhappiness
- Overwhelmed
- Burned out
- Loneliness
- Hurt
- Loss
- Rejected
- Anxiety
- Insecurity
- Grief
- Apathy
- Guilt
- Ashamed
- Fear
- Depression
- Hopelessness

We all need to have proton tools (which I will discuss in the later chapters) to assist us throughout our lives. We cannot predict or control how the world will treat us or what strangers may do to us or our loved ones. We can only control how we think and behave as a response. Since that evening, I have experienced my son's death, my brother's murder, my nephew's suicide, my father's deterioration from prostate cancer, my sister's painful struggle with postpartum depression before her untimely death, my eldest brother's death from a brain bleed, and myself being stabbed in the leg and in the arm and slashed across my face.

I have been to hundreds of funerals and shed buckets of tears over the years. Every morning, I gently massage my six-inch-long scar that runs from just below my navel to just under my sternum. I once rubbed that scar in frustration and anger, but now I caress my scar with gratitude and appreciation. I got my six-inch scar from a surgery after my appendix burst and caused peritonitis, which then poisoned my body, causing organ failure, and then once again, I was resuscitated back to life. I was once very depressed from my traumatic experiences, but now I am a positive and happy person overall.

From 2003 until today, I have made it my life's journey and mission to discover the reason, meaning, and purpose behind every emotion we feel, express, and deny on a day-to-day basis.

Did I want to be a psychologist growing up? No. How about a counselor? Never. I have never considered any of the above; even now, I do not consider myself a psychologist or a counselor. However, I believe we are all counselors and psychologists to our friends and loved ones in some way.

So, how did I get here, why am I writing this book, and am I even qualified to address such heavy subjects about human emotions, traumas, and behaviors?

There's a saying in the Caribbean community, "Who feels it, knows it," and I have felt it, known it, and survived it.

My own physically and psychologically traumatic events led me on a path and down a rabbit hole to things, scenarios, and situations I had not even begun to fathom existed. I guess it's like when a person who held no prior interest in the fight against cancer becomes a frontline advocate when they or their loved one becomes affected by cancer. I see the same commitments and behaviors with domestic abuse, knife crime, HIV, rape, and mental health.

Up until 2022, I have personally worked with well over two thousand people on a one-to-one basis from 2009. I have held workshops and seminars, lectured at universities, spoken at schools, held webinars, and have been interviewed on TV and radio many times. Since 2010, I have helped and empowered millions of people across different media platforms, helping those struggling with emotional or psychological trauma.

I discovered that some people just wanted to die because they didn't know how to live. Did I undertake formal education to be a psychologist or counselor to help, build up, and empower people? No. However, I made it my duty to read and study everything I could get my hands on to help people who are struggling with emotional trauma. Some of my favorites are *Affective Neuroscience* by Dr. Jaak Panksepp, *Feeling Good* by David D. Burns, MD, anything from psychiatrist Aaron T. Beck, Dr. Gabor Maté, psychologist Peter A. Levine, and many more great minds.

I watched thousands of case studies on human and animal behaviors. In hundreds of cases, I intensely scrutinized different traumatic experiences with people in my inner and outer community. I have extensive knowledge of spirituality, universal laws, spiritual frequencies, mindfulness, and more. I have spent more than ten thousand hours talking with social workers, doctors, dentists, real estate agents, electricians, pharmacists, teachers, and others, from what I now coin "electron occupations". Electron occupations are careers, jobs, or work environments with the highest stress, depression, and suicide rates.

I have traveled to many countries to study human behaviors of all types. I've interviewed once-millionaires who had lost everything in Las Vegas and then ended up homeless in the tunnels underneath the Vegas strip. I have sat and learned the mindset and behaviors of very happy people who had discovered purpose and happiness in the small things. I have also sat with people who just attracted positivity and financial abundance in countries such as Italy, Sardinia, Jamaica, Spain, Dubai, Bulgaria, France, Saint-Tropez, Egypt, Malta, and the United States, plus more.

"How do you feel?" I ask everyone I encounter.

"Why do you feel that way?" I inquire further, becoming more subtle and adopting an apologetic and respectful tone.

"Are you governed by your traumas or by your desires?" I ask this question in an attempt to discover the driving force and motivation of the person.

One of the most powerful techniques you can use when asking questions without actually asking the participant a direct question is:

> "It feels like ...?"
> "It seems like ...?"
> "It sounds like ...?"

I use these phrases to try to unearth answers without sounding as though I'm an interviewer or a nosey ass who just wants to invade the person's mind. That's a skill I learned from hostage negotiator Chris Voss. These phrases bypass the emotional defenses of the conscious mind and appeal directly to the subconscious mind.

After more than 14 years of observing human behavior and seeing many parts of our society suffer for many reasons, I wrote and designed this book to support, build up, and empower those suffering in silence.

Oh, and as for the question, "Am I qualified to write this book?"

My answer is simply, "Yes! I am!"

Who Helps the Helpline, When the Helpline Needs Help? is a solutions-based book about amazing people who help others while often suffering in silence themselves.

We will discuss how to make bad aspects of your life good by understanding how your feelings, traumas, and emotions work.

We will approach the controversial topics of how planets, materials, gold, stones, colors, prayers, and even how rats can help you improve your mind, body, and spirit.

In the first chapters, I will present stories and case studies of working professionals who carry home the electron (negative) vibrational frequencies of their occupation. Or do they? Maybe it is them who take their electron vibrational frequencies to work. I will leave that to you to decide.

In the later chapters, I will address how good and bad vibrational frequencies work and how to use them to harness your potential power.

Throughout this book, stress, burnout, depression, trauma, suicide, and other emotions, feelings, and behaviors will be looked at in depth to assist our helplines — you. Whenever you see the term *helpline*, I'm talking about those people who dedicate their lives to serving, fixing, and saving others. You may be a nonprofessional who helps people out of the goodness of your heart or a working professional who does it for a living. A helpline is a helpline regardless of the job title or financial reward. A helpline is a person who loves, cares, and serves from their heart. We will examine helpline careers in this book, such as physicians, nurses, firefighters, farmers, social workers, police officers, teachers, and others.

This book also discusses mental health awareness and active strategies and methods to empower individuals to combat depression, stress, and trauma. By reading this book, I also want governments to be aware of the disadvantages of their bureaucracy and how their bureaucracy can silence our helplines when our helplines are screaming for "HELP!".

Being a servant of God, I pray that I have presented compelling arguments in the coming chapters of this book that will shed light on the anchors and triggers of friends, family members, and loved ones' mental health challenges in the work environment. I also shed light on how the pursuit of having letters before or after your name can be the cause of your mental illness. Sometimes all that we pursue in the name of happiness may be the antithesis of our joy.

The worksheets in this book can be used to keep you on track and guide you to your own mental health and excellence. There are also external add-ons to this book, such as our KBenaire Life Board and App, that you can purchase separately.

The KBenaire Life Board and App are designed to help you with your:

Career / Vocation
Education / Knowledge
Family / Relationships
Feelings / Emotions
Finances / Wealth
Health
Legacy
Lifestyle
Mastermind groups
Mentors
Self-development
Spirituality
And Networks / Associations

I will also discuss how to use The 12 Universal Laws to help you on your life journey.

We will cover the following laws:

The Law of Energy
The Law of Rhythm
The Law of Inspired Action
The Law of Divine Oneness
The Law of Gender
The Law of Polarity
The Law of Relativity
The Law of Transmutation
The Law of Compensation
The Law of Cause and Effect
The Law of Attraction

The Law of Correspondence

Now let's start with Dr. Alex Hellman—a good man who decided he was not good enough to live.

Who helps our doctors when our doctors want to die?

CHAPTER 1

WHO HELPS THE PHYSICIAN WHEN THE PHYSICIAN NEEDS HELP?

"I am a killer. That's a fact! That thought goes through your head; that thought doesn't leave," says Dr. Alex Hellman, as he stares into his bathroom mirror, his tone of voice sad, low, and matter-of-fact. While shaving and shaping the outline of his thin beard, he continues, "Actions of mine contributed to a man's death".

Dr. Hellman's eyes are reflective. He has much more to say despite his great emotional pain.

"I was paged to take this patient to the operating room so we could repair his bleeding. We put a breathing tube in to enable surgery to find the bleeding. When I put in the new breathing tube, his heart rate went down to zero, and it became clear". Hellman stops and shakes his head, then he said, "He was not going to wake up".

Dr. Hellman is an anesthesiologist. He is a frail white man, 5'9" in height, about 154 pounds, with a low-cut beard, receding hairline, and clear-framed glasses a window to his regretful, hopeless and dark soul. Dr. Hellman speaks slowly and softly, sometimes pausing poignantly between sentences by looking at the floor or straight through you and into the distance.

An anesthesiologist is a doctor (MD, Doctor of Medicine, or a DO, Doctor of Osteopathic Medicine) who practices anesthesiology. They are physicians who specialize in perioperative care, developing anesthetic plans, and administering anesthetics. Their job is to give patients anesthetics during operations and medical procedures. They make sure patients are safe and comfortable before and during surgery. Following surgery, they closely monitor patients to ensure that they recover well. Such a medical specialty is fraught with responsibilities, overwhelming stress, and pressure.

While preparing patients for surgery, the anesthesiologist establishes a rapport with patients; they learn about their needs, their family, and their medical history and spend a large part of their time reassuring the patients. Often, patients fear surgery and being placed under anesthesia, so anesthesiologists must have a strong sense of empathy for their patients and develop a trusting relationship. Dr. Hellman had all of these characteristics in spades, but sometimes things just go wrong, as they did in this case.

So, what does it take to become an anesthesiologist?

According to careerexplorer.com, a person's educational journey to become an anesthesiologist in the United States typically involves eight stages.

Stage 1: Graduate from high school, taking biology, physics, physiology, and chemistry.

Stage 2: Get a Bachelor's Degree from a university, which will take four years. Although there are no requirements for specific majors, choosing to major in biology, chemistry, nutrition science, or neuroscience is a good idea.

Stage 3: Prepare for a Medical College Admission Test (MCAT). Your scores and university transcript will determine whether you are accepted to medical school.

Stage 4: Study at medical school for four years to earn a Doctor of Medicine degree or a Doctor of Osteopathic Medicine degree. Both degrees will qualify you to become an anesthesiologist.

Stage 5: Complete an anesthesiology residency, which will take four years. Residents work under supervision to receive clinical training through working in a hospital and providing medical care to patients. After four years, they are eligible for the American Board of Anesthesiology examination.

Stage 6: After residency, many physicians complete an additional year of training to get a fellowship, which allows them to learn a specialized type of anesthesiology, such as cardiac or pediatric.

Stage 7: Obtain a license to practice in the United States by taking the United States Medical Licensing Examination. Or the Comprehensive Osteopathic Medical Licensing Examination, or both.

Stage 8: Obtain an optional board certification. About 90% of all anesthesiologists are board-certified. Board certification indicates a physician's expertise, commitment to the practice, mastery of anesthesiology, and commitment to abide by the ABPS Medical Code of Ethics.

According to the National Careers Service, to become an anesthesiologist in the United Kingdom, students must first complete at least five general secondary education certificate programs, including English, Mathematics, and Science, in addition to three A-level courses in Biology, Chemistry, and Physics.

Students must then complete a five-year degree in medicine recognized by the General Medical Council, a two-year foundational training program, then up to eight years of specialist training before working as an anesthesiologist.

According to Christopher Troianos, MD, a Professor and Chair of the Anesthesiology Institute of the Cleveland Clinic, "In the 1960s and 1970s, it wasn't uncommon to have a death related to anesthesia in every 1 in 10,000 or 20,000 patients". Dr. Troianos continued, "Now it's more like 1 in every 200,000 patients; it's scarce".

Dr. Alex Hellman spent many years committed to his education and career. Now, why would Dr. Hellman have been so bewildered and hurt that a patient died under his care? And more importantly, why did Dr. Hellman take his patient's death so badly, as thousands of other doctors do globally every year?

From Belief to Knowledge

There are five stages between believing something to be true and knowing something to be true. Both belief and knowledge can be either positive or negative.

In Dr. Hellman's case, his five stages between belief and knowledge were negative. We will address the positive sides of belief and knowledge later in this chapter, but first, here are my five stages between belief and knowledge:

Stage One - The Belief System

Stage Two - The Meaning System

Stage Three - The Action System

Stage Four - The Results System.

Stage Five - The Knowledge (knowing) System

So, let's start with Stage One - The Belief System

Dr. Hellman torments and blames himself for killing a man—which is his belief— instead of accepting that there are limitations to medical sciences. The details are unknown, but Dr. Hellman's patient died shortly after placing his breathing tube. It was a tragedy, but it doesn't mean he killed the patient—rather, it was a sad, freak accident. The problem with doing God's work is that you, I, or any physician is not God. When it's time for someone to pass on, no amount of technology, skill, or educational qualifications can change that reality. Life is on God's timetable, not ours. Yet, it's often easy to overlook that and think that we have absolute control over our life's timetable and that of others.

I continuously ask myself and the people I work with whether it would help physicians if they were religious or atheists? Should they study energy or spirituality? Should they incorporate prayer and faith into their practice? What should physicians do, or who should they become within themselves in order to accept that not every operation or surgery will result in their favor? Some of the heartbreakingly high depression and suicide rates of physicians are caused by burnout, guilt, and self-hate.

The Belief System and then self-talk of many physicians after losing a patient is *"I am a bad person"* and *"I am not good enough"*—and in Dr. Hellman's case, "I am a killer," this is a dangerous and ruinous set of beliefs to have as Dr. Hellman is a good, qualified, caring man with good intentions – he wants to save lives but has branded himself as a killer, which is a heavy burden to carry. So how should one relinquish such negative beliefs and thoughts? We will address this in the later chapters to come.

Stage Two - The Meaning System

The Meaning System connects our relationship with ourselves to the world around us. This is our self-talk—the conversations we have within ourselves before we express ourselves to the outside world. Dr. Hellman said, "I definitely cried about this every day going to work and going home". Consumed by guilt, he purposefully read his patient's obituary to discover that the man had a wife and very young children.

"Where's the justice in this situation?" Dr. Hellman said. "There's only one way to make this situation right," he affirmed sternly. He then slowly, after gazing down and taking a small gulp, proclaimed, "Suicide!"

The contemplation of Stage Three, The Action System, was now forming in his mind—he didn't want to live anymore. He was broken, he needed help, and he needed to be reassured that he wasn't evil or a danger to his patients. Dr. Hellman's meaning (his self-talk) was that of hopelessness, and his thoughts of suicide were gaining momentum. Let's touch on Dr. Hellman's thoughts and suicidal behavior more as we delve deeper into this chapter.

In early 2018, it was estimated that more than one million patients in the United States would lose a physician that year through suicide.

Two-thirds of US doctors are either burned out, overwhelmed, depressed, suffer from anxiety, or all of the above. Often, doctors, by nature, place the welfare of others above their own. They give, and give, and give again until they have nothing more to offer.

When comparing colleagues who had never endured a complaint, medical practitioners in the United Kingdom who had received a complaint were 77% more likely to develop moderate to severe depression. Complaints would also double the risk of anxiety and double the risk of thoughts of suicide or self-harm. (Bourne et al. 2015).

According to Dr. Clare Gerada, medical director of the National Health Service's Practitioner Health Program, "Female doctors have up to four times the risk of suicide in comparison to people in the [general] population". The Office for National Statistics revealed that 430 health professionals committed suicide in England between 2011 and 2015. These are the sad truths about many people who spend their lives saving other people's lives while ending their own.

The question is, how do they sustain a depleted emotional bucket when their well of self-belief and positivity has run dry? Most physicians feel they cannot discuss their problems with their peers. I mean, who should the helpline go to when the helpline needs help? Who trusts a broken physician? People expect their physicians to have all the answers. They are skilled, smart, and, in most cases, extremely gifted. If only skills, smarts, and innate gifts from God could fix negative beliefs that lead to negative behaviors.

Depressed and suicidal physicians in many countries run the risk of losing their licenses because of their own mental and emotional turbulence. When doctors carry heavy burdens and bottle up their emotions, something occurs within them—it's an electron, it's dark, and it's dangerous. It's Stage Three: The Action System.

Stage Three - The Action System

The Action System can manifest in multiple ways, such as suicide attempts, self-harm, excessive alcohol or drug use, or any combination of the three. Stage three can be a cry for help. But, in many cases, the cries can go unseen, unheard, and unanswered.

The wife of Dr. Hellman, Dr. Charlene Hellman, recollected that her husband was withdrawing from her and their children. This was an early stage three behavioral sign of Dr. Hellman's depression.

Dr. Hellman explained how he mapped out his plan to commit suicide. "I had all the materials; my plan was to commit suicide. I would just start an IV on myself, inject the medicines, and I'd stop breathing. Things would take their course in 20 minutes and that would be that". His plan was clear.

Dr. Katherine Gold of the University of Michigan explained that the numbers that we use for physician suicide does not have great data about them. They are mostly based on expert opinion. Suicide is a hard thing to track down because it's stigmatization.

As a result, when a physician commits suicide, it could be reported as something else. Sadly, Dr. Hellman was not alone in being confined within the dark prison of his mind. Dr. Mitchell Hardison drove down a small ravine, pulled into a cul-de-sac, parked, and shot himself in the heart. Dr. Hardison died on September 10, 2015. He was only 63 years old.

Dr. Mitchell Hardison left behind a loving family. He was concerned that if he said anything about his depression and burnout, there would be a devastating outcome from the medical board. He felt hopeless, and hopelessness is dangerous. Patients sent dozens of letters to Dr. Hardison's family after his death. They all hailed him as a great doctor and a loving, kind, remarkable man. I cannot help thinking that had Dr. Hardison received those letters of love, support, and appreciation while he was still alive, they could have been the very thing to save his life.

Stage Four - The Results System

The aftermath of Dr. Mitchell Hardison's actions resulted in his unfortunate and untimely death. Those who end their lives early never get to experience Stage Five.

Stage Five - The Knowledge System — knowing that things can and will get better.

So, the million-dollar question is, Who Helps The Helpline When The Helpline Needs Help?

You may assume that doctors would be able to tap into their peer networks, from counselors to psychiatrists. But doctors often face barriers such as embarrassment, stigmatization, and penalization that would prevent them from accessing interventions. The fear of being ousted from their respectable positions or careers due to being 'incompetent' or 'unfit to work' stops thousands of physicians from seeking professional help. Firefighters, scientists, police officers, nurses, surgeons, and anesthesiologists all suffer the same fear of penalization due to their belief that they are not permitted to show even a trace of mental collapse.

So why is expressing mental illness such a significant taboo among these sectors?

One word: licensing.

The fear of losing their licenses or the right to work due to their mental illness is enough for most professionals to either suffer in silence or go incognito in seeking professional help. It has been reported that thousands of professionals use aliases and pay cash only for their treatments, so they don't leave any digital footprint that could identify them.

In the minds of many, even the idea of sharing their mental and emotional challenges with colleagues can be too much of a risk to explore. On top of that, they don't want to be perceived as weak or having lost control.

This situation is not limited to healthcare workers, public service workers, and first responders. There are others who suffer in silence. Actor and comedian Robin Williams entertained us, made the world laugh, and smiled while he was dying on the inside. His depression went unnoticed by most people until his death by asphyxiation. Robin Williams' sunrise was July 21st, 1951, and his sunset was on August 11th, 2014.

Over the years, I have discovered that different occupations carry different "frequencies"—positive and negative. I call these frequencies proton (positive) and electron (negative). Some jobs and careers are positive, proton jobs, in which job satisfaction and overall happiness spread among the workforce. Other jobs are negative, electron jobs with high rates of stress, depression, and suicide. It's no accident that surgeons, veterinarians, scientists, pharmacists, farmworkers, electricians, real estate agents, police officers, lawyers, dentists, and doctors have the highest rates of suicide of any profession. It's also no accident that some occupations and industries are proton-happy occupations, such as human resources, HR business partners, corporate recruiters, IT consultants, loan officers, and marketing consultants. So, how does your career or job make you feel? And what vibrational frequencies are you living in daily?

CHAPTER 2

FIREFIGHTERS ON FIRE

Question, who fights for our firefighters, when our firefighters are on fire?

A human conveyor belt of anxious helpers lined up along the first-floor communal way and down the creaking old stairs that led into the adjacent parking lot where the Brixton Soup Kitchen van and cars were waiting. They were to be filled with food, clothing, and other essentials. We were more than equipped with those essentials to help others, but, in hindsight, I realize we were not even close to being prepared or equipped for our own emotional traumas to come. Our destination—Grenfell Tower!

It was a date that people in the UK will never forget—June 14, 2017. It was 1 p.m.—three hours in, and finally, our tired hands were buttering the last of the bread in the Brixton Soup Kitchen. Jennifer and two of her assistants packed the hundreds of freshly cooked sweetcorn and tuna pasta meals they had spent the entire morning preparing. In another room, Solomon, Isaac, Hash, Micah, and dozens of helpers prepared and packed clothing donated by the local community. A mountain of men, women, and children's clothing was packed into bags and boxes, alongside drinks, personal hygiene products, and toiletries.

Hours earlier, at 12:55 a.m. on June 14, 2017, an emergency 999 call-out was made concerning a fire on the fourth floor of Grenfell Tower. North Kensington Fire Station dispatched two pumps to attend the fire. (Before I continue, depending on where you are in the world, there are different names for fire engines, in this book, we will refer to fire engines as *pumps* or *pumpers*.)

12:59 a.m. North Kensington pumps arrived at Grenfell Tower.

1:15 a.m. - More emergency call-outs were sent from Kensington Fire Station and Hammersmith Fire Station to assist with the Grenfell Tower fire—1:32 a.m. Paddington Fire Station assigned their aerial appliance and pump to the Grenfell Tower fire. This aerial appliance was essential; however, very late in the response timeline of this high-rise building block fire. Not all pumps have an aerial ladder, and not all aerial ladders are located in every fire station across the UK. An aerial ladder device is a mechanically-operated extendable ladder mounted on a pump to rescue people and extinguish high building block fires. At this time, only one station had an aerial ladder near Grenfell Tower, Paddington Fire Station.

On the night of the Grenfell Tower fire, the first of the first responders did not even begin to fathom that they would need an aerial appliance for a fourth-floor fridge fire. But because of the building's external cladding, the fire climbed to the 24th floor in a matter of minutes.

The firefighters tackled the blaze on the fourth floor, believing they had it under control. However, the fire raced up the building's external cladding, consuming everything in its path. Floor by floor, flat by flat, room by room, the fire and smoke savagely penetrated homes and eventually, the residents.

Shortly after 1:32 a.m., more fire appliances from Fulham, Wembley, Acton, Chiswick, Willesden, Chelsea, Park Royal, West Hampstead, and Euston fire stations arrived to fight the unprecedented disaster that was beginning to emerge.

Onlookers and neighbors witnessed screams and cries for help from men, women, children, and even babies, as the fire and toxic smoke engulfed their homes. A man saw trapped residents having to make the impossible choice between facing the flames and leaping to their death. Those who jumped died; others who stayed were consumed by the thick black smoke and flames.

A woman witnessed her best friend banging on her living room window, screaming for someone to help her as she helplessly looked up with dismay. She said, "I saw the flames creeping up behind my friend before she disappeared behind them".

What she and countless others saw will haunt them for the rest of their lives. We heard the accounts of friends, family, and neighbors. But what did the first and second responders experience? What did they see, hear, smell, touch, and taste?

Firefighters have been banned from discussing the Grenfell Tower disaster with the media. However, on UK's *BBC Newsnight*, some firefighters anonymously came forward to talk about their traumatic experiences and their harmful effects on their colleagues. Here are some of the accounts from the *Newsnight* report firefighters:

"I saw firefighters who I know are extremely fit, marathon runners, completely [messed up], throwing up". Firefighter D said.

Firefighter B recalls, "The fire floors we went in were helmet-meltingly hot".

"I stood up on the 10th floor to smash a door in and instantly felt heat on my head and shoulders. When I got down and removed my tunic, my shoulders were burned," Firefighter C remembers.

I spent two years after the Grenfell Tower disaster talking to best friends, family members, and colleagues of some of the first responders who attended that night. I can affirm that many of the friends and family members also suffered. They were suffering from secondary trauma.

The Grenfell Tower is located in the borough of Kensington and Chelsea on the west side of London, just a stone's throw away from the annual Notting Hill Carnival location. Grenfell Tower stands 24 stories high, and 21 of the stories were residential floors with 129 homes in the tower. The tower comprised of six flats per floor with narrow hallways and small elevators. According to the Royal Borough of Kensington and Chelsea, it is estimated that 203 families were living in the tower.

Imagine being on the 23rd floor of a high-rise building with a maniacal fire raging at your door. Imagine toxic, black smoke permeating through the cracks, gaps, and air vents, restricting your sight, sound, and breathing. Imagine not being able to use the elevators in a 24-story building block, where a fire is moving faster than you can run up or down the stairs. Firefighters had to climb each floor step-by-step, staircase-by-staircase, lobby-by-lobby, landing-by-landing, home-by-home, fighting the flames and investigating homes looking for survivors to save.

Firefighters who discovered trapped residents periodically shared their breathing apparatuses with those suffering from smoke inhalation. As a result, those firefighters also suffered from smoke inhalation, which has caused short-term and long-term health problems.

After talking to some of their family members and colleagues, I found out that many of the firefighters didn't anticipate the chaos that occurred due to the loss of radio communication as they went higher up in the building. They also didn't anticipate that they would have water pressure problems as they climbed to each floor. The firefighters suffered that night. A total of 72 people died as a result of the Grenfell Tower fire.

Back to 3:27 p.m., June 14, 2017, we crammed like sardines into the Brixton Soup Kitchen van. Solomon, Hash, Micah, Jennifer, Isaac, and several other Brixton Soup Kitchen members and I were within view of the Grenfell Tower. On approach, we started to truly witness the severity of what had happened hours before. What we saw on TV was not even close to the emotional disruption that we were about to experience from a mile away; as we looked up to a sky darkened by smoke and fire on a London summer afternoon.

As we got closer and turned onto Lancaster Road, approaching Silchester Road, about 700 yards away from Grenfell, we saw something hair-raising and heart-wrenching. Ash and debris covered all the cars, bikes, and homes surrounding the tower. It was like a modern-day apocalypse. Even more unsettling was the smell of burning flesh; I can smell it now as I write this sentence. Just thinking about it sends my mind into a tailspin.

People were walking around crying, lost, and confused. Sons were consoling mothers, fathers embraced daughters, and strangers hugged strangers. Devastated families and friends held photos of loved ones feared dead in the fire. Firm but extremely pensive police officers cordoned the building off with tape to prevent onlookers and distressed family members from getting any closer to the actively burning building.

People sat on the ground with their heads in their hands. Others stared at the building in disbelief. Screams and shrieks of pain in the distance reached us as the horrific reality of what had happened to the residents, survivors, friends, and family members started to seep in. Grief turned into anger; chaos turned into order. I sensed an incandescent protest looming, and it eventually happened three days later.

Firefighters were lying on the ground outside the tower after fighting to save other people's lives and preserve their own. They were tired, broken, and emotionally dejected from what they experienced.

Since the Grenfell Tower disaster, firefighters and other first and second responders have reported having post-traumatic stress disorder (PTSD), suicidal thoughts, self-harm, anxiety, and depression due to what they experienced that night and the following days.

They have spoken about remembering the screams for help and the yelps which faded to silence behind the flames. They also saw burning bodies and smelled the stench of death. No training can truly prepare anyone for what those firefighters saw that night, the magnitude of the disaster, and the many lives that were lost.

Most firefighters banter with their colleagues to navigate their emotional traumas. Others become distant, with bouts of melancholy outbursts. You cannot 'unsee' what's been seen, 'unsmell' what's been smelled, 'unhear' what's been heard, or 'untaste' what's been tasted. It is so easy to take all the deaths, pain, and traumas home with you and then impose it spiritually, emotionally, and even physically onto loved ones.

It is a non-negotiable ask from doctors, surgeons, police officers, and other public servants, such as, firefighters to remain in their positions and roles when they are deemed incapable, incompetent, or unfit to fulfill their roles due to PTSD, depression, or anxiety when other people's lives are at risk.

The problem behind a firefighter's curtain of "I'm OK. No, really, I'm fine!!!" is the inner demon eating away at the core of their happiness, confidence, sense of self, and relationships with their families and with life itself.

I have a question for you: Do you think a firefighter can be honest and share their deepest, darkest traumas without fearing discrimination or being branded as incompetent? It is known that first responders, including firefighters, are petrified to lose their rank, role, or even their jobs in some countries. So, what do they do? They hold back and suffer in silence. What would you do if your career and livelihood were at stake?

What do our firefighters need?

1. Our firefighters need to be in a safe space to express themselves without fearing judgment, ridicule, or penalization. It is imperative to change the global firefighting culture so that everyone working within that sector can express thoughts and feelings of stress, depression, suicide, and trauma.

2. Our firefighters globally need round-the-clock paid access to counselors, psychiatrists, social workers, and therapists to help them with what they can't 'unsee,' 'unhear', 'unsmell', or forget.

3. Weekly group therapy sessions in which firefighters can come together and share their thoughts, feelings, journeys, and experiences will most definitely help our firefighters to know that they are not alone. Group sessions will also lower their feelings of frustration, anxiety, stress, and anger. If these feelings can be nipped in the bud, the feelings and thoughts of hopelessness, chronic sadness, and even thoughts of suicide will decrease.

The most common word firefighters hear is "HELP," and the least common word firefighters use is "Help". It is tough for most helplines to ask for help when the world they serve only expects to be served.

Only if we can take the time to listen with our eyes and see with our ears will we hear the silent screams of those who work to help us when they need our help more than we need theirs.

Buildings will burn down to the ground, and lives will be lost if our firefighters cannot function properly. What will happen if our firefighters are too anxious, overwhelmed, or depressed to attend car crashes, chemical spills, floods, and other rescue missions?

Every tragic accident a firefighter attends will have a heavy electron effect on them. We must help our firefighters release the trauma we hand over to them before it metastasizes like cancer. We must help the helpline before the helpline cannot even help themselves.

Reach out to them, talk to them, and invest in their well-being, joy, and purpose. It is worth the investment.

CHAPTER 3

THE HELPLINES THAT NEED HELP?

Caution. Proceed with care. The raw truth of what nurses think and feel may offend you!

What are the thoughts of some nurses, and why do they get stressed out, burned out, and even depressed?

Let's start with Mary Dix: "I feel like an ER nurse, a social worker, a psych nurse, an ICU nurse, and even a counselor. I think the most stressful thing about nursing is knowing that people's lives are in my hands".

Olivia Taylor, "I don't want to sound ungrateful or like I hate my job. Being a nurse can be fulfilling and at times rewarding, with that said, my colleagues and I get stressed because some patients and their families have become so entitled and rude, with unrealistic expectations, coupled with the hospital's unrealistic expectations, of how many patients we nurses can safely care for. Sometimes I feel like I'm the emissary in the film *300*, being kicked into the bottomless pit for delivering news that is out of my control. I have been physically attacked, spat at, and spat on many times. Once,

I was told, "You bitch, I hope you die of the most painful cancer," spoken by a patient who was dying of cancer. Sometimes I cry myself to sleep at night and get anxious on my way to work, dreading what I may endure that day".

Whitley Cummins: "I think the most stressful thing is not taking home the emotional baggage from work daily. I feel like a hypocrite, always telling my workmates to have boundaries and not take work home or the emotions from home to work, but that's easier said than done. You cannot unsee what has been seen, and you can't unfeel what has been felt. Sometimes closing my eyes and seeing the day's traumas is more painful than being in the moment and witnessing the trauma because my mind starts to play tricks on me. It replays the screams, the blood, the deaths, and the families' broken hearts but with its enhanced version".

Charlie S.: "I'm a final year student nurse... What stresses me out about nursing is the terrible nursing ratio times. Caring for many patients and having so many things to do, I have recently made many mistakes due to feeling overwhelmed and exhausted. It really scares me that one day I will make an unforgivable mistake that may lead me to lose my job or, even worse, cause the death of my patient".

The above statements from Mary, Olivia, Whitley, and Charlie barely scratch the surface of nurses' experiences on their daily encounters at work or even the aftermath when they go home.

It takes a particular type of person to be a nurse—more than just qualifications and grades. You have to care. You have to have an innate caring system within you. But how much should one manage without it clouding judgment or having an effect on mental health? You have to be astute when monitoring and looking after patients, whether it's blood pressure, pulse, respiratory rate, oxygen saturation, or temperature. Observation is one of the most important parts of nursing.

There are other components to nursing, such as monitoring physical and emotional behavior. It's not just what you see and hear as a nurse, which is also a requirement, but what you sense and feel. Trends in patients and behaviors must be recorded and logged with accuracy. There is no space for error; a small mistake could mean the difference between life and death, chronic conditions, or an immediate cure. Mary said, "The most stressful thing about nursing is knowing people's lives are in my hands". Reflecting Olivia's words of frustration, "unrealistic expectations of families coupled with the hospital's unrealistic expectations of how many patients us nurses can safely care for. Sometimes I feel like I'm the emissary in the film *300*, being kicked into the bottomless pit". Charlie's statement is spine-chillingly reminiscent of many nurses' experiences, "I have recently made many mistakes due to feeling overwhelmed and exhausted"

Nurses listen when patients are angry, heartbroken, scared, confused, or in a state of hopelessness to the point of having suicidal thoughts. Nurses listen and sometimes even share their own stories to provide positivity and hope for many patients living through loneliness behind their nylon hospital curtains.

Doubt and fear seep into patients' already wavering thoughts when they hear screams, cries, and whimpers from the adjacent hospital beds. Nurses wear many hats to help, build up, and empower their patients. They wear the hats of counselors, a psychologist, and friends to express friendship in a fraught hospital environment. In 2020 and 2021, nurses

were pushed to the brink at the peak of the COVID-19 pandemic.

I now want you to brace yourself, and I want you to put yourself in the shoes of this particular nurse. You are about to read the assertion of what happens when gross negligence and medical mismanagement manifest in a hospital, resulting in dire consequences. You will be heartbroken and may even sob when you hear what a qualified RN Nevada nurse says about her time and experience working in a New York City hospital at the peak of the COVID-19 pandemic.

Now I must add that what you are about to read has been partly transcribed from a viral YouTube video and partly transcribed when I interviewed this nurse on my podcast, *Kevin Bennett's Trauma*. Both videos together exceed three hours of recording time. So, I have extracted what I believe is relevant to this book and this chapter.

With sleep-deprived eyes and a sniffling red nose due to frantic fits of lamenting, Nurse Nicole Sirotek was on the verge of her second emotional breakdown within only two days. With clear signs of compassion fatigue and secondary trauma, she sat in front of her phone on a cold NYC hospital floor, feeling emotionally drained. I would describe her emotions as helpless and frustrated. Nicole is another nurse who is about to be a whistleblower.

"Hey, everyone," Sirotek says as she starts her video diary. Now taking a deep sigh while shaking her head, she continued, "Great goodness. It is 8:42 New York time, and I got to my regular unit, and they took my patient away—my black guy," she announced, with pursed lips. "And now I'm getting switched units. This is exactly what happened before at the other hospital; as soon as I told somebody, like management, and tried to advocate for my patient, they took the patient away from me, and then they moved me".

Sirotek now takes an even deeper breath with an expression of sadness and anger. She went on, "I legitimately don't even know what to do anymore. Even the advocacy groups don't give a shit about these people. Like, literally, black lives don't matter here. I mean, that's pretty sad that somebody who is white and lives hundreds of miles away from the city gives more of a shit about these people than the actual people in this city". Sirotek proclaimed, eyes open wide, shocked, face drenched with astonishment and dismay.

"I had a complete breakdown yesterday because, you know, I missed an important email to do a revision on my proposal so my proposal got canceled because I was trying to advocate for my patient and talk to management here and get the care that he needs because he's being medically mismanaged... I just had a complete [flipping] breakdown because, you know what, my entire proposal got canceled because I wasted my time advocating for a [flipping] patient who's just going to die anyway; and sure enough, they take the patient away from me, and then almost two hours into the shifts they switch me to another unit". When I interviewed Sirotek, she reported that the patient later died. Every time she saw and experienced mismanagement in one form or another, they switched her to another unit to cover it up.

Further into Sirotek's video, she stated that patients were being reported as dying of COVID-19 when they were actually dying due to medical mismanagement.

Back to Sirotek, "A patient had a heart rate of 40 and the resident started doing chest compressions on him, which is not what you do. You just externally pace them or you give them some atropine, and then I ran in there to stop him from doing chest compressions on somebody with a [flipping] pulse. Then he decides to push epi [epinephrine], he throws some pads on him to defibrillate the guy in bradycardia... He f**king defibrillates him and kills him". Sirotek then ran to report what was happening to the director of nursing, but he shook his head and ignored her. Again, another patient died due to medical mismanagement.

This wasn't the only case Sirotek witnessed, "There was a nurse who placed an NG tube (nasogastric tube, which is designed to be inserted through the nose and down the throat to the stomach) into some guy's lungs and filled his lungs with tube feeding". That tube should have never been placed into his lungs; Sirotek once again witnessed another medical mismanagement and reported it, but again was ignored.

"There was a nurse who confused a long-acting insulin with a short-acting insulin and gave 30 units of a fast-acting insulin and killed the guy". Fatigued and exasperated, Sirotek concluded, "I'm not professing to be a doctor, by any means. But there are, like I said, basic standards of care that we have to do". So, who is Sirotek, and who helps the nurse when the nurse needs help?

Nicole Sirotek is a Nevada nurse who traveled to New York City to help with the coronavirus surge. Once she shared her horrifying accounts of what happened in at least two hospitals at that time, Sirotek was edged out of her job. Then hospitals and agencies across the country that would usually hire her stopped calling her and accepting her applications.

Government agencies then started to investigate and intimidate Sirotek into shutting up; black cars with tinted windows full of agents parked outside her house and followed her around town. Sirotek's family was affected, her income was affected, and friends and colleagues stopped taking her calls. Her nursing credibility was then challenged.

Sirotek told me on my podcast *Kevin Bennett's Trauma,* that she was banned and, at best, restricted across social media platforms. Nicole was told to "stop talking or else" via messages sent to her!

Kevin Bennett's Trauma podcast is about amazing people who are or were struggling with depression, stress, and trauma. On the episode with Nicole Sirotek, she shared even more flabbergasting accounts about her experiences before and after her video went viral. Listening to what she had to endure made me respect her bravery in standing up for what she believed in, knowing that those beliefs and fighting for them could lead to losing everything, including her life.

To be a helpline who extends their job and duty to pursue truth and justice to the point where they may lose everything must be respected.

We have seen this story play out many times before throughout the ages.

Some of the most extreme stories known to date are stories of Jesus on the cross, the fate of Mahatma Gandhi, Martin Luther King Jr., and William Wallace. It is a scary reality that plays itself out over and over again throughout time. People sacrifice themselves for the betterment of humankind. We do not need to go back in history to see the personal sacrifice of people trying to help us, build us up, fix us, and empower us. On a daily basis, our nurses, doctors, firefighters, police officers, and military personnel are helping others while losing their own lives in the process.

A nurse being attacked by his or her patients is not uncommon. Firefighters having stones and bottles thrown at them while trying to put out fires and save lives is not unusual. Military personnel being attacked by the same people they are trying to defend and keep safe, domestically, and internationally, is not uncommon.

I want to share more of what some of our helplines are experiencing so we can reflect on that and be more supportive of them.

Let's continue with surgeons.

Surgeons

Surgeons heal the world, but when they express signs that they need to be healed psychologically, they are in danger of losing their licenses, livelihood, purpose, respect among their peers, and eventually, their desire to live. Globally, many surgeons suffer in silence for these and many other reasons. Let's take a deeper dive and see what these reasons could be.

All surgeons are physicians, but not all physicians are surgeons. So, just for a moment, I want to think about our surgeons separately from the rest of our amazing physicians who tirelessly serve us.

Without our surgeons, there would be no operations, heart transplants, brain surgeries, spine surgeries, or lung surgeries. How would the fight against cancer fare with no surgical oncology?

Without surgeons and surgeries, where would you and I be? Well, if we remain ignorant and close our eyes to what is happening to our surgeons, we could be in a detrimental situation in which the helpline might not be as readily available to patients—us. Appointments could be backed up for weeks, months, and even a year or more. The private sector would become more expensive, and the public health service would be under immense pressure, causing a deleterious chain of events.

Government reports going back to the 1980s have shown that surgeons have incredibly high rates of suicide due to their occupation. What is happening to our surgeons that are causing such high depression and suicide rates? Why are our physicians suffering and even taking their own lives?

Data repeatedly points to surgeons and other physicians being chronically stressed and depressed due to difficult working conditions, heavy workloads, unpredictable schedules, unrealistic expectations, and emotionally charged situations and events.

Surgeons also suffer from a lack of sleep, which leads to irritability, insomnia, burnout, and anxiety. The fear of making detrimental mistakes when those feelings occur could lead to physicians mistakenly harming or—even worse—killing their patients. The fear of malpractice and car accidents due to fatigue are consistently at the forefront of our physicians' minds. Chronic hopelessness can easily lead to suicidal thoughts and behaviors. Many of our physicians fear losing their licenses, so they tend to self-medicate, which then spirals their well-being and mental health even more out of control and into a darker place. Painfully, many of our surgeons and other physicians—regardless of what they are experiencing—are not aware that they are in the midst of a nervous breakdown. The deeper and darker they spiral, the more they lose their sense of reality, the more they withdraw from friends and loved ones, and the more suicide becomes desirable to them.

We seriously need to help and save our physicians. Here's what we need to look for:

1. Behavior of extreme hopelessness
2. Withdrawal from friends and loved ones
3. Consistent conversations and murmurs about death or suicide
4. With feelings of hopelessness, trying to access pills, firearms, or other possible means of suicide
5. Inconsiderate and careless behavior
6. Giving away important belongings, saying goodbye for no logical reason, or both
7. Seeming unsettled, troubled, and not sleeping
8. Excessive alcohol and drug use.

Things work environments should consider or introduce:

1. Have an anonymous early prevention and support system for at-risk physicians.
2. Teach our physicians coping and problem-solving skills to help them manage challenges and concerns in their personal and professional lives.
3. Physicians **MUST NOT** be in fear of sharing their mental illnesses or challenges for fear of strikes against their names or losing their licenses.
4. In some countries, truck drivers must have a mandatory number of hours of sleep within a period. Physicians should have the same mandatory sleep and rest hours to function correctly.
5. Isolation, detachment, the feelings of loneliness, and feelings of hopelessness are the gateway feelings to suicidal ideation and behaviors. I believe there should be nonjudgmental and non-disclosure meetups where physicians can share their pains and journeys

together. Sometimes the helpline needs to help the helpline.

6. Friends, family, and loved ones should have the option of education and training in early warning signs and early prevention.
7. Under investigation, many of our physicians are treated as guilty. We need the law to adhere to the basic human right of being presumed innocent until proven guilty.
8. Work-life balance must be promoted and introduced into the workplace.
9. Reducing the number of health examiners' reports required for health assessments will reduce the workload and anxiety.
10. Introduce case conferencing for all health and performance cases.
11. On-site counseling and therapy services. Having on-site therapists will be cheaper than losing physicians to sickness and death. Our helpline truly needs help!

Ambulance Paramedics

Ambulance paramedics tend to get verbally abused and physically attacked by their patients.

They are also exposed to the worst kinds of human pain and suffering. What they see and experience in a day is more horrifying than the average person's worst nightmare.

For the best part, paramedics are unappreciated and looked down upon by the hierarchies in their sector and sometimes even the general public. As the first responders, they are the first contact with victims and the victims' family members. Sometimes the emotional connection with the victim or their family will cause secondary trauma to the paramedics, can you imagine the traumatizing horrific injuries paramedics see and experience?

Ambulance paramedics work irregular hours, which can cause personal and professional problems. It is not uncommon for these emergency workers to have high-stress levels when dealing with sickness, traumas, and deaths. The people who save us from ourselves are in grave danger from our pain and suffering. The ones who are the first to save us could be the last to be saved by us.

Globally, many of our ambulance paramedics struggle with the following while serving us:

1. Mixed moods and emotions
2. Compassion fatigue
3. PTSD
4. Depression
5. Alcohol abuse
6. Drug abuse
7. Chronic perceived stress
8. Feeling overwhelmed and burned out
9. Self-blame and guilt
10. Repeatedly experiencing traumatic events
11. Avoiding distressing thoughts, feelings, or external reminders of events and patients
12. Loss of interest in sex, romance, and activities
13. Aggressiveness, recklessness, or self-destructive behavior
14. Sleeping problems and sleep disorders
15. Hypervigilance, constantly assessing potential threats around them
16. Secondary trauma

Here are some solutions for helping our ambulance paramedics in some countries, but not all:

1. The option of taking a paid leave of absence when suffering from chronic stress, burnout, or PTSD
2. Anonymous early prevention and support systems for at-risk ambulance paramedics
3. Education in coping methods and problem-solving skills for managing exposure to traumatic events

Social Workers

Social workers tend to be seen as the bearers of bad news in most communities. According to the British Association of Social Workers, 10% of all social workers have been attacked more than ten times throughout their careers. When they take action, they are deemed wicked and the destroyers of homes and families. When they don't go far enough, they are penalized and looked down upon by everyone—including their superiors. Social workers tend to have unrealistic caseloads, and government bureaucracies exacerbating their situation. When things go wrong, social workers don't have a voice or the autonomy to represent themselves.

Social workers are on the frontline of government decision-making. When the decision-makers make bad decisions, our frontline social workers are the ones who suffer. Many social workers entered their profession because of their previous traumas. They are not in their job for money or recognition. They are there to stop and fight against cruelty and danger to vulnerable people. After becoming a social worker, they experience and witness traumatic events that could trigger them or tip them over the edge.

Our social workers tend not to be recognized globally as advocates for our communities. Instead, many of our social workers carry the burdened cross of cultural, community, and family resentment. But how important are our social workers to us and our communities?

Without our social workers, the vulnerable in our society would be in grave danger. Who helps the voiceless social workers when government bureaucracies wrap them up in red tape? Social workers get the backlash when governments make bad decisions behind closed doors. But what do our social workers experience when working with the vulnerable in our communities? Social workers often hear harrowing stories of what their clients endured, such as neglect, torture, abuse, and molestation. They see videos and photos of horrific injuries, death, domestic violence, and sexual abuse. Nothing is more painful than looking into the eyes of innocent children and then discovering that their innocence has been raped away from them. All that social workers see, hear, smell, and witness can cause them to suffer from compassion fatigue.

Compassion fatigue is a combination of secondary traumatic stress and burnout. To understand compassion fatigue, we must first look at secondary traumatic stress. Secondary traumatic stress is caused when a person, such as a social worker, is deeply affected and traumatized by the trauma or suffering of the victim they are working with. Secondary traumatic stress is like PTSD but without direct exposure to the trauma itself. One of the reasons for secondary traumatic stress is the constant exposure to suffering, murder, loss, and pain.

Burnout is physical and emotional exhaustion. When our helplines suffer from burnout, they feel tired and drained for most of their day. They feel overwhelmed, helpless, and defeated and have self-doubt. They start to procrastinate, not wanting to face another case or victim. They detach from friends, family members, and even their bodies. Their formerly positive outlook turns into cynical darkness, melancholy, and anxiety. Tearful moments become more frequent than happy smiles. What was once a career to do good and make positive change turns into an imprisoned mind and a traumatized body.

We need to have enough understanding and awareness to see the signs when our social workers are teetering on the edge of a mental health crisis.

Here are some characters to watch out for:

1. Loss of enthusiasm for work
2. Heightened levels of irritability with friends, loved ones, work colleagues, and clients
3. A decrease in energy and productivity
4. Inability to sleep and mood swings
5. Engaging in unhealthy stress responses, such as overeating, alcohol abuse, or drug abuse
6. Difficulty maintaining focus and memory problems
7. Physical, mental, and emotional exhaustion
8. Isolation from coworkers, friends, and family members
9. Loss of accomplishment or pride in work
10. Making dangerous statements about giving up, or not wanting to be alive anymore.

Dentists

Have you ever wondered what life would be like without our dentists?

First, we wouldn't know where to start with our dental health and oral hygiene. Our journey would begin with bad breath and decaying teeth. Constant oral neglect, bad breath, and decaying teeth would gradually escalate into tooth loss and gum disease. The diseases of the mouth would escalate from oral diseases to illnesses in other parts of the body. It would only be a matter of time until bad dental health became heart disease, diabetes, stroke, and even cancer. We need our dentists, but what do many of us do to our dentists who serve us and save our lives daily? Let's look and see...

We were taught from childhood that sticks and stones may break our bones, but words can never hurt us. That's so untrue. Negative words, comments, and remarks can provoke mental health problems. Bones can heal from sticks and stones. However, people do not always recover from threats, negative criticisms, and being told they are not worthy or good enough. Words vibrate into frequencies that transform into negative self-talk, feelings, and behaviors.

Dentists are constantly being told by their patients that they hate them. It's not uncommon for multiple patients to express their hatred for their dentist on a typical day. "Hey Martin, I hate you and your bloody treatments. It feels like you are raping my mouth. Be flipping gentle!"

"No offense Mrs. Patel, but I hate you dentists with a passion".

These kinds of statements are what dentists hear daily. It may be said with tongue-in-cheek humor to some patients, but energy doesn't play tongue-in-cheek games; the problem is that these kinds of statements are offensive to dentists.

They take it very personally when the people they serve say disparaging things to them. It's not just the words declared but the negative energy delivered. Dentists are not just the bearers of bad news; they *are* the bad news for many of their patients. An anxious, frustrated, angry, fearful patient transfers that energy over to their dentists, and, like a sponge, their dentists absorb the electron energy.

From one patient to another throughout the day, dentists take negativity home with them every night. They can't wash it off in the shower or sleep it off at night. It doesn't disappear in their dreams, and tea and coffee in the morning does not soak up the anxiety, worry, and fear as they dread facing yet another day.

Dentists tend to be very high achievers—most are perfectionists. Where there is the pursuit of perfection, by default, insecurities, and disappointments are lurking somewhere nearby. From dental school to working or owning their dental clinic, dentists put a lot of pressure on themselves when dealing with surgery and people's lives.

There is no room for an off day when dentists can make big or small mistakes, but mistakes are inevitable when tiredness or exhaustion seeps in.

Some patients are very litigious, and dentists are fully aware of it. The fear of being sued or given bad reviews and criticized across social media—sometimes with their name and picture up— is enough to raise one's blood pressure and anxiety levels. If that's not enough, many dentists also work alone and in isolation. Being in too much isolation can be emotionally dangerous for anyone.

But here's the thing: when you are stressed, worried, and depressed, these feelings and emotions can lead to sinister thoughts and feelings. Have you ever taken a step back and looked at the size of the average dental treatment room? Most of them are no bigger than a prison cell with the same mundane windows and colors. Now imagine being in this dull, confined space for hours on end, every day, for most of your adult career. Then there's the added pressure and stress of overwhelming paperwork, updated equipment, new training and technology, and government guidelines. Contrary to popular belief, most dentists are not sitting on a treasure trove and living in a mansion on the hills. Furthermore, many of them are still paying off their student loans, debts, and the costs of dental instruments and equipment.

Traumatized patients see and experience a dental treatment room differently than how other patients see and experience them. When the needles and drills come out, the screams and tension in the 'surgery cell' intensify, the dental chair becomes an electric chair, the dentist is the executioner, and drilling the teeth can cause the same bodily reaction as electrocution. No dentist wants to hurt anyone they are helping, and patients know deep down that dentists don't want to torture their patients. So where does it go wrong? Many people don't know that the mind recognizes that dental appointments are required for a better quality of life, while the body feels, stores, and recognizes only the pain and suffering. Trauma stored in the body can result in PTSD for the patient, which can lead to the patient's mental illness if not released. The patient's trauma then transfers over to the dentist as secondary trauma. This secondary trauma results in the following (in no particular order):

1. Feeling guilty
2. Impostor syndrome—feeling unworthy, unskilled, and incompetent
3. Emotional exhaustion
4. Insomnia and headaches

5. Nighttime teeth grinding
6. Difficulty with connections, intimacy, and sex
7. Increased anxiety
8. Difficulty sleeping
9. Lack of appetite or binge eating
10. Frustration and anger at home and work
11. Resentment toward their demands in their professional and personal affairs
12. Irritable bowel syndrome (IBS)
13. Rashes or breakouts
14. Dreading to go to work to perform treatments on specific patients due to how they may legally or violently respond
15. Negative self-image and self-perception
16. Emotional, psychological, and physical pain
17. Talking less and isolation at home and work
18. Problems in relationships
19. Depression
20. Emotional numbness and detachment from others
21. Feeling hopeless
22. Suicidal thoughts and talking about death with others.

Police Officers

Police officers are often seen as the enemy because of the bad press and the bad apples within the police force globally. We record and make reports about them when the corrupt cops are doing their worst. The corruption in law enforcement must be rooted out, and the general public must feel safe and protected from those hired to protect us. However, there are also fantastic police officers who keep our communities and societies safe and together.

They root out the bad, the wicked, and the evil in our society. They save us and protect us from tragic events, either at the hands of others or by our own hands. Sometimes our pain, mistrust, and fear of law enforcement could make us look past life without the good law-abiding officers who contribute to our society daily.

So, what would our lives be like without our police officers?

First, nothing would deter the bad and the wicked from committing crimes. In a very short period, there would be anarchy in the streets. There would be home invasions, blatant robberies, and murders. Businesses and people's livelihoods would be threatened, and violent attacks and abuse of the worst kinds would skyrocket.

Eventually, self-government and vigilantes would appear, and the weak and the vulnerable would-be prey to the strong and the dominant. What was once a democracy would quickly turn into tyranny.

As you are aware, we need a police service to sift the bad and the dangerous out of our society.

Police officers and military personnel are two of the three occupations (firefighters being the third) in which the employees are asked to face physical dangers and put their lives on the line throughout their careers.

The army is the helpline for our country, and the police are the helpline for our society.

I have an interesting question for you: Who helps our security when our security is feeling insecure?

When these sectors of our helplines need help, it tends to cause significant disruption and a ripple effect of insecurity throughout our homes, communities, country, and even the world.

There is a saying that “misery loves company”. I say, “Frequency loves frequency”. Many employees join the police force or the military because of a traumatic event or trauma they have experienced or witnessed in one form or another.

Let me explain.

There are two types of people who normally want extreme change in the world. There are hurt people who hurt other people. They want to see the pain in others match the pain in themselves. They are the Adolf Hitler type of personality. Then there are hurt people who heal other people. These people are like Nelson Mandela-type personalities. Mandela used his pain of apartheid to promote forgiveness and togetherness worldwide. I don’t believe most hurt people who hurt other people set out to be that way. I believe most of them cannot overcome the pain they experienced, so they live in an electron frequency of hurt, anger, depression, suicidal thoughts, and destructive behaviors.

The frequencies of pain are bad enough. But when a lower vibrational frequency is coupled with an angry mind, the hurt people who hurt other people start to plot their first sinister plans like Hitler. Hurt people who heal other people experience the same electron frequencies. However, their thought processes are different. They devise plans to feel better and do better for the world, like Mandela.

Most of our helplines started their journeys because of an experience they encountered directly or indirectly. Doctors, nurses, firefighters, police officers, military personnel, or anyone could be a Hitler or a Mandela if their traumas are not treated. All of our helplines want change because of a previous or current trauma they are trying to figure out.

You will tend to discover that people who are our societies' savers or destroyers have treated or untreated emotional traumas.

We must treat our police officers' feelings, emotions, and minds by investigating and investing in their traumas.

So, what happens when the traumatized helpline goes untreated?

More police officers die by their own hands than are killed in the line of duty. According to the King's Centre for Military Health Research, "New research, carried out by King's College London and Imperial College London with a large sample of over 40,000 police officers, found that around 10% of police officers reported symptoms of probable depression compared to approximately 4% who were reporting symptoms of probable Post-Traumatic Stress Disorder (PTSD) ".

The report also found that "probable anxiety disorders were more common than probable PTSD (8.5% vs. 3.9%)".

In the same report, it found that "poor mental health was related to changes in blood pressure". If not managed, high blood pressure (hypertension) can lead to disabilities, poor quality of life, a deadly heart attack, or even a stroke.

Many police officers have recurring nightmares about what they have seen or experienced. Insomnia is the aftermath, which then leads to them becoming irritated and quick to anger in their professional and personal lives. Many police officers globally say they receive zero supervisor support for their depression. Some say their supervisors are suffering even more than they are.

I asked a police officer about occupational stress and depression. He said, "There is no place to show weakness or vulnerability in the Met [Metropolitan Police]". He continued, "We smile, go for drinks after work, and start again the next day". I asked, "What happens when you can't start again the next day?" "Oh," he said, nodding his head back and raising his eyebrows. "That's called burnout. I have one of those every few months. But I have to drag myself back to work and deal with conflicts and car accidents, domestic violence, deaths, and tragedy overall". He tucked his hands into his bulletproof vest and shrugged his shoulders while gently kicking an invisible ball. "We are expected to look normal and remain sane in the process of our madness," he concluded.

Police officers are torn between their annual leave and taking sick days due to their depression and PTSD. Too many days off could lead to pay reductions or even worse in certain countries. There have been cases in which police officers were unable to cope to the point where they applied for disability retirement but were refused by senior health practitioners.

Many of their stories ended tragically; they gave up and then committed suicide.

Due to the nature of police officers' jobs, reports and studies have shown that years of dangerous threats and physical confrontations with arrestees have resulted in many officers suffering from hypervigilance and paranoia. Even shopping with their families or clubbing with their friends could result in panic attacks.

In 2010, suicide was the 10th leading cause of death in the United States.

The 2017 National Survey on Drug Use and Health stated that 4.3% of adults reported severe thoughts of suicide in that past year.

In 2018, more than 48,000 Americans died by suicide, and almost half of the suicides were caused using a firearm.

The nonprofit organization Blue H.E.L.P (Honoring the Service of Law Enforcement Officers Who Died by Suicide) records show that in 2017, 124 law enforcement officers were lost to suicide. In 2018, there was a rise of 25.8% to 156 law enforcement officer suicides. Another increase of 26% happened in 2019, with 197 suicides. In 2020, there was a decline of suicides by 27.4% to 143 suicides. In 2021, there was another decline to 138, down by 3.5% of law enforcement suicides.

Let's hope that the numbers decline even further, but I hypothesize that COVID-19 was also within that period of the decline in suicides. The lockdown may have contributed to the reduction in workplace stress and suicidal ideation. I don't know yet; time will reveal all, so let's see.

The Law Enforcement *Officer Suicide: 2020 Report to Congress* indicated that police officers' have higher exposure to stress and trauma, which makes them more susceptible to suffer from post-traumatic stress disorder [PTSD], depression, anxiety, cardiovascular disease, and experience addiction problems. Now factor in their access to firearms; it doesn't take a rocket scientist to see how events can end. Police officers are at higher risk of suicide than the general population. In fact, "at least one study has suggested that suicidal ideation is more prevalent among law enforcement officers than the general population". If a person with mental health problems is armed with a weapon, they are a danger to themselves and others!

A split-second decision can result in someone's life being taken away from them and their loved ones when a stressed and depressed mind cannot decipher between a threat and a benign person. It unbalances the world. If we are not careful, the electron spiritual entity of FEAR will govern us all. We need to fight this FEAR with the proton spiritual consciousness of LOVE.

We need to help, build up, and empower our police officers, or everyone will suffer, including the general public – you and I.

I have some suggestions:

1. An anonymous early prevention and support system for at-risk police officers.
2. Educate officers in coping and problem-solving skills to help them manage challenges and concerns in their personal and professional lives.
3. Have an on-site counselor at every police station. It will be more cost-effective than having police officers take paid leave and mental health early retirement.
4. Build a group message platform where police officers can express their fears, concerns, and trauma. Officers could choose to do this anonymously.
5. Friends, family, and loved ones should have the option of taking education and training in early warning signs and early suicide prevention classes.
6. Work-life balance must be promoted and introduced into the workplace.
7. Wellness programs should be introduced into the workplace.

8. Peer support is significant in helping with feelings of detachment, loneliness, and isolation.
9. Give police officers access to culturally competent mental health services.
10. Each police officer should be required to have a mandatory counseling session at least once every quarter.
11. The power of prayer. Your knees are made to bend and adjust; we must drop to our knees and pray for change, health, and LOVE.

A conclusion for you to ponder, here's a very short story.

Once upon a time, on one of the coldest winter nights recorded in Russian history, a man lost deep in the boreal forest, barely equipped for the freezing winter night, holding the last of his fire torch to keep him warm, stumbled across a group of wooden sticks and logs.

As his torch rapidly burned down; he frantically turned to the group of wooden sticks and logs and said, "Hey, logs, if you heat me because I am freezing, I will light you with the fire torch I am holding". The logs responded, "If you light us first, we will heat you and keep you warm throughout the night". But the man disagreed and stubbornly said, "NO, serve me first, and I will light you after". The two sides debated all night until the man died of hypothermia.

Sometimes, we must serve our helpline first before our helpline can serve us in return. I believe we need to light the logs of our helpline before our helpline can warm us up. Servitude and empowerment go both ways.

Farm workers

Farm workers are not the backbone of our societies. They are not even the backbone of our communities. They are the backbone of our planet. Without farm workers, life would stop, markets and supermarkets would close within weeks, factories would close before the markets, and restaurants would close even sooner. Unprepared people would stop functioning within a matter of a week, then 28 days later, the death toll would begin. Life as we know it would drastically change forever. Farmworkers suffer frequent crop failures due to pest attacks, crop diseases, and the unpredictability of rainfall.

Farm Workers tend to suffer a very high percent rate of health problems and relationship breakups due to their lifestyles, financial problems, and loss of work. Hopelessness is the gateway emotion to suicide, and farmworkers have an extremely high rate of feeling helpless and hopeless.

Let's picture what hopelessness looks like through the eyes of a farmer.

Across the world, there is a generational legacy regarding farming, farms, and farmers. Farms and farming are more than just agriculture—they're a form of identity for farmers. Farms tend to be handed down from fathers to children through many generations. There is immense stress and pressure on farmers not to lose their farms. Farmers carry an unrealistic legacy to maintain their farms among their peers and communities. Losing their farms is almost impossible for them to bear.

A farmer losing their farm is a farmer losing their identity. It is like discovering you are not the color you thought you were or finding out after 50 years that your parents are not your birth parents. It is the equivalent of you being responsible for your last 100 years of generational legacy and losing it all over a poker game.

Farmers are, for the most part, isolated away from their friends and family members when working the farm. They are very proud people; they work in silence, and suffer in silence. For some reason, farmers are taught from a very young age not to complain and just to suck it up and get on with it. That's what their fathers and their fathers' fathers did before them. Farmers feel overwhelming shame if crops fail or they don't have enough money to provide for their families. Farmers tend to have little to no concept of the world outside and away from their farms. Mornings become days, and days become onerous nights.

In India, farmers are dying by suicide at such an astronomical rate that India now has a suicide epidemic, with more than 300,000 farmer suicides since 1995.

A September 2020 article published on the site DownToEarth by Rajit Sengupta, entitled "Every day, 28 people dependent on farming die by suicide in India," shocked me to the core. This article alone broke my heart, and what I researched after reading this article almost brought me to tears.

The article reports that 7.4 percent of suicides in India are people in the farming sector, according to the *Accidental Deaths and Suicides in India* Report 2019 by the National Crime Records Bureau. This is only slightly lower than the number of deaths by suicide in 2018.

So, what the hell is going on over there? Sadden and astonished, I had to read even more articles, reports, and statistics, I then watched over thirty hours of documentaries. I eventually discovered another article and video on the platform called The *Insider* entitled "India has a farmer suicide epidemic, and farmers are protesting new laws they fear will make things worse," written by Yasmina Hatem, Lisa Desai, and Mark Abadi. It reads, "India has some of the highest farmer suicide rates in the world, with more than 10,000 deaths yearly, and numbers expected to have reached a record high in 2020. In Punjab, three to four farmer suicides are reported in the local news daily.

"Across India, farmers are demanding an end to new laws they say are not just threatening their livelihoods, but costing lives.

"Protests that erupted in Punjab have spread throughout the country as farmers demand a complete rollback of the three laws passed in September. Collectively, the laws deregulate the buying and selling of agricultural goods, exposing farmers to the uncertainties of an open market and potential exploitation by corporations.

"Meanwhile, record numbers of farmers in India are committing suicide, and experts fear the farming laws could drive even more people to the brink.

"The new laws that they have passed, we call them death warrants of farmers and laborers," farmer Kewal Singh of Punjab said.

So, what are the three farm bills?

1. Farmers' Produce Trade and Commerce (Promotion and Facilitation) Bill, 2020
2. Farmers (Empowerment and Protection) Agreement on Price Assurance and Farm Services Bill, 2020
3. Essential Commodities (Amendment) Bill, 2020

Because these three bills are very complex and have historical significance with many moving parts, I will address them in a later book.

Here are some suggestions:

1. Governments globally must set aside an annual budget to secure cultivation, agriculture farming, and farmers.
2. A further investment must be made in mental health support and emotional well-being programs for farmers.
3. Kickstart investments need to be made to incentivize farmers to introduce new crops and new ways of farming to follow the changing eating and dietary habits.
4. Loan sharks in many countries (including India) prey upon vulnerable farmers and their lands. Farmers and their lands must be protected at all costs.
5. Mental health education and training must be available to farmers and their loved ones.
6. Climate change is destroying agriculture and massively affecting farms. Something needs to be done to protect agriculture.
7. A farmer's charity should be set up for visiting lonely and depressed farmers. The goal would be to talk, inspire and comfort farmers.
8. Governments must protect farmers from being priced down by corporations.
9. There needs to be easy access to support farmers and counseling for vulnerable farmers in rural areas.

Teachers

I believe that one of the greatest songs of all time is Whitney Houston's 1986 number-one hit song, "Greatest Love of All".

In that song, Houston is explicit about the key to a successful future for our children and society. The key word in her song is "teach". Children are our future, and our teachers are at the helm of their education, inspiration, and sense of pride. When parents and guardians send their children to school, they expect results, and rightfully so. Teachers are the epitome of the helpline; this is exactly what this book is about. Without our teachers, what would society look like? What would our children's future look like? What would our higher education look like?

Without our teachers, there would be no math education, which means no accountants, financial analysts, economists, or physicians.

Without our teachers, there would be no science education, which means no biologists, chemists, engineers, or veterinarians.

Without our teachers, there would be no geography lessons, which means no commercial and residential surveyors, environmental lawyers, weather forecasters, or landscape architects.

Teachers are the gatekeepers to our generational future. If our gatekeepers are not in good stead, our future is bound to be in jeopardy. But let's look at our gatekeepers and see if they are being kept, nurtured, and in good stead.

Teachers are intrinsically loving and caring people. They do not choose to be teachers to become financially wealthy; they want to help, build up, and empower people. But it's very hard to be positive and loving when experiencing stress, emotional exhaustion, anxiety, and depression.

According to The Office for Standards in Education, Children's Services and Skills (Ofsted), the teacher well-being research report published on July 22, 2019, stated that "Working hours in schools and FES (further education and skills) providers are long. Full-time school teachers reported working 51 hours on average during the given week, while senior leaders worked even longer, 57 hours on average. Our findings show that teachers spend less than half of their time teaching, while lesson planning, marking, and administrative tasks take up much of their non-teaching time. Many respondents in both sectors do not have enough time to do the important aspects of their job. Therefore, they work in their free time: evenings, weekends, or annual leave".

Back to the Ofsted report:

"The main causes of heavy workload are:

1. The volume of administrative tasks
2. The volume of marking
3. Staff shortages
4. Lack of support from external specialist agencies such as for special educational needs and disabilities (SEND) or behavior
5. Challenging behavior of pupils
6. Changes to external examinations
7. Frequently changing government policies and regulations
8. In some cases, lack of skills or training"

Due to the above causes, teachers suffer from burnout, anxiety, a lack of sleep, and are prone to infections and illnesses. But it doesn't stop there. Parents want the best for their children, and sometimes their passion for their children's education spills over to teacher abuse and violence. When schools lack funding, teachers are expected to do more with less. That alone can cause even more stress and depression.

Student and family poverty can also cause pressure in the classroom. Teachers of yesteryear never needed to police children and their families. Now teachers must be highly diligent and report neglect and potential abuse of their pupils, which strains their relationships with parents, caregivers, and pupils.

The voices of our teachers, like those of our social workers and nurses, are muted by bureaucracy and politics.

I've been talking to and helping teachers since 2009. Over that time, I've heard some horrifying stories of teachers' experiences with depression and attempts at suicide because of their feelings of stress, melancholy, depression, and hopelessness.

A ship tends to sink when water enters, and people mentally drown when electron feelings do the same. Like the ship, water must remain on the outside, and negativity must do the same for our mental health. We must not invite the feelings and behaviors of doubt, worry, and anger into our world. It will only lead to sleep deprivation, fatigue, weight gain or loss, dark thoughts about self-harm, or even worse.

I will start with the following, and I suggest you add to this list with a plan of action.

1. Our teachers need to get sufficient sleep. A sick, burned-out, depressed teacher is helpful to no one, not even themselves.

2. Teachers should get mental health support, a therapist, counseling, and make regular visits to their doctor.
3. Teachers must be actively listened to, and changes must be made due to the Ofsted findings and report.
4. Teachers need to be able to spend more time with their friends and family members. We are social beings, so being around happy friends and family is vital for our psychological and spiritual health.
5. Teachers must be more financially compensated when given extra workloads and responsibilities.
6. Teachers should receive counseling support and open, frank discussion platforms to voice their concerns and problems.
7. Teachers need to feel protected to carry out their job without fearing violence and abuse from others. There needs to be zero tolerance for violence against teachers.
8. Parents should be aware of the roles of pupil safeguarding and government responsibilities that teachers must enact. Teachers are not the enemy and should not be treated as such by some parents or caregivers.
9. Early identification of SEND should be consistent throughout the country. SEND must be explored to ensure teachers have the proper support and help for that cohort of pupils.
10. Teachers need to know when to go home from work. They need a decent work-life balance. Teachers need to maintain relationships with their friends and loved ones. They also need that time away from work to maintain a proton mental health.

Our Helplines

Please see the table below and have a good look at the different occupations with the highest stress, depression, and suicide rates. I have collated this list from many different sources. If you want more information on my sources from this list, please refer to the Notes and References section at the back of this book.

When reading about our support workers and other professionals covered in this book, you may have noticed that they all have some things in common. They are all occupations of servitude. Most professionals in our covered occupations are either disrespected, hated, or heavily disliked by the same people they serve—the general public. But it doesn't just stop there. Most of these professionals either went into their selected fields because of previous emotional traumas, or will have traumas by the time they leave their occupation. It's still a hypothesis, but I believe that an occupation's vibrational negative or positive frequencies attracted the person well before they knew they wanted that particular job or career. Their pull toward their occupation is based on their vibrational energy. The moment their stress, depression, or trauma, takes control of their life, their job or career becomes preordained.

But what is trauma? And why do traumas have such an effect on people? Trauma is an overwhelmingly painful experience that the mind and body have difficulty dealing with and processing. Emotional trauma is built-up trapped negative energy that stores in the body's memory. Trauma in the body happens when our physical and psychological abilities to respond effectively to a threat, harm, or danger becomes too overwhelmed, helpless, and powerless to deal with that tragedy.

When trauma is trapped in the body, the body will react under the immense stress and pressure of being unable to release the negative energy. That then causes neck pain, back pain, migraines, headaches, syndromes such as IBS, and even diseases. Traumatic events are unique to us all. What may be a tragedy to me, maybe thrilling to you! A traumatizing experience that isn't dealt with will then form into trauma which can prevent a person from wanting to receive or express love, passion, joy, and fun; the effects of trauma will make the person want to forget, push away, and erase anything connected to the trauma they experienced. This is where drugs and alcohol abuse can easily seep into a person's life.

Drugs and alcohol, for many people, numb their excruciating emotional and physical pain. Self-harm also becomes an 'option.' Trauma can lead people to isolate themselves from their friends, loved ones, and life itself, leading to suicidal thoughts and behaviors. People who have trauma tend to be disconnected from their bodies and intimacy. Yoga, tapping techniques, and emotional freedom can reconnect people with their bodies and intimacy.

Where there is a trauma, there was once the feeling of helplessness. Helplessness derives from the inability to effectively defend or protect oneself or others in a traumatic situation. When people feel helpless, they tend to feel powerless and hopeless. Hopelessness can then lead to giving up on life itself—not wanting to be here anymore, not wanting to be a 'burden' to others.

As a society and even among many cultures and communities globally, we try to sweep our traumas under the rug, hoping they will somehow sort themselves out and disappear. When in fact, traumas don't just sort themselves out, and traumas never just disappear. Built-up, trapped negative energy must be carefully and strategically released from the body and the psyche.

For example, the traumas of rape, sexual abuse, and child abuse don't somehow sort themselves out and disappear. For the abused child, the child turns into an adult while the trauma remains the same age. For victims of rape and sexual abuse, the electron frequency of the trauma vibrates and attracts other electron frequencies through people, relationships, circumstances, events, situations, and occupations. Misery loves company, and frequency loves frequency.

The transgenerational traumas of the holocaust and slavery don't just somehow sort themselves out and disappear. Unless people deal with the negative energy of their transgenerational trauma, that trauma is stored within them and then passed down to their children, and their children's children, etc. People then unintentionally end up in negative vibrational relationships with friends and lovers. They also get drawn into unhealthy environments, professions, and hobbies. That will then cause them even more pain and harm, repeating the negative cycle of their mothers and fathers.

Problems start to occur when people in positions of power who haven't dealt with their emotional traumas are given guns and legislative control over the general public. This is where gross misconduct, racism, bigotry, corruption, and murder become the new normal in society.

This is where the relationships between the general public and police officers, politicians, military personnel, social workers, financial service workers, and even lawyers start to fracture. When my ex-girlfriend and I broke up after discovering her cheating, I said, "I trust you, but I don't trust your emotional trauma. Your trauma uses your body as a host to express itself via promiscuity." I also believe this to be true with many (not all) of our police officers, politicians, military personnel, financial service workers, and lawyers. They are good people with good intentions, but undealt trauma will use their minds and bodies as hosts to make bad decisions and see the world in a dark, sinister way. Our fight is not against our helpline professionals and workers; it's against the parasite of trauma living within some of them. Here's a list of occupations where traumas tend to take host in people and cause havoc in their lives:

Stress by Occupation	Depression by Occupation	Suicide by Occupation
Enlisted military personnel	Nurses	Surgeons
Firefighters	Nursing home and childcare workers	Medical doctors
Physicians	Social workers	Dentists
Airline pilots	Healthcare workers	Police officers
Police officers	Artists, entertainers, writers	Veterinarians
Event managers	Teachers	Financial services
Senior corporate executives	Administrative support staff	Real estate agents
Taxi drivers	Maintenance and grounds workers	Electricians
Construction workers	Financial advisers and accountants	Lawyers
Paramedics	Salespeople	Farmers
Financial analysts	Food service staff	Pharmacists
Sales managers	Construction workers	Military personnel and veterans
Mental health counselors		Scientists
		Construction workers

CHAPTER 4

THE 7 BRAIN SYSTEMS - UNDERSTANDING MIND AND EMOTIONS

Do you have a solution for when you are in a dark place?

I am incredibly passionate about how people receive active knowledge on how planets, stars, prayers, and intentions can change one's life and circumstances forever.

It will be my life achievement and success if I have somehow persuaded you through reading this book that suicide is not the only way out and that living with depression is not the only way to live. Stress is not your last name and should not be adopted into your life like a surrogate for your happiness.

I would like to put forward another compelling reason fervently, but this time, about the power of your brain and mind. I would like to convince you somehow that you can make yourself happy regardless of your current circumstances or any other previous traumatic experiences that may be negatively controlling your daily life.

To do this, I had to research neurologists, psychologists, people of faith, nutritionists, counselors, therapists, and neuroscientists. I eventually discovered a neuroscientist and psychobiologist by the name of Dr. Jaak Panksepp, this man and his discoveries blew my mind away.

Dr. Jaak Panksepp was born in Estonia on June 5, 1943. His family escaped the post–World War II Soviet occupation by moving to the United States. In 1940, Estonia was formally annexed by the Soviet Union under the rule of Joseph Stalin. Tens of thousands of Estonians were forced into the war by Adolf Hitler and Joseph Stalin. Many of them were killed, and even more were traumatized. I'm assuming Jaak's parents fled the tyranny in Estonia to give their son and their family a better life. Panksepp initially studied electrical engineering, then switched to clinical psychology in the early 1960s. He worked in the back ward of a psychiatric hospital as an undergraduate student, where he saw "human tragedies" he said in a TEDx Talk.

In the same 2013 TEDxRainier Talk, Panksepp proclaimed, "No one knew what emotions were... how we get these feelings. So, I shifted to neuroscience—first clinical psychology, then neuroscience. That is the only path to understanding how we feel." Panksepp looked sternly into the packed auditorium with well over two thousand people gazing back, mesmerized by every word he said.

Panksepp is special. He is exceptional. He is the epitome of a game-changer. Panksepp experienced massive pain many times throughout his life, which further propelled him to understand how to combat depression and trauma. One time in particular, as a single parent, Panksepp experienced the death of his 16-year-old daughter.

You wouldn't be mistaken if you thought he looked like Santa Claus with a short beard, a warm-toned voice, and a receding hairline. His aura is one of trustworthiness, and his body language exudes an air of calm. Panksepp had been inspired by pioneers such as Walter Rudolf Hess, who shared the 1949 Nobel Prize in Physiology or Medicine alongside Portuguese neurologist Egas Moniz.

At a previous talk at the University of Notre Dame in 2010, Panksepp stated, "I decided the only way to understand human emotions was to understand animal emotions."

In Zurich, Switzerland, in the 1930s, Hess was the first to discover the emotion of ANGER in cats (this emotion is capitalized because it's being referred to from a scientific perspective). However, that wasn't what he was looking for or what his Nobel Prize was for. He received his Nobel Prize for mapping the areas of the brain involved in the control of the internal organs of mammals. Hess initially set out to look for the nervous system in the brain that controlled the viscera, stomach, and other internal organs in mammals.

Hess eventually discovered that the "autonomic nervous system" controlled mammals' heart rate, digestion, and blood pressure. Hess electrically stimulated different parts of the brain in animals, and over a period of time, he found that by probing certain areas of the brain, the animals' heart rates would increase. Probing other parts of the brain would increase their blood pressure or increase and decrease salivation. Hess also discovered something huge—when he electrically stimulated the same brain regions, the cats he was experimenting on behaved angrily. This discovery changed the medical profession forever.

But let's not celebrate his achievements too quickly! Before he could be recognized for his discovery of animal emotions, there was a problem that he had first to overcome that took many years.

Hess feared his work and reputation would have been negatively critiqued, marginalized, or, at best, restricted if he wrote about his discovery that cats have feelings. Back in the 1920s and 1930s, American behaviorists would have shunned or ousted Hess for his discovery. The focus was on the behavior of mammals at that time in the 1900s, but not the emotions of cats, nor were they ready for such discoveries.

The American behaviorists back then controlled the American academic psychology world, and they weren't interested in their beliefs and work being challenged by some Swiss physiologist. Plus, they didn't believe in anything they couldn't see, and feelings couldn't be seen in an animal's head.

Hess believed this, so he changed the term 'ANGER' in cats to the term 'SHAM RAGE.' According to Panksepp, "SHAM RAGE is like a puppet pretending they're angry. So it's just a motor manifestation and not the psychological component." Years later, once Hess retired and was writing his last books toward the end of his life, he then stated in his autobiographical work that he was sorry for not being honest with the public. "He was not true to his convictions," Panksepp said. He went on to say, "He said he always thought the animals were angry. But he did not want his work pushed to the side by the American behaviorists."

Panksepp, inspired by Hess's previous discoveries and accomplishments, decided to build upon Hess's work years later. But Panksepp wanted to take it further; first, he would experiment on rats instead of cats.

"That was one of the first experiments I replicated in another species. Instead of cats, I did rats.," Panksepp said in a *Braincast* interview, "And I found that the anatomy of the rat ANGER system was similar to what Hess and others had described in cats. But I went one step further." Panksepp said, now more ardent, "I asked the animal, 'Do you like this feeling? Do you dislike this feeling? Or perhaps it doesn't matter to you?'"

Listening to this part of Panksepp's *Braincast* interview confused me. How do you ask a rat how it feels? They don't talk or communicate in our language, do they? I tried to keep an open mind, as it is Dr. Jaak Panksepp we are talking about; after all, he is major league. No, he is a game-changer in mammal emotions, so I kept listening to his interview. Panksepp went on to explain, "The only way you can ever ask an animal whether it has a feeling is whether it's a reward or a punishment. And I asked the question whether this kind of stimulation is good or bad for the animal's feelings." So, from what I understand of what Panksepp was saying, the rats used a wooden box with a metal pedal attached to it to express their likes and dislikes about their experiences.

In the 1950s, James Olds and Peter Milner created a wooden box device with a metal pedal lever. A single light and long leads with electrodes suited for rats' heads were attached to the box. The electrodes were placed in the rats' heads that penetrated parts of their brain. The rats were left to roam around or inside the box until they discovered the metal pedal lever. Curious rats eventually pressed the lever; the light lit up then the device caused the rat to feel a sensation of pleasure.

Tiny jolts of current went through the electrodes implanted deep within the nucleus accumbens of the rats' brains, which stimulated the brain's pleasure or reward system. These rats would press the lever up to 2,000 times per hour for their pleasurable stimulation. The 'horrible' rats many of us loathe not only have feelings but also have similar feelings to us human beings.

Years later, Dr. Panksepp emulated the same process. "The first animal I did was a great success," he said, beaming from ear to ear. "I had to build my equipment, learned how to do surgery, and then I put the electrodes in the right place, then I dropped the animal on the lever." Panksepp now found his first love and future successes that would, in due course, cement his legacy. Panksepp was the first to discover the ANGER emotion in rats. Other scientists before him discovered anger in cats and monkeys. Then Panksepp asked a second question, what other feelings do rats have?

Panksepp furthered his experiments by mapping the brains of rats. He discovered that rats also felt anger and pleasure in the same parts of the brain where humans felt anger and pleasure. Panksepp then realized they could understand human feelings in the brain because the rats' systems for feelings were almost the same as in other animals. The mapping of mammal feelings was a major breakthrough. Another question was soon to be asked and answered: When humans are tickled, humans laugh. Is it possible that rats would do the same?

Panksepp and his team observed the rats playing among themselves for about five years. As the rats played, they noticed they were making chirping sounds that appeared to be laughter. Panksepp and his team then studied the sounds but weren't quite sure what to make of them. One morning,

Panksepp had an epiphany. We will continue with Dr. Panksepp later.

Rats make all their sounds out of the range of human hearing; the typical hearing frequency range of a human being is between 20Hz to 20,000Hz. Rats vocalize between 20,000Hz to 100,000Hz.

The lowest vocal range of rats is higher than the highest range humans can hear. When rats are scared, annoyed, or going through negative emotions, they make long chirping sounds at 22,000Hz. When rats socialize and interact with other rats, are happy, or are given food, they make short chirping sounds that start at 50,000Hz. For Panksepp and his team to hear the rats chirp and communicate, they had to use transducers that are called bat detectors.

Bat detectors pick up frequencies from 15,000Hz to 125,000Hz, then lower the audio frequency for humans to hear.

Panksepp's epiphany was that perhaps the rats' high chirping sounds were laughter. If they are, let's tickle some rats, Panksepp concluded. He went down to his laboratory and made history. Panksepp said, "We tickled the first rat, and ultrasounds came on outrageously. It was the highest level we have ever seen." Dr. Panksepp tickled animal after animal, and the results were overwhelmingly the same. The rats loved to be tickled so much that when Panksepp and his team members moved their hands away from the rats, they chased them around until they continued to tickle them again. It was like children playing games with their parents and not wanting to stop. They were excited!

Panksepp and his team tried the tickling experiment on every animal, and the results were identical. They laughed and played, they were excited, and it made them happy. Antidepressants are designed to reduce psychological pain; however, antidepressants are not designed to make you feel happy, joyful, or exuberant. The part of the brain that can fight depression can get people back to a happier, psychologically healthier place.

You may, at this point, ask yourself, "Why did I just read about rats, cats, and other animals?" Others may have a light bulb moment on self- and animal discovery. To help and understand the helpline, we need to have some form of psychological understanding of how feelings and emotions work.

It is impossible to understand feelings and emotions without learning neuroscience. To even start helping the helpline, I want you to know how neuroscience and the history of neuroscience with animals can assist us.

Some of us are helplines at some point in our lives, but all of us need helplines throughout our lives. However, we can be forgetful, disrespectful, or apathetic toward our helplines. The helpline is seen as a non-emotional perfect entity that must serve and fix us. However, we tend to declare war on our helplines when they can't or don't know how to figure it out. Many of us have an attitude that they are 'perfect,' and we expect them to fix our imperfections.

We demand surgeons to reverse God's will in operations (or else) and farmers to provide more than we can possibly consume, with farmers suffering due to climate change. Our feelings and thoughts toward our helplines make our thought process even more distorted. Our helplines are more likely to be crucified by the majority than celebrated.

I have a question for you, as a people and a community as a whole, when do we celebrate our helplines apart from during or after a potential apocalyptic dawning? We honor them only when our helplines are on the brink of collapse. Only then does the general public appreciate our frontline helplines; for example, in the UK, parts of America, and other parts of the world, people acknowledged and appreciated their health workers during the COVID-19 pandemic.

On March 26, 2020, communities from across the UK united together at the request of the government to acknowledge our frontline workers.

Every Thursday, people stood on the streets and applauded. Others leaned out of their windows, banging pots and pans, expressing empathy in a moment in time by clapping and cheering for burned-out NHS workers who risked their lives daily was a good start two years ago. Two years later, in 2022, the claps stopped, and the pots and pans were safely back in their cupboards.

People stepped up when they discovered that healthcare workers were at the breaking point due to stress, depression, and burnout. But, to most of our helplines, it felt fake—like when someone wants to borrow something but first asks, 'How are you? How is your family?' but doesn't really care for you, or interested in your answers. They just need something from you. That is how a lot of our helplines feel today; now that people feel more secure and no longer feel like the world will end, there are no claps, cheers, or pot-banging. Furthermore, abuse against frontline workers is back on the rise again.

If some of you were to say, "But Kevin, they get paid to serve us. They get paid to do their jobs," I would respond by asking,

"How much is one's psychological pain worth? Or relationship breakup? Or suicidal thoughts? Or PTSD? Or death because of duty?" I will leave two spaces below for you to write your answer.

So, if we are serious about helping ourselves and our helplines, we need to understand how we are all controlled by how our feelings and emotions work. We need to understand why we have become what we are today. I truly don't believe our helplines just woke up one day and decided that their jobs, roles, and positions were just a good idea because of pay and benefits or because it was something their family or culture expected them to become or do. I believe there are moving parts that lead our helpline workers to their paths and situations today.

They are cultural, emotional, traumatic, and psychological reasons that lead people to where they are today. I believe there are frequency and spiritual reasons why people do what they do and become what they are. To be in an electron mindset and environment, you must have been vibrating at a particular frequency for some period of time. For example, I don't believe a social worker is in that role solely because they want to help people. I believe almost all social workers took on that role because they were vibrating at a social worker frequency, which led them to that job.

I hypothesize that most—maybe all—of our current helplines were vibrating at a particularly negative or positive frequency—which led them to their current positions in life. Most of us may envy surgeons for the amount of money they make, but the money they are making is not stopping them from committing suicide. If anything, the money they are making is an added factor and reason why they commit suicide. Do you know how hopeless many people feel when they discover that after all the years of studying, practice, and stress they endured, that there is no gold (i.e. happiness) at the end of the rainbow?

I believe Panksepp's term 'affective neuroscience' will help all who read the remainder of this chapter.

Through his research and experiments with animals and their brains, Dr. Panksepp discovered what can now help our psychological pain, such as depression, suicidal thoughts, and other negative feelings. In his experiments and animal testing, Panksepp discovered that there are seven basic emotional systems that psychologically governs us all. He coined it "affective neuroscience."

"Affective neuroscience" is a term named by Dr. Panksepp and is the psychological side of emotions and other powerful feelings such as hunger, thirst, and sensory feelings. These include good tastes, bad tastes, and feelings of pain in the body. But then you have emotions. Your emotions are built into your brain. There are seven primal, basic emotions that we are born with, located far down in the middle of our brains. We feel deep, intense emotions in our body because our emotions are in the visceral nervous system part of the brain. That is why when we feel intense emotions, we feel it in our hearts, our stomachs, and in the tightness or looseness of our bodies.

Whenever you see the full capitalization of the words SEEKING, RAGE/ANGER, FEAR, LUST, CARE, PANIC/GRIEF, and PLAY, we refer to them from a scientific perspective by capitalizing each emotional system in the brain.

The seven primal emotions systems:

1. The SEEKING System
2. The RAGE/ANGER System
3. The FEAR System
4. The LUST System
5. The CARE System
6. The PANIC/GRIEF System
7. The PLAY System

Can we use our seven primal emotions systems to help control and combat suicide, depression, worry, and fear, to name a few? The answer is 100% yes. Can we also use our primal emotions for happiness, connection to others, and self-love? Once again, 100% yes!

Emotions control the way we think, the way we feel, and the way we govern our results. Our results then affect how we connect with the world and treat ourselves and others. Each of our emotions is sensitive.

Emotions are like muscles we exercise in a gym. The more you exercise being fearful, the greater the chance that you will become terrified in general. The more you exercise joyfulness, the more you become even more joyful. What you introduce into your emotions will become your daily feelings and thoughts. It is essential to manage what you watch, your conversations with people, the music you listen to, how you talk to yourself, and how you allow others to talk to you. The more positively you think and act, the more positivity you introduce into your emotions. This is what spiraling up looks like. From today, set rules and boundaries with your self-talk and the conversations you entertain with people. Be clear with them, "Positive conversations only please!"

The SEEKING System

The SEEKING system in our brain is what Panksepp believes "is the most important emotion system in the animal brain. Without the SEEKING system, you cannot be happy and experience joy, fun, and excitement. You cannot emotionally go into the world with enthusiasm if you lose the ability to win and be motivated. If the SEEKING system is damaged, you and I cannot do anything. The feeling of self comes from the SEEKING system," Panksepp says.

The SEEKING system provides the feeling of rewards. It deals with the desire of wanting. Some people use cocaine because the drug is a seeking molecule. When people use cocaine, they feel ardor with massive energy. They feel like superheroes who can save the world until the high wears off. Then they struggle, and the FEAR, PANIC, or GRIEF system kicks in. The feelings of loneliness, isolation, and unhappiness start to take over.

Feeling down, sad, depressed, frustrated, and even angry can result from the low after the high from drugs such as cocaine and amphetamines. Then the desire to control the lows with marijuana or heroin becomes the next chase for some drug users.

We do not need drugs such as cocaine to feel enthusiasm, energy, or euphoria. But I understand that psychological pain or traumas can be so painful for some people that they just want to escape, even for a moment. Once they experience such drugs, the desire for more causes anxiety, irritation, and a need to escape from the unresolved traumas.

This is when the FEAR and the PANIC/GRIEF systems kick in. Guilt, worry, loneliness, sadness, depression, and even suicidal thoughts can quickly rear their ugly heads at this low point.

I don't want you to think that drugs are the only downside of the SEEKING system. It can also be watching excessive porn, self-harm, or extreme activities.

I hope that some of the suggestions, techniques, and tools in this book will help you discover natural and healthy ways to stimulate your SEEKING System.

I want you to write down alternative methods or preventative measures you can use to wean yourself off your unhealthy addictions or habits. But first, you must know your triggers. What triggers your moments of desire or addiction? It could be loneliness, remembering what happened as a child, or the picture of a loved one.

Write them down here.

What triggers you?

____

____

____

____

____

____

____

____

Now I want you to write down the preventative measures you can use to wean yourself off your unhealthy addictions or habits. For example, you could avoid places where you know drugs and alcohol will be available. You could go to therapy. You can exercise to release stress and excess energy and then meditate with relaxing meditative music if the urge for porn kicks in.

Write your list here.

The RAGE/ANGER System

The RAGE/ANGER system exists in us because we have to compete for resources. Resources are not always given to us. Sometimes you have to go out and fight for your resources. Sometimes we need this system to protect us and our family. If not managed properly, this system can be a significant part of our downfall and mental illness. The RAGE system deals with anger, irritability, resentment, hatred, and intermittent explosive disorder. As discussed earlier in this chapter, the ANGER part of the system was the first emotion Walter Hess mapped in cats and what Dr. Panksepp mapped in rats.

When angry, what can you do to prevent you from making bad decisions you may regret? For example, count to 10 before you take action in a moment of rage or anger. Or sleep, pray, or meditate before making that big decision that could cause harm or death. How about having trusted, level-headed advisers who help you see sense in a moment of rage?

Write down ten prevention methods you could use in a moment of anger or rage that may save you or someone else's life.

The FEAR System

The FEAR system is the fight or flight response. When we feel fear, it radiates throughout our body and affects our organs, blood pressure, and heart. Fear weakens the immune system. Too much fear can cause cardiovascular damage, ulcers, IBS, and decreased fertility. Fear and worry will give us anxiety, trepidation, and PTSD. Fear will age you and even lead to premature death.

Worry derives from imagination, and imagination of worry derives from fear and anticipating the worst-case scenario. Constantly worrying about the same thing will manifest as truth and reality. REMEMBER: Where your focus goes, your energy flows.

Here are my suggestions for helping you deal with your fear and worries:

1. Take a Moment to Breathe in the Face of FEAR

It is virtually impossible to think clearly when you are overwhelmed with FEAR. The spiritual entity of FEAR can easily lead you to a panic attack. The first thing you must do is take a moment to breathe and not be reactive but instead be responsive. You must physically calm yourself down to see the forest from the trees.

REMEMBER: FEAR is "False Evidence Appearing Real."

2. Deep Breaths Through the Attack

Sweaty palms, rapid heartbeats, and not feeling as though you can breathe could be a panic attack.

Don't run, don't scream for help, just slow everything down in your head. Lay your palm on your stomach, and breathe slowly and deeply. Talk slowly. Think slowly. Breathe slowly.

3. Confront the Wizard Hiding Behind the Curtain and Face Your Fears.

Running from your fears is natural. However, the faster you run, the stronger and scarier your fear becomes. First, make peace with the worst-case scenario. Then deal with each part of your fear in small bites as quickly as possible. The longer you leave it, the more 'powerful' it becomes. Build teams and fearless educated advisers around you who will nudge you to deal with your fear fearlessly.

4. Shadows Only Exist When You Are Looking for Them

Too many negative thoughts can make shadows appear real, catastrophizing your life, dreams, and future will lead to mental pain. This can lead to analysis paralysis, self-sabotage, and not wanting to connect with others due to feeling like a failure.

Our minds can be our wings, or our minds can be our ball and chain. To set your mind free and let it fly among the greatest thinkers and achievers, you must:

a) Truly believe that you are a blessing of and from God/your creator.
b) Get your life and mindset into a proton happy state before making decisions.

c) Surround yourself with the people, places, and things that will inspire you and positively influence and invest in you. Your environment is critical.

d) Dream big but start small. Don't paralyze yourself by getting overwhelmed by all the components to your success. Start small, celebrate each small win, and grow with gratitude.

e) Do not try to be interesting, but instead focus on being interested. Become interested in people, places, and things that you care about. You will discover that you get out whatever you put into it.

f) Realize that readers are leaders. Read, read, read, and read some more. Become friends with the greats of the past and become a visionary with the leaders of the future. Those who fail to understand the past are bound to repeat the mistakes in the future. That's not evolution; that is backward evolution.

5. Help Others to Combat Your Own Fears

In helping others with their fears, you will automatically discover solutions for your own fears.

6. Anytime fear presents itself, investigate it. The more you learn about it, the less power it has over you.

Write down your ideas that will combat your fears and worries.

____

____

____

The LUST System

The LUST system is all about your sexuality, eroticism, libido, and desire to connect with others physically. Undisciplined lust due to psychological pain, loneliness, developmental trauma, and other electron feelings can cause people to make bad decisions sexually. The need for a hug, sex, and other comforts due to electron emotions and feelings will more than likely align you with the wrong person, leading to drinking tea with the devil. Not managing lust can drive you down a dark path where sexual and relationship mistakes can cause long-term pain and trauma.

For the desire for oxytocin and endorphins, people will sleep with people they would normally never want to connect with if they weren't negatively lusting. Lust, coupled with the PLAY system, can result in unwanted pregnancies. Everybody then suffers. Children developmentally traumatized from birth to age 6 become angry teens, then depressed adults. The relationships between the mother, father, and children also don't stand a chance. On the other hand, lust is good when the connection is genuine, your vibrational frequencies are protons, and you can control your lust. It is important for courting before sex. Being addicted to the wrong type of person is as dangerous as drugs and alcohol. Toxic relationships tend to stem from toxic frequencies before meeting that particular person. The LUST system can be both good and bad, based on your frequency.

I want you to write down five things you must not do when negatively lusting. For example, calling or sexually connecting with someone you know is bad for you.

Here, you will write down five ways you can build a healthy relationship with someone in a proton way before sex. For example, courting and building a genuine connection.

The CARE System

The CARE system becomes active in women's brains due to pregnancy hormones. Panksepp explains that several days before the baby is born, the mother might be scared and worried if she can take care of her first baby. But after the hormones become active, the mother develops courage, her belief and attitude change, and she starts to believe she can do it. The CARE system is also a system of confidence. A mother needs confidence, devotion, and love to connect with her baby.

If the child doesn't receive love and devotion from the mother/parents, that child will have psychological problems growing up.

The CARE system is social emotions. These emotions depend on the thoughts, feelings, and actions of others. The CARE system is critical for baby emotions and maternal care. Within the nine months of gestation, how a mother thinks and feels and the frequencies she's vibrating at will affect how she expresses her love, or the lack of love, for her baby. This will inadvertently shape the relationships the baby will have in later life.

Touching, hugging, holding, and showing the baby love after it's born will release oxytocin and endorphins for the baby and mother. If the baby feels love and security and doesn't feel overwhelming psychological pain, the baby will have a psychologically healthy relationship with humans and mammals in the future. Children with psychological pain tend to be the people who end up hurting other people or healing other people, all while they are hurting internally.

I have two questions:

1. What can you and your partner do during pregnancy to help the mother and fetus be emotionally, physically, and psychologically healthy and happy?

For example:

a) Keeping stress and arguments to a minimum.
b) Eating the right foods, listening, reading, and watching all that is positive.

What can you and your partner do after pregnancy? Once the baby is born, how can you help the mother and baby emotionally, physically, and psychologically become healthy and happy? For example, lots of hugs, expressions of love, connection, bonding, and positivity. Add to this list here.

____

____

____

____

____

____

____

The PANIC/GRIEF System

The PANIC System

When a baby cries and is left alone for long periods by the parents or guardians to the point of debatable neglect, the baby eventually will stop crying. However, something else happens, the baby starts to feel abandoned and sad, and then it slowly but surely becomes dejected, feeling the psychological pain of knowing or assuming that no one will come to fulfill its needs or wants. Over a period of time, developmental trauma will seep in.

Babies become toddlers, toddlers become teens, and teens become adults. Throughout the journey from baby to adult, the feeling of neglect and abandonment never disappears. It is almost impossible for that feeling to leave that teen and adult because the brain was not fully developed when that trauma was forming within it.

The baby needed to be held, hugged, and loved, in order to learn how to love and form connections and bonds with others. It needed to emotionally know that care, love, and connection were there in times of its needs and wants. A lack of trust eventually becomes frustration, anger, anxiety, isolation, and depression.

When the PANIC system is activated too much, it suppresses the SEEKING system, which suppresses enthusiasm and euphoria. For the neglected baby, who is now a teen or an adult, relationships and trusting people become a massive problem.

This adult may not even know that they have developmental trauma. The feeling and self-conversations of neglect become everyday occurrences. They will say to themselves, "If I don't love, I can't be hurt, so I will not allow anybody to get too close to me." These people spend their lives jumping from one potentially great relationship to another, running away from anyone willing to love them. Feelings of guilt, shame, shyness, embarrassment, and a poor self-image become their 'identity.'

Suggestions:

1. Hug as much as possible and love people as much as possible to release endorphins and oxytocin.
2. Seek psychotherapy, for example:
    - Cognitive Behavioral Therapy (CBT)
    - Dialectical Behavioral Therapy for teens with emotional dysregulation
    - Trauma-Focused Cognitive Behavioral Therapy (TF-CBT)
    - Mindfulness-based therapies
    - Play therapy
3. Self-conversations can be dangerous. Express your thoughts and concerns within relationships to prevent misunderstandings and communication problems.

4. Work on skills for enhancing resiliency and social integration.

Add more ideas that you believe will help your GRIEF/PANIC System

The GRIEF System

The GRIEF system is also built into our brains and can badly affect us if not managed properly. We are social creatures, so isolation, grief, and too much sadness can harm our mental health. This system deals with grief, sadness, psychological pain, and depression.

So how can we make our lives happier, more fun, and more fulfilling while minimizing depression, sadness, psychological pain, and emotional trauma? How can we use the discoveries of people like Dr. Panksepp, Walter Hess, Egas Moniz, and others to benefit us?

Being sad is painful, being depressed is debilitating, and feeling hopeless and suicidal is dangerous. I want us all to be educated enough to deal with these emotions, feelings, and disorders.

Experiencing a loved one emotionally or physically dying before their time is heartbreaking. Giving up is death before God's will, and not wanting to live is believing no more blessings are coming your way. If I have to research even more cats, rats, and scientists to find ways to ease your pain and the pain of others, I will do so.

I have felt so much psychological pain in my life. It hurts. It really hurts. We will all feel life-changing emotional pain at some point in our lives. This can disconnect us from the world. The feeling that there is no hope can lead to very dangerous ideations. Seeing the world progress while you are stuck in quicksand or drowning can feel like you are being punished for a crime you didn't commit.

These feelings and thoughts can easily lead to no longer wanting to be alive. I want to help you or your loved ones to see and feel differently. Even me writing this here is a sad moment for me. My tears are welling up, about to spill over onto my keyboard as I type this sentence; my mind is wondering about the people I love and know who have committed suicide for these reasons.

Learning about the emotions of rats and cats is interesting, but my focus is on the results of what they can do for us. Our SEEKING and PLAY systems are the keys to our happiness, enthusiasm, and hope.

The SEEKING system is what we must focus on first to break our emotional pains, lack of desire, and not wanting to win in the world. The SEEKING system deals with happiness, joy, fun, and excitement. I want you to experience the SEEKING SYSTEM to brighten your world and build a happier and stronger relationship with yourself.

Here are some tasks to consider:

1. Go out into the world and discover new, fun, and exciting hobbies.
2. Figure out what makes you proud of yourself.
3. Take time out to go for walks in locations that inspire you.
4. Seek new friends and networks that are positive and progressive.
5. Try stargazing, seek out new planets, then write about them in a blog.
6. Go to the theater to watch a play, a musical, an opera, or a ballet performance.
7. Set daily and weekly goals that will make you proud of yourself.
8. Build a relationship with God or your Creator. There is power in prayer, meditation, and openness to being loved.
9. Seek out interesting cultural relics.

I want you to add more ideas for combating sadness in your life:

The PLAY System

The PLAY system is the subcortical part of the brain. The PLAY system deals with joy, fun, games, friendship, and euphoria. Play also influences the neocortex part of the brain. Physical and social play stimulates happiness, bonding, togetherness, and hope. The PLAY system will help you when you are experiencing depression, grief, and sad times. When Dr. Panksepp tickled the rats, they became even more joyful rats. When we play as humans, we are happier people. But for some crazy reason, the older some people get, the more they repel The PLAY system. So, in the name of The PLAY system, play more, be more open to fun experiences, and embrace the child in you.

It is important to change your emotional age to a younger more vibrate age. You can be young, but be old emotionally if you do not stimulate your PLAY system. The PLAY system will stop being stimulated, and the journey of unhappiness and not feeling joy, fun, or euphoria begins. Fun overrides loneliness and sometimes sadness. Having a loving pet can bring immense pleasure into your life. Families who play together tend to stay together, so play games with your wife, husband, children, and extended family.

Happy and joyful families can get through anything together; on the other hand, unhappy family members tend to want to be alone.

Your tasks:

What fun and games can you or your family introduce into your lives daily? I must add, the games you choose must not be computer games that will isolate you from people, or games that will cause hurt, harm, or loss to you, and others. That's counterproductive. The play needs to be fun, tactile, and social. Please note: be as childish as possible. Your happiness and feeling good depend on it.

The happiest children were and are those who socially play and enjoy themselves. Create your list of play activities and build your proton happiness, feeling good, and joy states. Childlike behavior can sometimes save your life. List at least ten games and where to find playful and joyful people to participate with you. Get started now.

Game 1.____

Game 2.____

Game 3.____

Game 4.____

Game 5.____

Game 6.____

Game 7.____

Game 8.____

Game 9.____

Game 10._______________________________________

Where and when will you play these games?

List where and when:

Game 1.____

Game 2.____

Game 3.____

Game 4.____

Game 5.____

Game 6.____

Game 7.____

Game 8.____

Game 9.____

Game 10.____

CHAPTER 5

BEAUTY, PAIN, AND TRAUMA

My understanding of depression.

As she leaped to her death, was she thinking, "It's time for me to sleep finally. No more 'perfect' smiles, no more perfection, no more expectations, no more online bullying, no more discrimination, no more darkness, no more pain, no more feelings of hopelessness, no more disappointment. Just no more!" The death of another fantastic helpline, Sunrise: April 28th, 1991, Jackson, Michigan. Sunset: January 30th, 2022, Midtown Manhattan, New York. Cause of death: suicide. Rest in peace Cheslie Kryst, aged 30 years old.

Born to a Polish American father who was a bodybuilder and an African American mother who was crowned Mrs. North Carolina in 2002. Kryst had five siblings—four brothers and one sister. As a child, Kryst was an introvert and a nerd, as she proclaimed in one of her many YouTube videos. Kryst's family moved from Michigan to Charlotte, North Carolina, when Kryst was young. They later settled in Rock Hill, South Carolina, where Kryst attended Northwestern High School.

The family then moved a few more times over the years, and Kryst attended a number of schools. There was something special about Kryst. She was very smart throughout her life, and she was academically astute. In 2013, she graduated cum laude from the Darla Moore School of Business with a degree in marketing and human resource management. She was also a member of the Alpha Lambda Delta honor society, Gamecocks women's track and field team, and mock trial.

After finishing her undergraduate degree, Kryst enrolled in Wake Forest University School of Law in Winston-Salem, North Carolina, graduating with a Juris Doctor and Master of Business Administration in 2017. Following her graduation, Kryst became licensed to practice law in both North Carolina and South Carolina. She began working as an attorney at Poyner Spruill LLP, practicing complex civil litigation. She was practicing civil litigation, but not only that, she worked pro bono for prisoners who felt that they had been sentenced to excessive prison time. She was looking at whether there was any justification for leaving them in the federal system.

But there was even more to Kryst. She was gorgeous and had an athletic body from her earlier years of being an athlete; she was 5' 6" tall, with long, black, curly hair, pearly white teeth, flawless skin, and the personality and poise to match. She was so beautiful inside and out that Kryst was crowned Miss USA 2019. Millions celebrated her for who and what she was. Her intelligence, beauty, and stardom were inspirational for the world to admire, but if you know anything about Kryst, you will know she didn't stop there.

In October 2019, Kryst became a New York correspondent for *Extra*, after serving as a special correspondent in September 2019. Her interview with actor Terrence Howard broke the news that the actor planned to retire from acting following the final season of the television series *Empire*. She interviewed celebrities such as Denzel Washington, Gabrielle Union, Taylor Swift, Oprah Winfrey, Tom Hanks, and Rihanna, to name a few. Kryst fought for equality and against discrimination and racism. She was also a mental health advocate. On World Mental Health Day, Kryst made a video that she dedicated to people struggling with stress and mental health. She said, "The most important thing that I did is talk to a counselor. She's really easy to talk to. She gives me great strategies, especially if I'm sad or happy or have a busy month ahead of me." Kryst seemed self-aware and tuned in. Kryst was always laughing. She smiled at everybody all the time and came across as jovial and very, very 'happy.' On Sunday, January 30th, 2022, Kryst was last seen on the 29th floor of the Orion, a 60-story high-rise apartment building. She jumped to her death around 7:15 a.m.

Cheslie Corrinne Kryst was found dead on the street below.

Who helped the helpline, when the helpline needed help? Happy people don't just jump off buildings.

Kryst helped women concerning women's equality, she advised and helped models to be more confident and positive, she also advocated and helped many prisoners who were unfairly treated by the federal prison system. She advised tens of thousands of people and inspired millions more. So how was it possible that people who met her or were around her did not see the small micro signs of depression or her feelings of hopelessness? Maybe they didn't want to see it or did not take it too seriously. After all, she was pretty, intelligent, successful, celebrated, and always appeared happy. But that is the problem right there—no one can always be happy, and being pretty and successful can sometimes work against you when you are suffering in silence. I mean, you have nothing to be depressed about, right?

April Simpkins, Kryst's mother, in a statement said, "I have never known pain as deep as this. I am forever changed. Today, what our family and friends privately knew was the cause of death of my sweet baby girl, Cheslie, was officially confirmed. While it may be hard to believe, it's true. Cheslie led both a public and a private life. In her private life, she was dealing with high-functioning depression, which she hid from everyone — including me, her closest confidant — until very shortly before her death."

Huh? High-functioning depression? I thought when I read what Kryst's mother said. When I heard that term, I had to research it. To make sense of high-functioning depression, I read an article written by Steph Coelho on June 9, 2020, and reviewed by Timothy J. Legg, Ph.D., PsyD. It read, "Some people use the term high-functioning depression, but this is neither a diagnosis nor a clinical disorder. Many mental health professionals also disagree with the use of the term.

Some experts believe that the term comes from a lack of clarity surrounding Persistent Depressive Disorder (PDD), or dysthymia, an ongoing form of depression. PDD differs from Major Depressive Disorder (MDD), or major depression, as the symptoms tend to be less severe but have a longer duration."

So, the professionals believe she may have had PDD or dysthymia, or major depression.

Before Kryst died, she shared a photo on Instagram beside which she wrote: "May this day bring you rest and peace." Rest and peace?? Was she sending a cryptic message to someone in particular, or was that her cry for HELP?

Let's dig a little deeper. In an Allure.com article written by Kryst herself on March 4, 2021, she said, "Each time I say, 'I'm turning 30,' I cringe a little. Sometimes I can successfully mask this uncomfortable response with excitement; other times, my enthusiasm feels hollow, like bad acting. Society has never been kind to those growing old, especially women."

At the age of 29, Kryst said, "Each time I say, 'I'm turning 30,' I cringe a little." Cringe a little? Kryst dreaded getting older to the point of cringing. Thirty years old, in the grand scheme of life, is very young, but not to a model or someone who feels their relevance will diminish as they age.

Kryst then said, "Sometimes I can successfully mask this uncomfortable response with excitement; other times, my enthusiasm feels hollow."

To mask something is to cover or hide something you may feel ashamed about. And when Kryst said that she could "mask this uncomfortable response with excitement," is that why nobody around her picked up her silent suffering? She became so good at using her mask of smiles, fun, laughter, and joy, that everyone felt so excited by that and wanted more from the helpline that needed help herself.

Let's read more of her article. "After a year like 2020, you would think we'd learned that growing old is a treasure and maturity is a gift not everyone gets to enjoy. Far too many of us allow ourselves to be measured by a standard that some sternly refuse to challenge and others simply acquiesce to because fitting in and going with the flow is easier than rowing against the current. I fought this fight before, and it's the battle I'm currently fighting with 30." Kryst really disliked the idea of turning 30. To her, 30 was old. Did she feel as though it was like a punishment from God? She said, "You would think we'd learned that growing old is a treasure and maturity is a gift not everyone gets to enjoy."

Even though she said that “far too many of us allow ourselves to be measured by a standard,” what she was saying was that she was being measured by her age.

The question is, by who? The older people in our society? The younger people in our community? The trolls or the critics? Or maybe her belief system? Everyone has a part to play in our community—good, bad, or indifferent. The good will love you no matter what. The bad will hate or dislike you no matter what. The indifferent will decide how they feel about you on that day. It is said that Jesus was the purest person to walk the Earth, and even He was crucified. If that’s the case, we don’t stand a chance. Kryst wanted to be liked by everyone, which is impossible to manifest.

I researched publication after publication about Kryst. The more I learn about the life, journey, and legacy of Cheslie Kryst, the more admiration and love I have for her. She had been hurting for a long time, perhaps since childhood. She once said on one of her YouTube vlogs that she regretted closing the gap between her front teeth because it made her unique. But she didn’t want to be unique then—she wanted to fit in. Kryst desperately wanted to be liked and to be perfect. She wanted to be a model like her mother, an athlete like her bodybuilding father, and a lawyer like her stepfather. She compared herself to what she emotionally deemed as “perfect” celebrities with their “perfect” lives. She never wanted to age. She believed that to age was to become irrelevant.

Kryst saw the world through the lens of a young model, not a maturing, beautiful, intelligent, powerful woman. The king of pop, Michael Jackson, also saw the world through the lens of a child. That lens got Jackson into hot water many times before his untimely death in 2009. Sometimes a developmental type of trauma can be lying in wait deep down in the cortex of your brain. It forms destructive beliefs, emotions, and feelings about yourself and the world around you like a puppet master.

Panksepp confirmed this at a 2010 talk at the Notre Dame Symposium on Human Nature and Early Experience. He said, "All the emotional systems sensitize. If you have excessive fear, you will become an excessively fearful individual. Or if you have excessive anger early on, you will become an excessively angry individual. These systems learn like muscles—they get stronger depending upon what's happened to them." We addressed the seven emotional systems in Chapter 3. Just like millions of others, Kryst strengthened her emotional muscles of trepidation until it became psychologically unbearable. She felt what I would presume hopelessness.

How can we prevent what happened to Kryst from happening to someone else? How can we read and see the signs, no matter how faint they may be?

Since 2009, I have made it my life's mission to discover what makes successful people successful, happy people happy, and depressed people depressed? I wanted to know how people journey from the dark world of depression and anxiety to the bright lights of happiness and self-love?

To point at any depression that someone is going through and prescribe them some form of magical pill undermines the depth and complexity of what depression and anxiety are all about.

Depression is disturbingly on the rise due to several factors. It is essential to differentiate between depression and feeling depressed.

We are born with emotions, which can be strengthened or weakened by our focus and what we entertain psychologically, emotionally, and spiritually. We learn feelings throughout the journeys and experiences in our lives.

Emotions and feelings are different. The pleasure of eating a sweet cake or the pain of stepping on a sharp nail fall into the sensory "feelings" department. Feeling hungry, tired, and thirsty are bodily feelings. Emotions are not sensory. They are bodily and brain responses toward ourselves and the world around us. Emotional feelings tell us what is and isn't important to us. Our emotions warn us about what is good and what is dangerous. Emotions are deep value systems that, when unbalanced, can cause us great emotional harm and problems.

Everyone feels short bouts of depression from time to time from relationship breakups, loss of a job, weight loss or gain, or just simply having a bad day. The feeling of sadness is a part of our random rotational cycle of life. Sometimes we can identify what anchors and triggers our feelings and emotions, such as a photo of a loved one who has passed away or received a past-due notice that reminds us of financial problems. Sometimes our anchors and triggers are unknown to us until we investigate or seek help in some way, such as therapy.

But those feelings can all change. You can go from sadness to hope or gratitude within a second, based on a trigger or anchor, such as an uplifting song, words of encouragement, a quick burst of exercise, or even a prayer.

On the other hand, excessive FEAR can cause psychiatric disorders and problems. The entity of FEAR can lead to eating, mood, and bipolar disorders. This is where our dangers are more than likely to start for us. Excessive FEAR is dangerous and will likely result in a depression of some type. I am like one of those annoying children who repeatedly ask, "Are we there yet?" and "Why?" And in this case, "Why do people get depressed?" and **"What is depression?"**

According to the American Psychiatric Association, depression is a common and serious medical illness that negatively affects how a person feels, thinks, moods, actions, and behavior. Yes, this book is about navigating your emotions and feelings on your way to your personal and professional success. However, we need to identify many components of what makes you suffer from depression, worry, and suicidal ideation, to name a few.

By the end of this chapter, you will have sufficient tools, awareness, and the essential ability to combat depression, anxiety, and other disorders to help you live happier than you were yesterday. I strongly recommend you also seek professional help and advice from a psychiatrist.

There are different types of depression. I would like us to explore some of the main types together. I want you to pay diligent attention to each symptom as we go through the types of depression and see if you or a loved one are exhibiting any of the symptoms.

Next to each symptom are boxes you can circle or highlight to identify if you or a loved one could be struggling or suffering from depression. But before we start, I must state that the definitions and all the symptoms of the depression presented below came from multiple sources, not me. These sources are the NHS, The National Institute of Mental Health (NIMH), the Centers for Disease Control and Prevention (CDC), and some prominent doctors and psychologists.

I also must affirm that you should seek professional advice as soon as possible if you are concerned that you or a loved one may be experiencing depression. I am not a doctor, nor am I a therapist or a counselor. Ok, pick up a pen, and let's go.

1. Major Depression

Major depression is also known as clinical depression or MDD.

Major depression is one of the more severe depressions that truly concerns me when I discover that someone is struggling with it. I urge people to seek immediate help with this form of depression because I know that one of the symptoms of this disorder is hopelessness. When you don't see yourself in the future, you have no plans to be a part of the future. When you are experiencing major depression, you may feel very sad and lose interest in things you used to enjoy. The symptoms of this type of depression could persist for weeks or even months and tend to interfere with your work, social life, and family life.

If you identify with any of these symptoms, please circle or highlight them. If you circle or highlight most symptoms with 'Always' or 'Sometimes,' please seek professional help or advice.

Let's get started.

a) I feel a loss of interest or pleasure in my daily activities.
[Always] [Sometimes] [Never]

b) I'm experiencing weight loss or weight gain.
[Always] [Sometimes] [Never]

c) I have trouble getting to sleep, or I feel sleepy during the day.
[Always] [Sometimes] [Never]

d) I feel restless and sluggish constantly.
[Always] [Sometimes] [Never]

e) I feel drained, and I lack energy for no reason.
[Always] [Sometimes] [Never]

f) I feel worthless.
[Always] [Sometimes] [Never]

g) I feel extreme guilt.
[Always] [Sometimes] [Never]

h) I have trouble concentrating and making decisions.
[Always] [Sometimes] [Never]

i) I have thoughts of suicide.
[Always] [Sometimes] [Never]

Psychological symptoms of major depression:

1) I constantly have low moods and/or sadness.
[Always] [Sometimes] [Never]

2) I feel hopeless and/or helpless.
[Always] [Sometimes] [Never]

3) I have low self-esteem.
[Always] [Sometimes] [Never]

4) I'm constantly tearful.
[Always] [Sometimes] [Never]

5) I feel guilt-ridden.
[Always] [Sometimes] [Never]

6) I tend to feel irritated and intolerant of others.
[Always] [Sometimes] [Never]

7) I have no motivation or interest in things.
[Always] [Sometimes] [Never]

8) I find it difficult to make decisions.
[Always] [Sometimes] [Never]

9) I'm not getting any enjoyment out of life anymore.
[Always] [Sometimes] [Never]

10) I feel anxious or worried or both.
[Always] [Sometimes] [Never]

11) I have suicidal thoughts or thoughts of harming myself.
[Always] [Sometimes] [Never]

Physical symptoms of major depression

The physical symptoms of depression include:

1) I am moving or speaking more slowly than usual.
[Always] [Sometimes] [Never]

2) I have changes in my appetite or weight.
[Always] [Sometimes] [Never]

3) I have been constipated lately.
[Always] [Sometimes] [Never]

4) I have unexplained aches and pains.
[Always] [Sometimes] [Never]

5) I have no energy.
[Always] [Sometimes] [Never]

6) I have a low sex drive. (Loss of libido)
[Always] [Sometimes] [Never]

7) I have been experiencing changes in my menstrual cycle.

[Always] [Sometimes] [Never]

8) I find it difficult to fall asleep at night, or I wake up very early in the mornings.
[Always] [Sometimes] [Never]

Social symptoms of major depression

1) I avoid contact with my friends.
[Always] [Sometimes] [Never]

2) I take part in fewer social activities.
[Always] [Sometimes] [Never]

3) I have been neglecting hobbies and interests.
[Always] [Sometimes] [Never]

4) I'm having difficulties at home and in my work life.
[Always] [Sometimes] [Never]

2. Postpartum Depression

According to an NHS document published on December 10, 2018, 1 in every 10 women suffers from postpartum depression in the UK within a year of giving birth.

A May 2022 CDC study showed that "about 1 in 10 women in the United States reported symptoms that suggest that they experienced an episode of major depression in the last year." Another study showed that "about 1 in 8 women with a recent live birth experience symptoms of postpartum depression. Estimates of the number of women affected by postpartum depression differ by age, race/ethnicity, and state."

So, what is postpartum depression? Postpartum depression is a form of intense depression that occurs after giving birth to a baby. This form of depression differs from person to person. For some, the symptoms may be more frequent, may last for longer, or maybe more intense than for others.

Below is a list of more symptoms of postpartum depression.

If you identify with any of these symptoms, please circle or highlight them. If you circle or highlight most of the symptoms by marking 'Always' or 'Sometimes,' please seek professional help or advice.

1) I periodically have episodes of crying.
[Always] [Sometimes] [Never]

2) I have no energy.
[Always] [Sometimes] [Never]

3) I'm suffering from anxiety and panic attacks.
[Always] [Sometimes] [Never]

4) I have a loss of appetite.
[Always] [Sometimes] [Never]

5) I'm eating much more than I usually do.
[Yes, I am] [No, it's normal]

6) I just can't sleep.
[Always] [Sometimes] [Never]

7) I'm sleeping too much.
[Always] [Sometimes] [Never]

8) I constantly doubt myself, and I don't honestly think I'm a good and worthy mother.
[Always] [Sometimes] [Never]

9) I feel worthless and guilty about my baby.
[Always] [Sometimes] [Never]

10) I think about harming myself.

[Always] [Sometimes] [Never]

11) I think about harming my baby.
[Always] [Sometimes] [Never]

12) I think about death and suicide.
[Always] [Sometimes] [Never]

13) I lack the ability to think clearly.
[Always] [Sometimes] [Never]

14) I lack the ability to focus on tasks.
[Always] [Sometimes] [Never]

15) I'm extremely sad.
[Always] [Sometimes] [Never]

16) I have mood swings.
[Always] [Sometimes] [Never]

3. Psychotic Depression

According to the NHS, Psychotic depression is severe depression with some form of psychosis. According to the NIMH, a person who is psychotic has lost touch with reality. Psychosis is a mental health problem that causes people to perceive and process the world differently from others. They will have hallucinations, delusions, and even disorganized thinking and speech. They may have difficulty figuring out what is or isn't real.

So, what can cause psychosis? For some people, it is possible that the person was susceptible to it. They may have inherited their psychosis from a family member. The genetic markers for psychosis runs within families, so there seems to be some form of a genetic component to the psychosis.

Chronic stress, hardship, traumatic events, and childhood adversities could cause psychosis. Social adversities such as violent crime, poverty, sexual abuse, domestic violence, psychological abuse, and physical abuse could all be the causes of psychosis.

How people are treated can traumatize the body and brutalize the mind. When a person is traumatized, feeling hurt, broken, or vulnerable, they tend to think and act in a vulnerable way. They can be hypersensitive to everything around them, causing paranoia and then psychosis.

Even alcohol abuse and drug abuse can contribute to a person having psychosis. Severe, prolonged sleep deprivation and sleep disorders can cause the brain to biologically change negatively, which can result in psychosis as well.

Let's look at some symptoms. If you identify with any of these symptoms, please circle or highlight them. If you circle or highlight most symptoms by marking 'Always' or 'Sometimes,' please seek professional help or advice as soon as possible.

First, hallucinations:

Sight – Seeing colors, shapes, people, or animals that aren't there, or objects moving that don't ordinarily move.

[Always] [Sometimes] [Never]

Sound – Hearing phantom voices that may give orders to do things or could cause anger, fear, or paranoia.

[Always] [Sometimes] [Never]

Touch – Hallucinations of being touched when nobody is actually there.

[Always] [Sometimes] [Never]

Smell – Hallucinations of strange or unpleasant odors that nobody else smells.

[Always] [Sometimes] [Never]

Taste –Noticing unpleasant tastes in the mouth when nothing bad-tasting has been eaten.

[Always] [Sometimes] [Never]

Next,

Delusions

Delusions are false beliefs that don't go away, even after the person's delusions have been proven to be untrue. For example, a person with psychosis is sure that people are listening to their thoughts and plotting to cause them harm. It's also not uncommon for people with psychosis to believe others are poisoning their food.

Here are more symptoms:

1) I tend to talk rapidly and constantly.

   [Always] [Sometimes] [Never]

2) I seem to switch from one topic to another mid-sentence randomly.

   [Always] [Sometimes] [Never]

3) I seem to suddenly lose my train of thought, which causes me to pause in my conversations and activities abruptly.

   [Always] [Sometimes] [Never]

4) I feel very tired and overwhelmed.

   [Always] [Sometimes] [Never]

5) I've been feeling anxious, scared, threatened, and even confused at times.

[Always] [Sometimes] [Never]

6) I get really agitated.
[Always] [Sometimes] [Never]

7) I have anxiety.
[Always] [Sometimes] [Never]

8) I am constipated.
[Always] [Sometimes] [Never]

9) I believe I may have hypochondria; I always worry that I am ill and worry about getting ill.
[Always] [Sometimes] [Never]

10) I have insomnia. I find it hard to fall asleep, and then I wake up several times throughout the night. I feel exhausted throughout the day.
[Always] [Sometimes] [Never]

4. Bipolar Disorder

According to NIMH, “Bipolar disorder [formerly called manic-depression] is a mental illness that causes unusual shifts in moods, energy, activity levels, concentration, and the ability to carry out day-to-day tasks.”

The word *bipolar* has two parts to its meaning. The first part, *bi,* means “two”—in this case, referring to two sides to a person’s moods. The other part is *polar* means “opposites,”—in this case, referring to the extreme high and low moods. In medicine, a disorder is a disturbance of the normal functioning of the mind or body. Disorders may be caused by diseases, trauma, or even genetic factors. Bipolar disorder is defined and discovered by the presence of mania and hypomania.

According to the Substance Abuse and Mental Health Services Administration, mania is “a period of abnormally and persistently elevated, expansive, or irritable mood,” and “abnormally and persistently goal-directed behavior or energy” lasting at least one week and present most of the day, nearly every day.

When looking into a person’s mania, abnormality and persistence are a part of the problem. First, the abnormal behavior that negatively presents itself can be beneficial in identifying that the person has a problem. For example, a person without any flying experience getting into the cockpit of a plane to fly the plane may be showing symptoms of mania. Or a person planning to take over the world and wanting all the world leaders to bow down to them can also be a symptom of mania. These symptoms include inflated self-esteem or grandiosity, excessive involvement in pleasurable or dangerous activities such as unrestrained spending sprees, sexual licentiousness or indiscretion, or unwise business investments.

The abnormal moods, energy, behaviors, and actions that are way over the top and negative are signs that professional help is needed.

Hypomania is a milder mania with extreme mood and energy changes. Hypomania lasts for a shorter period than mania. These changes need to be seen for at least four days to be recognized as hypomania. Mania is more severe; the extreme mood and energy changes last at least one week and could last much longer.

To have mania or hypomania, you must have three or more of the following symptoms that last a minimum of four days. Please note this is not a diagnosis. It is for awareness and educational purposes only. If you circle or highlight three or more of these symptoms by marking 'Always' or 'Sometimes,' please seek professional help or advice.

1) Abnormally jumpy, upbeat, wired behavior for a minimum of 4 days.
[Always] [Sometimes] [Never]

2) Talking unusually fast and constantly for a minimum of 4 days.
[Always] [Sometimes] [Never]

3) Increased agitation and energy for a minimum of 4 days.
[Always] [Sometimes] [Never]

4) Extreme grandiose behavior for a minimum of 4 days.
[Always] [Sometimes] [Never]

5) Having racing thoughts and thinking and talking about many topics, one after another, for a minimum of 4 days.
[Always] [Sometimes] [Never]

6) Being easily distracted for a minimum of 4 days.
[Always] [Sometimes] [Never]

7) Being easily irritated or agitated for a minimum of 4 days.
[Always] [Sometimes] [Never]

8) Being delusional, having hallucinations, and disturbed or illogical thinking for a minimum of 4 days.
[Always] [Sometimes] [Never]

9) Getting just a few hours of sleep and feeling rested or not sleeping at all for a minimum of 4 days.
[Always] [Sometimes] [Never]

10) Eating more or less than usual and possibly eating foods you wouldn't normally eat for a minimum of 4 days.

    [Always] [Sometimes] [Never]

11) Doing activities that have disastrous consequences, such as spending sprees, sexual indiscretions, or foolish business investments for a minimum of 4 days

    [Always] [Sometimes] [Never]

12) Taking on too much work or making too many plans with friends, colleagues, or family members for a minimum of 4 days.

    [Always] [Sometimes] [Never]

What goes up must come down. Bipolar disorder is characterized by extreme mood swings, from highs (mania) to lows (depression). After the manic highs come the lows, and after the lows of depression come the manic highs. The lows of depression can be very dangerous if not diagnosed and treated by a professional. This is why I continually state that if you have any concerns about mental illness concerning yourself or a loved one, please contact a professional who can help you. This book is for awareness and educational purposes only, not to diagnose you or give you any form of medical direction.

Now let's have a look at the lows of bipolar disorder. Bipolar disorder can first present as mania, hypomania, or even depression. You can have a depressive episode, which may be seen as a form of depression that is not bipolar disorder. However, when you experience your first manic or hypomanic episode, you will likely be diagnosed with bipolar I disorder (BP-I) or bipolar II disorder (BP-II).

BP-I involves episodes of mania and depression, whereas BP-II involves episodes of hypomania and depression. If a person is having delusions and hallucinations, that is BP-I. If a person has BP-II, there is a good possibility that they will never be hospitalized. However, BP-I is a different case. With BP-I, manic episodes can be extremely dangerous and destructive for everyone. People with BP-II, spend more time being depressed with low moods than people with manic highs of BP-I. People with BP-II have frequent long episodes of severe depression. People with BP-II may have many more episodes of depression over their lifetime than people with BP-I.

People with BP-I and BP-II need to keep their mania and hypomania under control. But they must also work to avoid falling into debilitating feelings of hopelessness and suicidal thoughts. The difference between BP-I and BP-II is the mania—the delusions, hallucinations, disruptive illogical thinking, and potentially the psychosis. Psychosis can also occur within the severe deep darkness of BP-I and BP-II depression.

Here are some of the symptoms of a depressive episode of bipolar disorder. These depressive episodes may include several of the following at once. If you identify with any of these symptoms, please circle or highlight them.

1) Feeling extreme sadness

[I have only this symptom]
[I have this and other symptoms]
[I do not have this symptom]

2) Feeling of hopelessness

[I have only this symptom]
[I have this and other symptoms]
[I do not have this symptom]

3) Irritable most of the time

[I have only this symptom]
[I have this and other symptoms]
[I do not have this symptom]

4) Lacking energy and loss of interest in daily activities

[I have only this symptom]
[I have this and other symptoms]
[I do not have this symptom]

5) Major difficulty concentrating and remembering the basics

[I have only this symptom]
[I have this and other symptoms]
[I do not have this symptom]

6) Feeling overwhelmed and empty

[I have only this symptom]
[I have this and other symptoms]
[I do not have this symptom]

7) Feeling of worthlessness

[I have only this symptom]
[I have this and other symptoms]
[I do not have this symptom]

8) Feelings of guilt and despair

[I have only this symptom]
[I have this and other symptoms]
[I do not have this symptom]

9) Feeling pessimistic about everything encountered

[I have only this symptom]
[I have this and other symptoms]
[I do not have this symptom]

10) Self-doubt

[I have only this symptom]
[I have this and other symptoms]
[I do not have this symptom]

11) Having delusions, hallucinations, and disruptive, illogical thinking

[I have only this symptom]
[I have this and other symptoms]
[I do not have this symptom]

12) Lack of appetite or not wanting to eat

[I have only this symptom]
[I have this and other symptoms]
[I do not have this symptom]

13) Difficulty sleeping and waking up too early

[I have only this symptom]
[I have this and other symptoms]
[I do not have this symptom]

14) Suicidal thoughts and behavior

[I have only this symptom]
[I have this and other symptoms]
[I do not have this symptom]

What exactly causes bipolar disorder is unknown, however, some factors could be the cause, or put someone at risk of bipolar disorder. Please circle or highlight any of the factors you believe you may be experiencing or have experienced in the past.

1) Have you experienced extreme life-changing stress?
[Yes] [Possibly] [No]

2) Have you experienced abuse that has negatively changed your life forever?
[Yes] [Possibly] [No]

3) Have you been suffering from psychological trauma because of a car, bike, or any other accident?
[Yes] [Possibly] [No]

4) Do you have overwhelming problems?
[Yes] [Possibly] [No]

5) Has a negative, life-changing event severely affected you?
[Yes] [Possibly] [No]

6) Does one or both of your parents have bipolar disorder?
[Yes] [Possibly] [No]

5. Seasonal Depression

Seasonal affective disorder (SAD)

Seasonal affective disorder is also known as SAD or winter depression. It is a type of depression that affects some people during particular seasons and times of the year, around the same time every year. For example, SAD tends to start in late fall, peak in winter, and subside in spring. However, there is a less common seasonal depressive disorder that affects some people in the spring and summer seasons instead. This depression starts in the spring, peaks in the summer, and subsides in the fall. People with SAD tend to find themselves in persistent depressive moods, have a loss of pleasure in their sex lives, have no interest in normal daily activities, and have feelings of irritability, despair, guilt, worthlessness, and even low self-esteem.

People with SAD will more than likely have outbursts of tearfulness and anxiety, the lack of desire to be sociable, insomnia, and hypersomnia. This depression can be so severe that some people with SAD will even consider suicide and think a lot about death.

With the winter variation, people are more likely to gain weight because of carbohydrate cravings. Too much processed unhealthy carbohydrates will cause negative moods and health problems, affecting a person's mental health and well-being. According to Dr. Vanessa Patel, a psychiatrist, if you notice that your depression occurs at the same time every year for two consecutive years, you are meeting the criteria for seasonal depressive disorder. Some call SAD the "winter blues" or "cabin fever." Cabin fever is long confinement or isolation indoors during the winter periods, accompanied by feelings of irritability, frustration, and low energy. SAD is a more severe disorder than cabin fever and affects people's ability to function daily.

Here are some of the possible factors that can cause SAD. If you identify with any of these symptoms, please circle or highlight them.

1. A lack of sunlight and vitamin D in the winter

   [I have enough]

   [Could do with more]

   [I do not have enough sunlight]

2. Less socializing in the winter than in the summer

[I have enough]
[Could do with more]
[Not enough]

3. Diet tends to be unhealthier in the winter than in the summer

[Poor diet]
[Moderate]
[Healthy diet]

4. One or both of my parents, or a sibling have had SAD

[My parent(s) have/had SAD]
[My sibling(s) have/had SAD]
[Not sure]
[Never had SAD]

If you have SAD, you may experience some of the following symptoms and signs.

Let's discover them together. If you identify with any of these symptoms, please circle or highlight them.

1) Do you lack energy more often in the winter months?

[Always] [Sometimes] [Never]

2) Do you feel lifeless, sad, or down for most of the day in the winter?

[Always] [Sometimes] [Never]

3) Do you find it hard to concentrate and communicate with others in the winter?

[Always] [Sometimes] [Never]

4) Do you avoid or not want to see or socialize with people in the winter?

[Always] [Sometimes] [Never]

5) Do you sleep more than usual or not enough during the winter?
[Always] [Sometimes] [Never]

6) Do you feel melancholy, angry, tearful, guilty, or hopeless in the winter?
[Always] [Sometimes] [Never]

7) Do you gain or lose weight through changes in your appetite in the winter?
[Always] [Sometimes] [Never]

8) Do you suffer from more physical and emotional health problems or immune system disorders in winter?
[Always] [Sometimes] [Never]

9) Do you lose interest in sex or physical contact with your partner in the winter?
[Always] [Sometimes] [Never]

10) Do your arms and legs seem heavier, to the point where everything feels like an arduous task?
[Always] [Sometimes] [Never]

6. Situational Depression

Situational depression, also known as 'adjustment disorder,' is a specific type of mental disorder. This adjustment disorder can be brought on by several different factors, for example, the death of a loved one, divorce, financial difficulties, serious illness, abuse in a relationship, or even legal troubles.

Situational depression follows a traumatic situation or an event that has left a person chronically stressed. Please note that not everyone who suffers from chronic stress will end up with situational depression. People with situational depression tend to be prone to or highly vulnerable to other types of depression. This type of disorder then seeps in because of stressful experiences or even genetics.

Situational depression is a group of symptoms lasting anywhere from two weeks to several months. Here are some of the symptoms after a traumatic event or chronic stress. Please seek professional help or advice if you identify with the group of the symptoms of situational depression. Please put an [X] if you identify with any symptoms.

1) I have difficulty adjusting or getting used to life again because I am sad or hopeless. [ ]
2) I have difficulty adjusting or getting used to life again because I am tearful and I frequently cry. [ ]
3) I have difficulty adjusting or getting used to life again because of changes in my appetite. [ ]
4) I have difficulty adjusting to life because I have trouble sleeping. [ ]
5) I have difficulty adjusting or getting used to life again because of my increased worry and anxiety. [ ]
6) I have difficulty adjusting or getting used to life again because of my headaches and stomachaches. [ ]
7) I have difficulty adjusting or getting used to life again because of my low energy, fatigue, or both. [ ]
8) I have difficulty adjusting or getting used to life again because I am withdrawn from my loved ones, social activities, or both that I previously enjoyed. [ ]
9) I have difficulty adjusting or getting used to life again because of my increased absence from work or school. [ ]
10) I have difficulty adjusting or getting used to life again because I have trouble concentrating and making decisions. [ ]

7. Atypical Depression

Welcome to one of the more common types of depression. This depression is very interesting because of some associated symptoms and how they affect people. Atypical depression, also known as (major depression with atypical features) is similar to major depression. However, a person with atypical depression can have good days and mood lifts, unlike other types of depression. These mood lifts could be in response to positive events such as a party, a fun day out in the park, or going to the cinema to watch a movie. Other presentations of depression, such as melancholic depression, would respond negatively with low moods when a positive event occurs.

There are little to no high moods with the other types of depression, unlike atypical depression.

With atypical depression, people tend to have more of an appetite and are more likely to gain weight. With other types of depression, like melancholic depression, people lose their appetite and will lose weight.

With atypical depression, people tend to nap and sleep for long periods. With other types of depression, people sleep less and wake up very early.

With atypical depression, people's bodies will feel as though they're weighed down like they've been cemented to the ground, called 'leaden paralysis.' With other types of depression, such as bipolar disorder, people feel like they're either speeding up or slowing down but not cemented in place.

With atypical depression, people are extremely sensitive to criticism or rejection from others and have an intense reaction to it. With other types of depression, such as melancholic depression, people focus on their feelings of ruminating guilt more than their sensitivity to being rejected by others.

With atypical depression, people tend to feel worse in the evenings. With other types of depression, people tend to feel worse in the mornings.

Atypical depression can last longer than most other types of depression and cause people to sleep a lot through an episode.

Here are the symptoms of atypical depression. If you are depressed and experiencing any of these symptoms, please circle or highlight "Always," "Sometimes," or "Never."

1) When I am depressed, my mood temporarily lifts in response to good news or positive events.
   [Always] [Sometimes] [Never]

2) When I am depressed, my appetite increases, and I gain weight.
   [Always] [Sometimes] [Never]

3) When I am depressed, I sleep too much but still feel sleepy in the daytime.
   [Always] [Sometimes] [Never]

4) When I am depressed, my arms and legs feel heavy and leaden, and that feeling lasts an hour or more in a day.
   [Always] [Sometimes] [Never]

5) When I am depressed, I become more sensitive to rejection and criticism, which affects my relationships, social life, and job.
   [Always] [Sometimes] [Never]

8. Persistent Depressive Disorder (PDD)

PDD, also known as dysthymia, is a type of chronic depression that is less severe than other depressions but lasts a minimum of two years. The reason why I say dysthymia is not as severe as other depressions is that people who have dysthymia can still function in their lives with it. High-functioning depression is not an official diagnosis but more of a descriptive term that people use to describe functioning with depression daily, going to work, school, and even socializing with people. A low-functioning person cannot function in their life. They struggle to get out of bed and go to work or school. It is almost impossible for them to socialize with people.

According to the *Diagnostic and Statistical Manual of Mental Disorders*, Fifth Edition (*DSM-5*), the patient must have had a depressed mood for at least two years. For children or adolescents, the mood can be irritable instead of depressed, and the time requirement is at least one year. For both groups, symptoms cannot be absent for greater than two months at a time. In addition to a depressed or irritable mood, at least two of the symptoms listed below must be present.

Have you or a loved one suffered with at least two of the following symptoms for at least two years? If yes, please seek professional advice and help.

Please mark [X] in the box beside any symptoms you believe you may be experiencing or have experienced.

1) I have been depressed for at least 2 years, and I have a poor appetite or overeating. [ ]
2) I have been depressed for a minimum of 2 years, and I have insomnia or hypersomnia. [ ]

3) I have been depressed for a minimum of 2 years, and I have low energy or fatigue. [ ]
4) I have been depressed for a minimum of 2 years, and I have low self-esteem. [ ]
5) I have been depressed for a minimum of 2 years, and I have poor concentration or difficulty making decisions. [ ]
6) I have been depressed for a minimum of 2 years, and I have feelings of hopelessness. [ ]

My Conclusion

First, prevention of depression is better than a cure.

There's no sure way to prevent atypical depression, but these strategies may help.

- Take steps to control stress, increase your resilience, and boost your self-esteem.
- Reach out to family and friends, especially in times of crisis, to help you weather rough spells.
- Get treatment at the earliest sign of a problem to help prevent depression from worsening.
- Consider long-term maintenance treatment to help prevent a relapse of symptoms.
- Enthusiasm can defeat depression.
- Brisk walking can defeat depression.
- Get some exercise.
- Challenge negative thoughts.
- Regularly eat wholesome foods.
- Get adequate sleep.
- Drink plenty of water.
- Make a change in your routine.
- Get into a routine.

CHAPTER 6

SELF-BLAME AND RESENTMENT KILLS

"Why am I so flipping angry all the time?" Amy said as she leaned forward with an intense glare. Her eyes searched for meaning while she rubbed her sweaty palms on her ripped jeans.

I replied, "Why are you so flipping angry all the time?" I then leaned forward, matching and mirroring Amy's tonality and body language.

Pensively, Amy leaned back in a moment of stillness, biting her bottom lip to the point of redness. She lowered her glare, shifting from anger to sadness. She muttered, "I have everything, but yet I have nothing."

"Nothing?" I replied.

"Nothing" She echoed.

"You have sweaty palms," I jokingly countered. Amy's belief system and her regular pattern of behavior would typically spiral her down from sadness to depression to guilt to anger, then back to sadness again.

Amy chuckled. "I do have sweaty palms" she admitted as she rubbed her hands together in a self-comforting motion as the energy in the room lightened.

I cannot quite describe it, but it felt like Amy did not belong in her home. She seemed unsettled, like a stranger who had never experienced this environment before. "How long have you been living here?" I asked.

"36 years," she replied. "We moved here when I was 6. Mum died five years ago, leaving the house to Shawn and I."

"So, you've lived here for 35 years?"

"Yes, something like that," Amy said, counting the years on her fingers.

"Do you like living here?" I asked, now in full investigative mode.

"I do, I think," she responded.

"You think?" repeating her last words back to her.

"Hmmm, I'm not sure".

"What's bothering your spirit?" I asked, now digging even deeper but also really intrigued.

"That's a good question" she said, laughing, then bursting into tears. "I love this house, but I hate this home." She continued, now on the verge of an emotional breakdown. "This house flipping gives me the creeps nowadays." Amy's expressions transitioned into fear, then anger, then it stabilized into sadness. "Some rooms give me anxiety, and others suck the flipping life out of me."

"Suck the flipping life out of you?" I assertively replied.

"Yes, it drains my energy," she said. "It's like an energy vampire living in my house and taking over my home."

My instincts were to comfort her, but I knew professionally I had to stay on course. We were close, but close to what? And where? Is this a conversation about spirits and ghosts? Is she just experiencing loneliness or the stages of mourning due to the loss of her mother? I didn't know, but we were close to the real problem and solution.

"How many rooms do you have in your beautiful home?" I asked fervently.

"Four bedrooms," Amy replied, "three upstairs, one downstairs, two reception rooms, one we are in and the other beside us. That was Mummy's knitting room. It was her comfort room in the house. Oh, and the kitchen is through there (pointing down the long corridor). Also, there are two bathrooms," she said while turning around on her chair and now pointing toward two closed doors.

"That's a lot of rooms for one person," I said, provoking further explanation.

"Yes, my mother, father, older brother and I moved here in 1985."

"Tell me about life in your home here," I enquired.

"Well, we moved from a two-bedroom flat in Notting Hill Gate. I was six, and my brother Shawn was nine. My parents decided that Shawn and I were coming of age and needed our own space and bedrooms, so we moved here to Muswell Hill.

"My father was a scientist," Amy continued. "If I remember correctly, he was a cytologist. His job was to research diagnoses and treatments for human diseases. He used to say that his role in the world was to help humans live longer and better lives. He would always say, 'In everything, do unto others as you would have them do unto you.' He called it the 'golden rule.'

"All he wanted to do was help people. He spent so much time helping and serving others that he neglected himself and his health. He was constantly traveling and always stressed. He had burnouts but tried to hide them from us.

He died on a work trip in Singapore. It was in 2010 when he suffered his first stroke. Then, three days later, he had another stroke in hospital. Shortly after, Daddy had a massive heart attack which killed him. He died alone, no family, no friends, no one; That's so sad. He must have been so scared.

I sometimes wonder if in his last days, did he still believe that bull crap he used to tell Shawn and I, 'In everything, do unto others as you would have them do unto you.' What did others do for him apart from bloody burning him out, demanding so much from him that he was always away from us—his family. When he died, he was alone and stressed. His workplace sent cheap flowers and a condolence card to his funeral. In the reception room beside us was Daddy's man cave; he was a ferroequinologist."

"Ferroequinologist?" I replied.

"Yes". Amy said "Just another name for a person who studies trains as a hobby. Every chance Daddy would get, he would take us all to spot trains. Mummy wasn't interested in it but would tag along anyway just to please us. The trips would excite Shawn, which in turn, excited me. Shawn was my hero back then, and Daddy was Shawn's hero. In Daddy's man cave, he has hundreds, maybe thousands of pristine model trains. I think they're called Z scales, N scales, G scales, scales, scales, scales…," Amy rolled her eyes playfully.

She continued, "When Daddy died, Mummy kept his room the same. That was her way of keeping him alive I guess. I would hear her in the room sometimes crying for hours. She became very despondent over the years. Then one day, Mummy died of a brain aneurysm in Daddy's man cave after having a nasty migraine. I will never forget that day. It was November 3rd, 2016—six years after Daddy died."

Amy was now sobbing, reverting back to rubbing her palms on her knees while tapping away. "If I wasn't so self-absorbed," she continued, "I could have saved Mummy."

"And what about Shawn?" I asked.

Amy sighed, then sighed again. "Who knows nowadays? When Daddy died, Shawn turned to drugs. When Mummy died, he was a full-fledged junkie. He couldn't even FLIPPING HOLD IT TOGETHER AT MUMMY'S FUNERAL!" Amy then shifted quickly from pensive pain into a rage, hurling her phone across the room (just missing my head) and smashing it against the wall behind me.

I startled and jolted back in my chair. I turned around to see the broken phone and a dented wall.

"I'm so, so sorry" Amy said, trying her best to compose herself, putting both hands up in a surrender pose.

"No, this is good" I responded, "Well, not for your phone," I quipped, once again trying to lighten the mood in the room.

"What is so good about that?" Amy punctuated. "I could have hurt you Kevin" she said, shifting from the surrender pose to both hands on her head.

I then reached into my backpack and grabbed my black trauma folder. I took out two copies of pages 7 and 8—the home and feelings assessment sheets. "Amy, I'm going to ask you a series of single questions," now writing the days date on the feelings assessment sheet.

"Yeah sure. Go ahead Kevin," Amy replied, raising her head.

"I will say one word, you give me one emotion connected to that word," now ready to investigate Amy's raw emotions.

"Ok, no probs" Amy replied.

I started reading out the words.

"Shawn." I said.

"Betrayal." Amy said.

"Daddy." I said.

Amy looked down and whispered, "Too soon."

"Mummy." I said.

"Broken." Amy said.

"House." I said.

"Jinxed." Amy said.

"Amy." I said.

Amy paused, then answered, "Drained."

Now that I had opened Amy up emotionally, it was time to operate on her feelings. Highlighting the first column of Amy's feelings assessment sheet titled, 'How do you feel?' I was ready to ask her a series of 'How do you feel?' questions. These questions are designed to enter the gateway into the emotional relationship between oneself and the world around them. This is good practice for all of us to self-assess regularly.

The first few responses to the questions will typically be guarded, self-protective, or surface responses from the mind to shut the questioner up or eliminate them. That's normal and perfectly fine, expect it. The conscious mind will always protect itself from invaders—the people who may cause harm, loss, or pain to the mind. The mind will try to sort out the good people from the bad people by first giving any surface answer to those who are not invested in the person's well-being and happiness. But when you keep digging, the subconscious feelings and emotions will start to express themselves and tell you all that you need to know about the person.

Now let's get back to Amy.

"How do you feel when 'betrayal' comes to mind?" I asked.

"Angry," Amy replied.

"How do you feel when you think about 'broken'?" I said.

"Guilt," Amy replied.

"How do you feel when 'too soon' comes to mind?"

"Sad," she replied, eyes now welling up.

"How do you feel when 'jinxed' comes to mind?" I asked

"Anxious," Amy said, now expressing signs of fear.

"How do you feel when 'drained' comes to mind?"

"Depressed," Amy said succinctly, tears trickling down her red cheeks and smearing her eyeliner into her makeup.

How Do I Feel?	Why?	Behavior	How Would I Love to Feel?	Why?	My New Behavior	What I MUST DO NOW!
Anxious →		SELF-TALK			NEW SELF-TALK	
Depressed →		MUSCULAR PAIN WHEN			MUSCULAR PAIN NOW	Start Date: Complete Date:
Betrayal →	Shawn					
Shawn should have stepped up. He should have been the man of the house. He ran away and left Mummy and me to pick up the pieces.						Start Date:

How Do I Feel?	Why?	Behavior	How Would I Love to Feel?	Why?	My New Behavior	What I MUST DO NOW!
Angry →		TRIGGER WORDS Shawn – Betrayal Daddy – Too soon Mummy – Broken House – Jinxed Amy – Drained			TRIGGER WORDS	1.Get contact details for Shawn. Start Date: Complete Date:
Guilty →	Mummy	MOOD Morning Afternoon Night			MOOD Morning Afternoon Night	2.Write down on the Home Assessment sheet dark energy from jewellery, trinkets, ornaments, colors, and clothes Complete Date:
Mummy gave up on life. I was too self-indulged; I was drinking and partying while Mummy was suffering.						
Sad →	Daddy	MEDICATION			MEDICATION	
Daddy died trying to give us a better life.		SMOKE? (What?)			SMOKE	

With Amy's previous responses, her patterns of behavior and emotions started to make perfect sense to me. From sadness to guilt, guilt to anger, and anger to sorrow governing her life. But her body language when sitting in her chair, talking about her home, exuded fear, and anxiety. So, what was anchoring her self-talk and triggering such emotions? I also wanted to know about Amy's anger towards Shawn.

Her sadness connected to her father and feelings of guilt attached to her mother were becoming more apparent. But I also needed to investigate more on that. The unresolved issues were collectively causing Amy's depression and outbursts. There's a saying, 'Pressure burst pipes,' and Amy was seriously about to explode very soon. I was picking up that the energy in her home was a reminder of her painful past. And there's an energy that is disconnecting Amy from her home. I thought I needed to find out what it was very soon, or she wouldn't survive there much longer.

"Now I'm going to ask you a series of 'why' questions, if you don't mind, Amy," I said.

"Ok, shoot," she said.

I then highlighted the second column on Amy's feelings assessment sheet titled 'Why?'

"Why do you feel such sadness when you think about your Daddy? I asked. I noticed that Amy used the terms 'mummy' and 'Daddy,' not 'father' or 'mother,' like she did when her guard was up. She became childlike. It was as though she was six years old again. She is a grown woman but emotionally stuck at the age that her trauma took hold of her.

"Daddy killed himself trying to give us a better life," Amy began. "He worked all the hours God sent to provide us with this flipping house and a better life, but instead, it killed him and screwed us in the process. Mummy's dead, Shawn's a junkie, and I'm depressed. Great life huh? People say I'm 'blessed' to have this big expensive house, but they don't see the pain and sacrifice behind it. Hence me saying, 'I have everything but nothing at all.'

I can see now why Amy's resentment toward her home is connected to her mother and father.

Amy continued. "Daddy's man cave became Mummy's prison."

"Mummy's prison?" I said, repeating her last words back to her.

"Yes, she would come out of the cave to go to bed, cook, clean, take toilet breaks, and back in the cave to carry out the rest of her life sentence."

"Her life sentence?" I repeated.

"Yes, yes, yes" she iterated "Mummy was outgoing, beautiful, and vibrant before Daddy died," Amy said. "She then became a shadow of herself. She stopped doing her hair, stopped talking to her friends, and grew old very quickly."

Stroking my chin while writing the last words of Amy's 'why' answers about her mother, I then moved on to Shawn. Not wanting to burn Amy out or have her shut down before I gathered enough information, I asked, "Why do you feel betrayed by Shawn?" circling 'betrayal' in the first column titled 'How do you feel?'

"Shawn is my older brother, not my younger brother, and definitely not my child." Amy said now sating upright and becoming professionally stern, with an injection of energized anger. "When Daddy died, he should have stepped up. He should have been the man of the house, but noooo. Not Shawn. Selfish Shawn ran like a bitch and left Mummy and I to pick up the pieces. Mummy did not just lose her husband when Daddy died; she also lost a son the day he chose to use crack (Crack cocaine) over his family. And, for that, I will NEVER FORGIVE HIM!"

I wanted to challenge her narrative at that point, but the first lesson of understanding is the understanding itself. It's never good to prematurely challenge. God gave us more ears than mouths for a reason. Exercising the art of listening is a skill, and I was listening intently with enthusiasm.

To make someone feel comfortable, unjudged, and not looked down upon (which is never my intent or desire), I use terms such as 'it feels like,' 'it seems like,' and 'it sounds like.' Ok, let me explain. If I say, "It feels like you have a lot of love inside of you," I'm not saying that person has love inside them. I'm just saying it's my feeling, not my fact. If I say, "It seems like you're unhappy," I'm not stating that the person is unhappy. I'm just saying it's a vibe I feel without using the word *vibe*. People can interpret 'vibe' as bad energy if they have a negative mind or belief.

Stage two of the success cycle is 'meaning.' The meaning you give to things is based on your belief system, which is stage one. If your belief system is negative, by default, what you translate as meaning becomes negative.

When I say, "It sounds like you have more to share," the words 'It sounds like' are not specifically saying 'share more,' but urging the person to share more (with the right tonality) without saying it. All the previous terms are not demands or judgments but are effective persuasion tactics. They are brilliant terms to try to make sense of another person's statement, situation, or self-conversation while seeking more information without asking a question. For example, if you said to your spouse (in the right tone of voice), “Honey, it feels like you're upset.” They may respond by saying, “No Hun, just tired.” See, not only would they have given you all the information you need, but they wouldn't take your feelings statement personally. In this case, they would have likely been happy to give you all the information you needed while not feeling judged or accused.

If the question were ‘Why’ are you upset?’ that would carry a different type of energy and response—usually a negative one. People don't like being judged or told what's happening within their thoughts without confirmation or permission. When in any sensitive or—even worse—hypersensitive communication with anyone, use any or all of the following phrases with the right tonality. Remember, ‘it feels like,’ ‘it sounds like,’ and ‘it seems like.’

Now back to Amy.

“It feels like you have resentment toward yourself as well Amy.” I said.

“I do. Massive resentment,” Amy said. “Mummy needed me until her last breath, and I was too self-indulgent even to see it.”

“Too self-indulgent to even see it?” I repeated.

Nine times out of ten, repeating the last two or three words from the other person's sentence will urge that person to go further into detail without you needing to ask them to tell you more.

Asking people "to tell you more" can sometimes cause the other person to put up barriers or limit the conversation. People can quickly feel when you are becoming too intrusive or encroaching into uncomfortable territory in their minds if you keep pushing for more. Repeating the last two or three words, then become silent, will subconsciously kickstart the other person into sharing more information with you without even realizing it. The next part of the science is silence. People usually don't like silence when it's their turn to reply in a conversation. The best negotiators and interrogators use this science to extract vital information from a prospect or a suspect. My side note request: Please be ethical when using this science and tactic. This book is designed to help, build up, and empower people, not to cause harm, pain, or loss.

Amy admitted, "I was so stressed at the time.

I was drinking and partying to drown my sorrows. I would stagger in at 3 a.m. drunk, crashing out on the floor and sometimes on the sofa. I would wake up to see that I was lying in vomit. Mummy would clean me up and tuck me into bed. She loved me to the end," Amy sobbed. "I'm so flipping irresponsible," she concluded as she snapped back into her chair.

I sensed Amy was becoming too drained and tired to continue the day's session. I didn't want her to fall too deep down the emotional well. When you open someone up, you must be responsible and know when to repair and when to close them back up again. It's just like surgery. To conclude the day's session, we meditated for about eight minutes and did some affirmations for five minutes to raise her emotional vibrations. I then had her jump on my small portable trampoline for three more minutes. We did some stretching exercises, then I gave Amy weekly tasks and goals to do.

Task 1: Get contact details for Shawn.

Amy scowled but then agreed reluctantly.

Task 2: Anytime you encounter dark energy or vibe from any of your jewelry, trinkets, ornaments, colors, or garments in your house, I would like you to write them down on the 'Home Feelings Assessment' sheets.

Amy agreed. I thanked her and congratulated her for her courage and for working with me. I then bid her a farewell until our next session at the same time on the following Saturday.

The two tasks that I set for Amy are the same tasks I will set for you.

Task 1: Think of someone you love or care for deeply, such as a family member, a friend, or an ex-partner, who you feel may have done harm, loss, or offense to you. Gather their updated contact information and follow the instructions as we continue our adventure with Amy.

Name of person 1..

Email..

Phone number...

Name of person 2..

Email..

Phone number...

Name of person 3..

Email...

Phone number...

Name of person 4..

Email...

Phone number...

Name of person 5..

Email...

Phone number...

Task 2: Use our feelings assessment sheet to measure the energy or frequencies in your home to discover what may be giving you good or bad energy or vibes in your life.

1. Name the item.
2. Who or where did you get the item from?
3. Remember what you were experiencing when you got the item. For example, you were depressed or lonely when you purchased or received it.
4. How does the item make you feel? Or how do people treat you when you wear or have that item on your person?
5. Decide if the item is good energy and should stay, or a bad energy and must go. Get started.

Amy and I met at 1 p.m. the following Saturday for our weekly session.

“Good afternoon, Amy” I said, smiling.

Amy smiled back. She looked fresh. I cannot describe it, but the closest word to Amy’s vibe and energy was ‘fresh.’

“Hey Kev,” Amy said while giving me a formal La Bise kiss on each cheek while on tiptoes. “I feel much lighter and better than last week Kevin. Thank you.”

“That’s brilliant,” I replied. “

“Here, have a seat,” Amy said, directing me to our seating arrangement from the week before.

“What’s different with you?” I asked.

With her posture perfectly straight, sitting up in her seat, Amy said, “To know.”

“To know?” I repeated.

“Yes,” she said. “To know.” Amy continued, “When you left last week, I became very reflective. I thought about what we spoke about. And without you telling me the answers, you led me toward self-discovery. I connected with my cousin Patricia to ask her for Shawn’s number. They are very close, going back to our childhood. While Patricia gave me his number,” she added, ‘Shawn loves you Amy. Don’t block your incoming love for outgoing anger.’ For four days, I thought about Shawn. ’Is he OK? Is he healthy? Is he lonely like our father was before he died in the hospital alone?’

“Kevin, may I ask you a question?” Amy said.

“Yeah sure,” I replied.

"Why did you ask me to get hold of Shawn's contact details, but you did not also request that I call him? Why?" she asked.

"Why?" I echoed.

"Yes," Amy said.

"When my mother cooks her meat and fish dishes, she will always season the meat the day before, sometimes even days before she cooks it," I said. "The longer the meat would marinate, the better it tasted. I wanted Shawn's importance in your life to marinate before you entertained the idea of a conversation with him."

"Wow," Amy said, laughing and rolling back in her chair. "I would love to taste Mummy Bennett's home cooking!" She continued, "I couldn't wait Kevin. I spoke to Shawn yesterday."

"You did?" I exclaimed.

"Yes, crazy right?"

"When was the last time you spoke to Shawn before yesterday?"

"Two days after Mum's funeral," Amy said. "That was June 10, 2016. Five years ago now. He turned up at Mummy's funeral, off his head on drugs. I was so angry, embarrassed, and hurt; I called him two days after to tell him to never talk to me again. I wanted him to know that he was a disappointing mess-up and to drop me out and never talk to me again, and I meant it."

"So, how did it go yesterday? What happened? I'm intrigued, sensing good news. I want the full low-down Amy." I said, smiling from ear to ear and rubbing my hands excitedly.

“Well, it was about 8:30. I just got in from having my nails done. Nice, right?” Amy said, showing off her multicolored nails in a playful fun motion. “Anyway, I normally pay homage to Mummy when I step through the door by saying, ‘I’m home safe Mum.’ Shawn would do the same. When I said it yesterday, it hit me like a ton of bricks. Thoughts and feelings came flooding in. ‘Is Shawn home and safe? Is he dead?’ I would know that much; family members would tell me. But ‘home’ and ‘safe?’ I’m not sure. Then my mind started racing. If I feel so guilty about not being there for Mum when she died, what if Shawn died? I couldn’t live with myself. Then it crossed my mind—who says Shawn would even want to talk to me now after what I said to him? I contemplated if I should even call him for about an hour. Then I called Patricia.”

“Patricia?” I repeated.

“Yes, my cousin Patricia. Remember?”

“Oh yes, I remember now.”

“Come on Kev, keep up!” Amy said rolling her eyes playfully. “When I spoke to her, she told me that when she gave me Shawn’s number, she then called Shawn to give him the heads-up that I might call. She said Shawn sounded dumbfounded and happy, so that prompted me to call Shawn.”

“As soon as he said ‘Hello’ and I heard his voice, I burst into tears. He bloody cried too. We cried like babies for close to 5 minutes, before we could even string a full sentence together. We both kept saying ‘Sorry’ and ‘I love you.’”

“Oh my gosh,” I said, leaning forward. I almost slid off my chair, observing Amy’s moment of joy and happiness. I motioned for her to tell me more while holding back my emotions.

Amy continued, “We spoke about the good old days. We reminisced about Mummy and Daddy and joked about who was their favorite child. I was so happy when Shawn told me he’s been drug-free for the past two years. He has a fiancé now, and they are three months pregnant.”

“This is great news!” I said. “So task one is completed. But I want you to have further understanding Amy, so you don’t relapse with Shawn when this feeling you are experiencing blows over.”

“Okay,” Amy replied.

“May I ask you some questions?” I said. (Always ask for permission to enter someone’s emotional space.)

“Yeah. Go ahead Kevin,” Amy replied.

“Do you believe that the older you are, the more you should be able to manage the pain and trauma of the death of a loved one?” I asked.

“I don’t quite understand the question Kevin,” Amy replied.

“Ok, the loss of a parent. Do you believe the trauma of the untimely death of a parent should be felt any differently if you were 5, 15, or 50 years old?” I asked, readjusting my question.

“Pain is pain, regardless of age,” Amy responded.

“Yes, I agree. Do you believe that the trauma and loss of a loved one can cause psychological and physical damage to the mind and body?” I asked.

"Yes, it can," Amy responded.

She continued, "My friend Paul became ill with IBS when his mother died. He told me that the trauma and stress of his mother dying caused his IBS."

I then gently nudged in. "When your father died, what do you believe young Shawn was experiencing?" I asked.

"Depression," Amy said.

"Yes," I replied.

Amy continued, "I heard Shawn say several times that he wanted to die. Sometimes, he would say he wanted to kill himself and be with Daddy."

"Okay," I said, nodding slowly to get Amy to see that we were close to the point I wanted her to discover.

"Who did Shawn admire more than anyone on this planet?" I asked.

"Daddy," Amy replied.

"Who did Shawn turn to for advice and direction when your Daddy was alive?"

"Daddy," Amy replied again.

"Who did Mummy turn to when your Daddy was alive?"

"Daddy," Amy again replied, slowly piecing the puzzle together.

"Who did you turn to when your Daddy was alive?"

"Mummy and Daddy. Mummy would express that innate mummy love, care, and comfort I was always badly in need of, so I went to her for that. Daddy was a man's man; he was my educator, security net, and confidant."

"Okay," I said, "who did you turn to when your Daddy died?"

"I wanted to turn to Mummy, but I saw she was hurting too much to give me the comfort, security, and necessary answers I really needed. She tried at times. She often said, 'God has a greater plan for us.' Mum didn't even believe that statement herself." Amy then looked up at her chandeliered ceiling and sighed, "We were all trying to make sense of our emotional traumas without Daddy. I get it now; Shawn was seeking his answers in the drugs and anyone who would entertain or pay attention to him. His support system was gone. Mother's support system was gone. My support system was gone. He died alone. The man that was there for the world died alone, without any of his loved ones beside him."

"As for Mummy, she was seeking refuge in Daddy's man cave. And as for me, I wanted Shawn to replace Daddy. I wanted him to be my father and have all the answers, knowledge, and masculinity dad did. When he couldn't meet my unrealistic expectations, I blamed Shawn; then I blamed my boyfriends—one relationship after another. I blamed my best friends and eventually my mother. I even hated and blamed myself. This was my reactive illness, like Paul's IBS," Amy said. "We were all emotionally ill. Life just happens to us. We have to find positive tools to manage life's circumstances when pain comes to visit," she concluded.

As I did with Amy, asking the right questions at the right time with the right tonality will always allow a person to discover the answers for themselves. It will also allow you, the reader, to do the same. The tone, the words, and the meaning you give the words will help you to discover your unanswered questions.

Let's move on to Task 2. I now want you to monitor the energy and vibes in your home.

Task 2 is to discover if your jewelry, trinkets, ornaments, colors, or garments give you and your home good or bad energy. Concerning Amy, there was an energy in her home that was freaking her out and stifling her growth. I wouldn't rule anything out. I needed her to investigate anything in her home that could be causing such pain and problems.

"So, Amy, how did Task 2 go for you?" I asked.

"Oh, lord God Kevin. Now that was an interesting task!" Amy replied.

"Why was it interesting for you?" I interrupted. "What did you discover?"

"Hmm. Well, I acknowledged that I have a beautiful house. But my home is not in a good harmonious state. To be honest Kevin, I started the process. But some of the rooms, areas, and stuff in this house are way-too painful and overwhelming to deal with alone."

"Ok," I said, understanding where Amy was going with her reasoning. "Let's do this together."

I reached into my backpack and grabbed three packs of colored stickers. The red stickers were for bad energy, the yellow for undecided, and the green for good energy. I then collected the House Feelings Assessment sheets I gave Amy the previous week.

"Amy, we are going to go from room to room, area to area, and item to item in your home. I will ask you a series of questions about your items and rooms. You tell me your feelings and the relationship you have with them. Fair enough?" I asked.

"Sounds good to me," Amy said, with a hint of nervousness and panic.

"Ok, let's start here in this room Amy. What is that there?" I said, pointing to an item.

"It's a lion statue," Amy said.

I wrote 'lion statue' on the first line of the item sheet. "Okay, where did you get it?" I asked.

"Mummy bought it when we moved here. It is part of a pair. But Shawn and I broke the other statue play fighting," Amy laughed.

"How does it make you feel?" I asked.

"Positive," Amy said.

"I won't ask you the other questions on the sheet because it was your mother's, so let's move on," I said.

"Let's first put a green sticker on the lion statue to mark it as a keeper. It's good energy," I stated.

For the next 30 minutes, we zigzagged across Amy's living room and her kitchen, discovering what was vibrationally good, bad, and indifferent for her. A few pictures and a memorial book of Amy's mother's funeral stirred self-guilt for Amy and a bit of frustration toward Shawn. But we were working through those emotions, so I suggested putting a yellow sticker on them for now. Amy thought it was better to remove them, so we did.

I believe Amy's relationship with those items was more emotionally associated with what she was going through, but Amy felt they carried negative energy. She deemed them as unhealthy, so who am I to challenge what she was feeling?

The house was pretty stable frequency-wise, until we encountered three particular areas in the house. Amy became very jittery and even anxious approaching those areas. The first area was her father's man cave (also her mother's knitting room). The room sat untouched since Amy's father died 11 years prior. It was a dark British racing green colored room with closed blackout curtains and four layers of shelves in all four corners of the walls.

The room had a fairly big model train track skirting around the relatively small room. The four layers of shelves had hundreds, maybe more than a thousand model trains on them. Some were boxed, others were neatly placed out in the open. An old green Chesterfield armchair was in the center of the room with a small work table. The room felt old, with dust layers and a lingering smell of must and glue. Amy's mother's knitting needles and a ball of wool was lying on the table unattended since the day Amy's mother died in the room. The first feelings of pain and guilt running through Amy were triggered by her mother's knitting needles and ball of wool.

Amy jumped behind me as though she had just seen a tarantula.

"Get it out, please Kevin. Please!" Amy said, taking backward steps out of the room.

"How does it make you feel?" I asked.

"Scared, angry, anxious, and flipping hurt," Amy said, flinching and moving farther out of the room.

"Haven't you been in here since your mother died?" I asked, partly taken aback by Amy's response.

"Noooo," Amy said. "The last time I was in here was when Mummy died. She was slumped in that chair." Amy pointed at the Chesterfield.

"What is spiritually affecting you about it," I asked, following Amy out of the room.

"I used to see Mummy scream into that ball of wool to muffle her pain and cries," Amy recalled. "I would peek through the cracks in the door. The paramedics found threads of the same flipping wool in her mouth the day she died. Please, Kevin, I don't want to go back in there," Amy groaned, putting her hands over her eyes and mouth.

"When you think about that item, what comes to mind?" I asked.

"Mummy's pain, her brokenness," Amy replied. "I feel so much pain from this room, chair, and wool. Even with the door closed, I felt pain and anxiety radiating from the room. I did not even know what was affecting me until now."

"Mummy's last breaths are in that ball of wool," Amy said. I would normally get my clients to build a relationship with that energy, but on this occasion, I removed it from the house for Amy. Amy then calmed down. We reentered the room and continued. By the end of the day's session, we had discovered three more items that made Amy feel uncomfortable in the room where Amy's mother died. They didn't upset her to the point of frenzy as the wool did. They just made her uncomfortable. We decided to continue the following day.

At 1 p.m. the next day, we took up where we had left off. Amy had a gold ring that she purchased from a pawnshop in 2019.

She told me a story about when she bought the ring with the two diamonds. Sticking to the Items assessment sheet format, I asked Amy the following questions.

“How did you feel when you purchased this ring at that time?” I asked gently closing Amy’s eyelids, and slowly clutching her hand holding the ring.

“I remember breaking up with Andrew the day before getting the ring,” Amy said. “My girls and I went on a shopping spree. I was emotional that day. Looking back at it, I also purchased a silver charm bracelet with hearts, padlocks, dice, and other charms. This ring was a self-engagement gift to myself. I will commit to myself if Andrew is not interested in the commitment of marriage to me. I remember saying to myself, before I found out about him cheating on me. “Cheated on you?” I repeated. “Yes, if you saw this skank girl Kevin, what a damn shame. Once you go skank, you can’t come back; I used to sing to him,” Amy, reminiscently laughing out loud. “After having enough of one of my skank made-up songs,” Amy continued, “Andrew sarcastically replied and said, ‘I had to step up my choice of women when I chose that “skank” to sleep with over you.’”

“What is a skank?” I asked. “I only know about Skank the Dance,” I laughed.

Amy joined me on my moment of fun and laughter and then said “In our circle, we call a dirty, nasty person a ‘skank,’” Amy explained. “So, he was saying I was worse than a skank. I officially ended it that evening, and the day after, I purchased this ring.”

“Tell me why this ring makes you feel the way you do about it,” I enquired.

"Whenever I wore this ring, I would get into fights and arguments with women who looked like the girl Andrew cheated on me with. I am always drawn to anger and resentment when I put this ring on. Andrew also lingers in the back of my mind. I then would get even more angry and frustrated."

"When did you notice that this ring was your Achilles heel?" I asked.

"Last night," Amy replied. "The only reason I stopped wearing this ring was when one of the stones fell out," Amy pointing at the space where the stone was once placed. "Last night, when you left, I continued the item assessment in my room. I threw away old underwear, clothes, and bed sheets when I noticed I had the worst nightmares wearing them.

"I looked around the house and decided it was time to change the colors on most of the walls. I remember when you said in our second session that colors emit energy. Kev, I went into Daddy's man cave for the first time alone. Although it was nerve-racking, I did it," said Amy, raising her hands in a celebratory manner. "It's time for Daddy's trains to find a new home, and it's also time for this whole house to become my home again," declared Amy, sounding empowered and back in control.

"When I picked up this ring, old bad thoughts and energy started to seep back in," I never noticed it before, but, on reflection, I now can put all the pieces together. This ring and the charm bracelet are negative forces in my life that need to go. I feel happier and, more important. I feel like I am back in control again. Thank you. It's time for me and my home to have a refurb."

Item 1

Name of Item 1 Lion statue

What is Item 1 made of? Copper

Where did you get Item 1? Mummy purchased it

Estimated date of when you got Item 1 /

What were you feeling and experiencing in your life when you got Item 1? Please check all that apply.

I was feeling hopeless. [ ]
I was feeling depressed. [ ]
I was feeling guilty. [ ]
I was feeling ashamed. [ ]
I was feeling apathetic. [ ]
I was feeling insecure. [ ]
I was feeling fearful. [ ]
I was feeling lonely. [ ]
I was feeling sad. [ ]
I was feeling worried. [ ]
I was feeling jealous. [ ]
I was feeling angry. [ ]
I was feeling disheartened. [ ]
I was feeling doubtful. [ ]
I was feeling frustrated. [ ]
I was feeling overwhelmed. [ ]
I was feeling bored. [ ]
I was feeling upset. [ ]
I was feeling hopeful. [ ]
I was feeling positive. [ ]
I was feeling passionate. [ ]
I was feeling happy. [ ]
I was feeling loved. [ ]

Would you like to go into detail about your feelings when you got Item 1? What were you experiencing at that time in your life?

It was Mummy's

Based on your feelings, emotions, and experiences with the above item, how would you rate Item 1?

Negative item; not good for me [ ] Moderate; it's OK [✓] Positive item; it's a keeper [ ]

Item 2

Name of Item 2 Memorial book

What is Item 2 made of? Book / paper

Where did you get Item 2? WH Smith

Estimated date of when you got Item 2 /

What were you feeling and experiencing in your life when you got Item 2?

I was feeling hopeless. [ ]
I was feeling ashamed. [ ]
I was feeling fearful. [ ]
I was feeling worried. [ ]
I was feeling disheartened. [ ]
I was feeling overwhelmed. [ ]
I was feeling hopeful. [ ]
I was feeling happy. [ ]
I was feeling depressed. [✓]
I was feeling apathetic. [ ]
I was feeling lonely. [✓]
I was feeling jealous. [ ]
I was feeling doubtful. [ ]
I was feeling bored. [ ]
I was feeling positive. [ ]
I was feeling loved. [ ]
I was feeling guilty. [✓]
I was feeling insecure. [ ]
I was feeling sad. [✓]
I was feeling angry. [✓]
I was feeling frustrated. [ ]
I was feeling upset. [✓]
I was feeling passionate. [ ]

Would you like to go into detail about your feelings when you got Item 2? What were you experiencing at that time in your life?

Had to buy the book for Mummy's funeral

Based on your feelings, emotions, and experiences with the above item, how would you rate Item 2?

Negative item; not good for me [ ] Moderate; it's OK [✓] Positive item; it's a keeper [ ]

Item 3

Name of Item 3 Knitting needles and wool

What is Item 3 made of? Wool

Where did you get item 3? Mummy's

Estimated date of when you got Item 3 /

What were you feeling and experiencing in your life when you got Item 3?

I was feeling hopeless. [ ] I was feeling depressed. [✓] I was feeling guilty. [✓]
I was feeling ashamed. [ ] I was feeling apathetic. [ ] I was feeling insecure. [ ]
I was feeling fearful. [✓] I was feeling lonely. [ ] I was feeling sad. [✓]
I was feeling worried. [ ] I was feeling jealous. [ ] I was feeling angry. [ ]
I was feeling disheartened. [ ] I was feeling doubtful. [ ] I was feeling frustrated. [ ]
I was feeling overwhelmed. [ ] I was feeling bored. [ ] I was feeling upset. [ ]
I was feeling hopeful. [ ] I was feeling positive. [ ] I was feeling passionate. [ ]
I was feeling happy. [ ] I was feeling loved. [ ]

Would you like to go into detail about your feelings when you got Item 3? What were you experiencing at that time in your life?

Mummy had this when she died.

We found bits of the wool in her mouth.

Based on your feelings, emotions, and experiences with the above item, how would you rate Item 3?

Negative item; not good for me [✓] Moderate; it's OK [|] Positive item; it's a keeper [ ]

Item 4

Name of Item 4 Gold ring

What is Item 4 made of? Gold and diamonds

Where did you get Item 4? Pawn shop

Estimated date of when you got Item 4 /

What were you feeling and experiencing in your life when you got Item 4?

I was feeling hopeless. [ ]
I was feeling depressed. [ ]
I was feeling guilty. [ ]
I was feeling ashamed. [ ]
I was feeling apathetic. [ ]
I was feeling insecure. [ ]
I was feeling fearful. [ ]
I was feeling lonely. [ ]
I was feeling sad. [✓]
I was feeling worried. [ ]
I was feeling jealous. [ ]
I was feeling angry. [✓]
I was feeling disheartened. [ ]
I was feeling doubtful. [ ]
I was feeling frustrated. [✓]
I was feeling overwhelmed. [ ]
I was feeling bored. [ ]
I was feeling upset. [✓]
I was feeling hopeful. [ ]
I was feeling positive. [ ]
I was feeling passionate. [ ]
I was feeling happy. [ ]
I was feeling loved. [ ]

Would you like to go into detail about your feelings when you got Item 4? What were you experiencing at that time in your life?

Heartbroken, relationship breakup

Based on your feelings, emotions, and experiences with the above item, how would you rate Item 4?

Negative item; not good for me [✓] Moderate; it's OK [ ] Positive item; it's a keeper [ ]

Item 5

Name of Item Charm bracelet

What is Item 5 made of? Silver

Where did you get Item 5? Pawn shop

Estimated date of when you got Item 5 /

What were you feeling and experiencing in your life when you got Item 4?

I was feeling hopeless. [ ]	I was feeling depressed. [ ]	I was feeling guilty. [ ]
I was feeling ashamed. [ ]	I was feeling apathetic. [ ]	I was feeling insecure. [ ]
I was feeling fearful. [ ]	I was feeling lonely. [ ]	I was feeling sad. [✓]
I was feeling worried. [ ]	I was feeling jealous. [ ]	I was feeling angry. [✓]
I was feeling disheartened. [ ]	I was feeling doubtful. [ ]	I was feeling frustrated. [✓]
I was feeling overwhelmed. [ ]	I was feeling bored. [ ]	I was feeling upset. [✓]
I was feeling hopeful. [ ]	I was feeling positive. [ ]	I was feeling passionate. [ ]
I was feeling happy. [ ]	I was feeling loved. [ ]	

Would you like to go into detail about your feelings when you got Item 5? What were you experiencing at that time in your life?

Heartbroken, relationship breakup

Based on your feelings, emotions, and experiences with the above item, how would you rate Item 5?

Negative item; not good for me [✓] Moderate; it's OK [ ] Positive item; it's a keeper [ ]

		Home Feelings Assessment			
Date	Name Amy				
Item Name	Where did I get the item?	What frequency/mood was I in when I got the item?	What frequency/mood was the person/environment in when I got the item?	How does the item make me feel now?	Should I keep or get rid of the item?
Lion statue	Mummy purchased it	It was Mummy's	/	Positive	Keep
Memorial book	WH Smith store	Depressed. Lonely Guilty Sad Angry Frustrated Upset	/	OK	Keep
Knitting needles and wool	/	/	Depressed Fearful Guilty Sad	Negative	Get rid of it
	Pawn shop	Sad Angry Frustrated Upset	Low vibrational energy	Negative	Get rid of it
Silver charm bracelet	Pawn shop	Sad Angry Frustrated Upset	Low vibrational energy	Negative	Get rid of it

Dear reader, similar to what Amy was experiencing, this chapter is about you identifying what energies and frequencies you can either introduce into your life or bring back into your life. There is also the possibility that you may have negative energies you need to get rid of. You could be wearing items that are blocking your blessings. You could also own ornaments, statues, accessories, or trinkets within your household, office, car, or environment that may have a negative effect on your energy and emotions. I think it's time for you to investigate the items in your daily environment that are made from the following materials:

gold
silver
aluminum
zinc
nickel
brass
iron
steel
bronze
copper
stainless steel
lead
fabric

These materials are in your home. They are the accessories you wear; they interact with you at work and they play a part in your general life. The energy of materials vibrantly affects your happiness, sadness, luck, and misfortune. For example, the fabrics you wear and sleep on, such as cotton, linen, silk, wool, cashmere, and hemp, emit energy. A greater force can manipulate all energy. Your sheets, jewelry, clothing, and accessories can all alter your mood and feelings energy-wise if the handlers or energies before you are negative.

Here's my question: What items, fabrics, colors, and rooms must you assess for a better, healthier, and happier life? Use the worksheets below and start your assessments now.

When doing your energy assessment, here are some essential questions:

1. Do you know where your items were made and where they came from, or both? For example, blood diamonds, a place of bad intent, war, murder, sweatshops, etc.
2. What energy state were you in when you got your items? For example, were you frustrated, angry, upset, depressed, happy, or something else?
3. Did you get your items from someone else's pain or misfortune?
4. How did your life pan out after introducing the items into your life?
5. If you got these items as gifts or purchases, what mindset or energy was the person or environment in when you received the items from them?
6. Did your luck, mood, or behavior change when you owned the items?

These six questions are designed to observe what frequencies and energies have been introduced into your life through something you have purchased or received as a gift.

Start your item assessment log now.

Item 1

Name of Item 1____

What is Item 1 made of? ___________________________________

Where did you get Item 1? __________________________________

Estimated date of when you got Item 1 _________________________

What were you feeling and experiencing in your life when you got Item 1? Please check all that apply.

I was feeling hopeless. [ ]	I was feeling depressed. [ ]	I was feeling guilty. [ ]
I was feeling ashamed. [ ]	I was feeling apathetic. [ ]	I was feeling insecure. [ ]
I was feeling fearful. [ ]	I was feeling lonely. [ ]	I was feeling sad. [ ]
I was feeling worried. [ ]	I was feeling jealous. [ ]	I was feeling angry. [ ]
I was feeling disheartened. [ ]	I was feeling doubtful. [ ]	I was feeling frustrated. [ ]
I was feeling overwhelmed. [ ]	I was feeling bored. [ ]	I was feeling upset. [ ]
I was feeling hopeful. [ ]	I was feeling positive. [ ]	I was feeling passionate. [ ]
I was feeling happy. [ ]	I was feeling loved. [ ]	

Would you like to go into detail about your feelings when you got Item 1? What were you experiencing at that time in your life?

____

____

Based on your feelings, emotions, and experiences with the above item, how would you rate Item 1?

Negative item; not good for me [ ] Moderate; it's OK [ ] Positive item; it's a keeper [ ]

Item 2

Name of Item 2____

What is Item 2 made of? ____

Where did you get Item 2? _______________________________________

Estimated date of when you got Item 2______________________________

What were you feeling and experiencing in your life when you got Item 2?

I was feeling hopeless. [ ]
I was feeling depressed. [ ]
I was feeling guilty. [ ]
I was feeling ashamed. [ ]
I was feeling apathetic. [ ]
I was feeling insecure. [ ]
I was feeling fearful. [ ]
I was feeling lonely. [ ]
I was feeling sad. [ ]
I was feeling worried. [ ]
I was feeling jealous. [ ]
I was feeling angry. [ ]
I was feeling disheartened. [ ]
I was feeling doubtful. [ ]
I was feeling frustrated. [ ]
I was feeling overwhelmed. [ ]
I was feeling bored. [ ]
I was feeling upset. [ ]
I was feeling hopeful. [ ]
I was feeling positive. [ ]
I was feeling passionate. [ ]
I was feeling happy. [ ]
I was feeling loved. [ ]

Would you like to go into detail about your feelings when you got Item 2? What were you experiencing at that time in your life?

____

____

____

Based on your feelings, emotions, and experiences with the above item, how would you rate Item 2?

Negative item; not good for me [ ] Moderate; it's OK [ ] Positive item; it's a keeper [ ]

Item 3

Name of Item 3 ______________________________

What is Item 3 made of? ______________________________

Where did you get item 3? ______________________________

Estimated date of when you got Item 3______________________________

What were you feeling and experiencing in your life when you got Item 3?

I was feeling hopeless. [ ]	I was feeling depressed. [ ]	I was feeling guilty. [ ]
I was feeling ashamed. [ ]	I was feeling apathetic. [ ]	I was feeling insecure. [ ]
I was feeling fearful. [ ]	I was feeling lonely. [ ]	I was feeling sad. [ ]
I was feeling worried. [ ]	I was feeling jealous. [ ]	I was feeling angry. [ ]
I was feeling disheartened. [ ]	I was feeling doubtful. [ ]	I was feeling frustrated. [ ]
I was feeling overwhelmed. [ ]	I was feeling bored. [ ]	I was feeling upset. [ ]
I was feeling hopeful. [ ]	I was feeling positive. [ ]	I was feeling passionate. [ ]
I was feeling happy. [ ]	I was feeling loved. [ ]	

Would you like to go into detail about your feelings when you got Item 3? What were you experiencing at that time in your life?

____

____

____

Based on your feelings, emotions, and experiences with the above item, how would you rate Item 3?

Negative item; not good for me [ ] Moderate; it's OK [ ] Positive item; it's a keeper [ ]

Item 4

Name of Item 4____

What is Item 4 made of? _____________________________________

Where did you get Item 4? ____________________________________

Estimated date of when you got Item 4____________________________

What were you feeling and experiencing in your life when you got Item 4?

I was feeling hopeless. [ ]	I was feeling depressed. [ ]	I was feeling guilty. [ ]
I was feeling ashamed. [ ]	I was feeling apathetic. [ ]	I was feeling insecure. [ ]
I was feeling fearful. [ ]	I was feeling lonely. [ ]	I was feeling sad. [ ]
I was feeling worried. [ ]	I was feeling jealous. [ ]	I was feeling angry. [ ]
I was feeling disheartened. [ ]	I was feeling doubtful. [ ]	I was feeling frustrated. [ ]
I was feeling overwhelmed. [ ]	I was feeling bored. [ ]	I was feeling upset. [ ]
I was feeling hopeful. [ ]	I was feeling positive. [ ]	I was feeling passionate. [ ]
I was feeling happy. [ ]	I was feeling loved. [ ]	

Would you like to go into detail about your feelings when you got Item 4? What were you experiencing at that time in your life?

____

____

____

Based on your feelings, emotions, and experiences with the above item, how would you rate Item 4?

Negative item; not good for me [ ] Moderate; it's OK [ ] Positive item; it's a keeper [ ]

Item 5

Name of Item 5____

What is Item 5 made of? ______________________________________

Where did you get Item 5? ______________________________________

Estimated date of when you got Item 5______________________________

What were you feeling and experiencing in your life when you got Item 4?

I was feeling hopeless. [ ]	I was feeling depressed. [ ]	I was feeling guilty. [ ]
I was feeling ashamed. [ ]	I was feeling apathetic. [ ]	I was feeling insecure. [ ]
I was feeling fearful. [ ]	I was feeling lonely. [ ]	I was feeling sad. [ ]
I was feeling worried. [ ]	I was feeling jealous. [ ]	I was feeling angry. [ ]
I was feeling disheartened. [ ]	I was feeling doubtful. [ ]	I was feeling frustrated. [ ]
I was feeling overwhelmed. [ ]	I was feeling bored. [ ]	I was feeling upset. [ ]
I was feeling hopeful. [ ]	I was feeling positive. [ ]	I was feeling passionate. [ ]
I was feeling happy. [ ]	I was feeling loved. [ ]	

Would you like to go into detail about your feelings when you got Item 5? What were you experiencing at that time in your life?

____

____

____

Based on your feelings, emotions, and experiences with the above item, how would you rate Item 5?

Negative item; not good for me [ ] Moderate; it's OK [ ] Positive item; it's a keeper [ ]

Item 6

Name of Item 6____

What is Item 6 made of? ____________________________________

Where did you get Item 6? __________________________________

Estimated date of when you got Item 6 ___________________________

What were you feeling and experiencing in your life when you got Item 6?

I was feeling hopeless. [ ]	I was feeling depressed. [ ]	I was feeling guilty. [ ]
I was feeling ashamed. [ ]	I was feeling apathetic. [ ]	I was feeling insecure. [ ]
I was feeling fearful. [ ]	I was feeling lonely. [ ]	I was feeling sad. [ ]
I was feeling worried. [ ]	I was feeling jealous. [ ]	I was feeling angry. [ ]
I was feeling disheartened. [ ]	I was feeling doubtful. [ ]	I was feeling frustrated. [ ]
I was feeling overwhelmed. [ ]	I was feeling bored. [ ]	I was feeling upset. [ ]
I was feeling hopeful. []	I was feeling positive. [ ]	I was feeling passionate. [ ]
I was feeling happy. [ ]	I was feeling loved. [ ]	

Would you like to go into detail about your feelings when you got Item 6? What were you experiencing at that time in your life?

____

____

____

Based on your feelings, emotions, and experiences with the above item, how would you rate Item 6?

Negative item; not good for me [ ] Moderate; it's OK [] Positive item; it's a keeper [ ]

Item 7

Name of Item 7____

What is Item 7 made of? ____

Where did you get Item 7? ____

Estimated date of when you got Item 7__________________________________

What were you feeling and experiencing in your life when you got Item 7?

I was feeling hopeless. [ ]	I was feeling depressed. [ ]	I was feeling guilty. [ ]
I was feeling ashamed. [ ]	I was feeling apathetic. [ ]	I was feeling insecure. [ ]
I was feeling fearful. [ ]	I was feeling lonely. [ ]	I was feeling sad. [ ]
I was feeling worried. [ ]	I was feeling jealous. [ ]	I was feeling angry. [ ]
I was feeling disheartened. [ ]	I was feeling doubtful. [ ]	I was feeling frustrated. [ ]
I was feeling overwhelmed. [ ]	I was feeling bored. [ ]	I was feeling upset. [ ]
I was feeling hopeful. [ ]	I was feeling positive. [ ]	I was feeling passionate. [ ]
I was feeling happy. [ ]	I was feeling loved. [ ]	

Would you like to go into detail about your feelings when you got Item 7? What were you experiencing at that time in your life?

____

____

____

Based on your feelings, emotions, and experiences with the above item, how would you rate Item 7?

Negative item; not good for me [ ] Moderate; it's OK [ ] Positive item; it's a keeper [ ]

Item 8

Name of Item 8____

What is Item 8 made of? ____________________________________

Where did you get Item 8? ___________________________________

Estimated date of when you got Item 8___________________________

What were you feeling and experiencing in your life when you got Item 8?

I was feeling hopeless. [ ]	I was feeling depressed. [ ]	I was feeling guilty. [ ]
I was feeling ashamed. [ ]	I was feeling apathetic. [ ]	I was feeling insecure. [ ]
I was feeling fearful. [ ]	I was feeling lonely. [ ]	I was feeling sad. [ ]
I was feeling worried. [ ]	I was feeling jealous. [ ]	I was feeling angry. [ ]
I was feeling disheartened. [ ]	I was feeling doubtful. [ ]	I was feeling frustrated. [ ]
I was feeling overwhelmed. [ ]	I was feeling bored. [ ]	I was feeling upset. [ ]
I was feeling hopeful. []	I was feeling positive. [ ]	I was feeling passionate. [ ]
I was feeling happy. [ ]	I was feeling loved. [ ]	

Would you like to go into detail about your feelings when you got Item 8? What were you experiencing at that time in your life?

____

____

____

Based on your feelings, emotions, and experiences with the above item, how would you rate Item 8?

Negative item; not good for me [ ] Moderate; it's OK [ ] Positive item; it's a keeper [ ]

		Home Feelings Assessment			
Date	**Name**				
Item Name	Where did I get the item?	What frequency/mood was I in when I got the item?	What frequency/mood was the person/environment in when I got the item?	How does the item make me feel now?	Should I keep or get rid of the item?

CHAPTER 7

THE FIVE STAGES OF SUCCESS AND FAILURE

In Chapter 1, we talked about Dr. Hellman, the anesthetist, and spoke briefly about his five stages of success and failure. I would like to focus on those five stages again, but now about your success and the adventure towards it. I want to dedicate this chapter to you with worksheets to fill out and goals and affirmations to commit to. The first chapters of the book were about emotional pain and trauma. I want to now focus primarily on your happiness and growth and what it takes to achieve them.

So, let's do a quick recap. There are five stages to a powerful self-belief and knowledge system. These five stages will give you an unwavering desire to succeed in life. There are also five stages to point-blank failure. The science of these five stages of success and failure is in the same sequential order.

Let's explore again what those five stages are.

- Stage 1: your belief about yourself and the world at large
- Stage 2: the meaning you give to your situations and circumstances
- Stage 3: the action you take
- Stage 4: the results you get
- Stage 5: knowing you are great, powerful, and amazing. You have the knowledge to be, do, and have all you desire.

Before we start talking about the five stages of success, we need to clear your mind and your world of things that will take you far away from your excellence and your ultimate journey to success. In today's world, it is easier to be sad than happy, frustrated than contented, and to want to stop than keep pushing forward with vigor. Or is it?

The truth is, how easy or hard it is depends on your focus and energy. Where your focus goes, your energy will flow. This chapter is about giving you the energy and focus for you not just to be happy and self-confident but also to have the energy and flair to go with it. Please have your pen and thoughts ready, and let's get you started.

Minimize Your Clutter

A cluttered mind will create a cluttered world. A cluttered world can cause mental and physical health problems and forget about work and life excellence. How can you be in a place of excellence when your life is one big psychological junkyard? Your clutter internally will eventually manifest into your clutter externally. Internal and external clutter will affect your behavior, moods, attitude, and relationships with others for the worse.

Throughout this book, we have often seen this with amazing people like Cheslie Kryst, Dr. Alex Hellman, Dr. Mitchell Hardison, and all our other helpline workers. To think clearly, your mind, thoughts, and lifestyle must be as simple, minimalized, and clutter-free as possible. Being unable to think clearly during high stress and depression can be detrimental. Now, I'm not saying that clearing your mind solves your problems. I'm saying to think clearly without clutter will give you a better perspective.

People such as Mark Zuckerberg, Michael Bloomberg, and the late Steve Jobs discovered a new level of excellence when they simplified their minds and made their lives and lifestyles as clutter-free as possible. Many people cannot understand why Zuckerberg—the CEO of Facebook, whose net worth is around $78 billion—wears essential blue hoodies, T-shirts, and simple jeans as a clothing lifestyle. He will wear a simple black or blue suit if dressing for a formal occasion. Like many other heavy hitters, Zuckerberg does not want to spend his time coordinating outfits and wearing the latest trends when he could be focusing on his next chess move for world domination.

Former Apple CEO John Sculley spoke about visiting Steve Jobs' home. He said, "I remember going into Steve's house, and he had almost no furniture. He just had a picture of Einstein, whom he admired greatly, and he had a Tiffany lamp, chair, and bed. He didn't believe in having many things around, but he was meticulous and his environment."

Many highly successful people like the late Steve Jobs understood that a simple life creates more focus, clarity, and space to breathe and think. Clarity creates a headspace to problem-solve due to fewer distractions. Warren Buffet is not a minimalist like Michael Bloomberg and the late Steve Jobs, but his world is about simplicity. He doesn't use a computer or have multiple gadgets. He also doesn't own or have an excessive number of possessions that will distract him from the bigger picture. With an estimated net worth of $108.4 billion, the 91-year-old Buffet wakes up daily around 6:45 a.m., works out for about an hour, and doesn't have breakfast at home—he gets takeout from a local restaurant such as McDonald's.

Buffet prides himself in driving himself to work. He drives a simple car and lives in a simple house that he has lived in for six decades, which he purchased for $31,500 in 1958 in Omaha. Buffet has often said, "You can only drive one car at a time, you can only sleep in one bed at a time, and you can only wear one suit at a time." Buffett is one of the most intelligent investors ever to grace this planet.

So, how can you simplify your life before we look at your five-step journey to success?

I suggest you do the following:

1. Look in your closet and drawers. What old or unneeded clothing can you get rid of? Can you minimize your wardrobe to 10 to 15 outfits, including casual clothing and dressier wear?
2. Excess cups, glasses, plates, and cutlery will lead to high washing up and storage maintenance. How many of them can you get rid of?
3. Look at all the furniture and ornaments in your house. Do you need them all? Try to get rid of about 60–70% of them.
4. Paint your house in colors that give you the feeling and energy of openness and space.
5. Minimize the number of objects in front of your windows and anywhere else blocking light and fresh air.
6. A storage cupboard doesn't mean storing things you don't need. Get rid of those negative unwanted energies.
7. If you are not going to read all those excellent books you own, give them to someone who will. Looking intelligent by displaying books you've never read or never intend to read will not make you more intelligent than you already are. It just clutters your home and your thoughts.
8. If you can afford it, get a cleaner to come in once a week, then keep the house clean for the other six days of the week. The time you spend cleaning your home and your yard could be focused on your success and excellence. Don't waste precious time.
9. Clear all the clutter across all your business, personal, and social media platforms. Too much clutter will cause distractions and anxiety;

unsubscribe, unfollow, unfriend, and clean it all up. Cleaning up is a very empowering experience and should be done regularly.

10. Spend within your budget. The credit you get from others is for investments and business purposes. Do not spend what you can't afford on things that will cause you unnecessary pain in the future.
11. Delete all contacts on your phone and other devices that will cause you emotional stress and psychological pain.
12. Conduct a friend and family audit. Are all those around you good for you spiritually and emotionally? If not, time to reconsider who is in your new inner cycle.

Now that your world and mind are a bit clearer let's start with the five stages of your adventure towards your success and try to avoid as many unnecessary failures as possible.

The adventure begins with your belief system.

Stage 1: Belief

Your belief is a hypothesis to others but must be a fact to you. Extremely positive believers know that what they want to achieve is not currently in their possession or their peripheral. However, in their minds, they believe they have it already. They make love to their beliefs, romanticize them, and walk through the stages of how they will celebrate and own their moments of achievement.

Many successful athletes play the winning of a race repeatedly in their minds—they believe that they just have to turn up to the race to achieve it. Boxers foresee what round and what punch they will win their fight with. If the beliefs are positive, they will smile and get butterflies. If the beliefs are negative, they will become sad, discouraged, or angry. Either way, "As *a man thinketh in his heart, so is he.*" But beliefs go deeper than winning a race or that one knockout punch in a boxing match. Beliefs are also about what you believe and who you believe you are - so here are some questions for you to ponder.

Do you believe you are of or from God?

[Yes] [Not Sure] [No]

Do you believe some big bang created you?

[Yes] [Not Sure] [No]

Do you believe because of your color, race, gender, or ethnicity that, you will be a success or a failure?

[Yes] [Not Sure] [No]

Most highly successful people believe that they have been sent by a supreme being on a special purpose mission to do great things and to make a change in the world. Whether they believe in God or are atheists, they tend to have a strong sense of superiority about who and what they are in relation to others.

You will see these examples throughout history. The pharaohs believed they were the mediators between the gods and the world of men. European monarchies believe in the doctrine of the 'divine right of kings,' which asserts that no earthly being can rule over them. Presidents, prime ministers, emperors, and other world leaders believe themself to be the only path to salvation and a functioning society. It takes a special type of person to have that special kind of belief in themselves.

If you do not currently have the belief system that you need to be good, great, or even amazing, it's OK. This is the time to introduce a new belief system into your psyche.

So, let's do it; let's get you started.

Do you believe you are of or from God? Build that relationship with your belief system now!

Do you believe that you are much more than your current circumstances? You are, and you must emphatically state that you are. Do it!

Do you believe you are here on a mission to do good for yourself and your fellow living beings? I want you to believe, I want you to believe that you are here for that reason. You made it this far to be great and to be a leader over others. Believe it with your heart and soul.

I want you to write down now whatever you need to believe to discover your greatness, power, and purpose: "*As a man thinketh in his heart, so is he.*" Proverbs 23:7 KJV.

Current Belief 1________________________________

Current Belief 2________________________________

Current Belief 3________________________________

Current Belief 4________________________________

Current Belief 5______________________________

New Belief 1______________________________

New Belief 2______________________________

New Belief 3______________________________

New Belief 4______________________________

New Belief 5______________________________

Stage 2: Meaning

The way you think will result in the way you feel.

The way you feel will result in your behavior toward yourself and others. But how you think, feel, and behave derives from your belief system. Now that you have written down your new and existing <u>positive</u> beliefs, it is time to exercise them in your psyche.

The more you convince yourself that you are great, your attitude, behavior, and posture will strengthen. If you tell yourself, 'I am worthless, incapable of being, doing, or having,' your energy and body will adjust negatively. If you tell yourself, 'I am irrelevant. Why would that person like or love me?' The more you push the self-destruct button. Your body will begin to spiral down in health, your demeanor will start to erode, your luck will deplete, and the world at hand will treat you accordingly.

The energy of your thoughts can destroy your body while the universe helps to throw stones at you through your negativity. You will see this reaction in drug users, alcoholics, and people who have given up on themselves. Sad, but true, people can become more unpleasant toward you if you treat yourself negatively.

But you are different. You are special. Keep reminding yourself that you are. Keep telling yourself that you made it from all the other 200 million sperms who started the journey and wanted your place and the 100 thousand sperms who made it to the womb.

But you were specially selected and chosen to be here today, to be amazing, great, and to win in this game called life. You also made it through the turbulent journey of gestation, childbirth, potential crib death, infections, diseases, and all the other dangers you've experienced while growing up to where you are currently today. You are here for a positive, powerful reason. You just need to keep telling yourself that until it becomes who you are and what you are in your behavior, mindset, and relationship with yourself and others. When negativity comes to visit, and when the hard and bad times raise their ugly heads, your self-talk and the 'meaning' you give to your situations, circumstances, and events must be positive and powerful. You will know that everything will be OK—after all, you made it out of 200 million other sperms to be here. The stronger and more prominent your dreams, desires, plans, and beliefs, the more you will think, act, and confidently talk with others.

Now I want you to write affirmations to confirm and support your beliefs. I suggest you think of some reasons for your purpose here. I also want you to tell yourself repeatedly, when times are hard or bad energy is against you, say with absolute conviction, "No weapon formed against me shall prosper; and every tongue which rises against me in judgment I shall condemn."

When you spell your affirmations, incantations, and prayers into existence, powers beyond your mind and understanding will start working for and with you.

Write down what you must tell yourself repeatedly to reinforce your belief system, then end it with a prayer of gratitude.

What is the first positive, encouraging self-talk you must tell yourself over and over again?

1.____

____

____

____

What is the second positive, encouraging self-talk you must tell yourself over and over again?

2.____

____

____

____

What is the third positive, encouraging self-talk you must tell yourself over and over again?

3.____

Now I want you to consummate that positive, encouraging self-talk with a prayer of gratitude that will send a message to God or The Universe that you are ready for your new blessings to come.

You can write down an existing prayer of gratitude or a creative one.

My prayer of gratitude __________________________

Stage 3: Action

Now you are more of a believer (Stage 1). You believe you are here on this planet to do great things and change or improve the world.

Now your self-talk is more positive and stronger (Stage 2). Now you are starting to self-conversate like a president, a prime minister, an emperor, or a pharaoh. You are not 100%

there yet, and that's OK. You are going in the right direction and are in the early stages of your greatness. If you are now telling yourself, "I can do it," with conviction. You're pointed in the right direction.

Suppose you are now saying to yourself with power, faith, and poise, 'God (or a creator of your choosing) placed me on this planet to do what others are failing to do properly. I WILL MAKE LIFE BETTER AND HAPPIER FOR MYSELF AND OTHERS,' your role and position will start to present people, circumstances, situations, and events that will open the door to what is yours.

My mother used to say that her mother back in Jamaica used to say, "If you were born to drown, you are not going to hang." and "What is yours is yours." Believe what is yours, be unapologetic about what is yours, demand what is yours, and affirm what is yours.

To others, you may come across in a grandiose way. So it is up to you how you want to drip-feed your greatness down to others. Barack Obama, Donald Trump, Martin Luther King Jr., Mother Teresa, the Dalai Lama, and all of the other leaders and healers throughout history thought with such conviction of leadership and power. They all had, or have, an unwavering belief system and purpose that they are the one—they are uniquely special. You can express and act in a Jesus-type, firm but humble manner or in a loud and brash Donald Trump-type manner (which I 100% do not recommend, as it is both destructive and dangerous to people who are vulnerable and easily led).

I recommend that your outward behavior always be respectful, loving, empathetic, firm, and fair to all. Your inner conversations should be connected to God's and the Universe's laws and rules.

Then there's action. Taking action is the only path to your results and success. Start small; start with baby steps. The more you achieve the baby steps, the more your belief will become knowledge. The more you win small, the more your self-conversations will strengthen. Always be prepared for your bigger goals and the missions at hand.

In Chapter 8, I talked with my two good friends, Michael Pusey MBE, and the Tokyo 2020 Olympic BMX silver medalist, Kye Whyte. I wanted to know how Whyte became the second-best in the world at BMX racing and the stages of his success. In that chapter, he said, "I make sure I improve by working harder the next day than I did the day before.

If I train my legs on Monday, I will do five sets of 5 squats, with or without weights. Then on Tuesday, I would do six sets of 6 squats. If I do another five sets of 5 on Tuesday, the same as Monday, I will add more weights to my weight bar when doing squats. My goal is always continuous improvement." Whyte's continuous growth and excellence led him to achieve his goal. And his goal was mammoth—to be the Olympic BMX silver medalist out of the thousands of professional BMX competitors globally. Whyte first set himself small strategic bite-size goals. First, he set his sights on the BMX racing regionals. He won. Next, he set his sights on the nationals and won that, too. Then at the British championships, he did it again. On to the European championships, and he was the winner. World championships, victorious again, and then the Olympics. Kye Whyte, Olympic BMX silver medalist, is not a fluke. He uses the same five stages of success for his achievements.

Now I want you to put your actionable strategic steps and goals in place and get started. I suggest you read over all the questions and think about them before you fill in your answers.

1. What must you know to manifest your beliefs, dreams, and goals? For example, I need to know where all the investors meet or hang out.

2. Who must you know to manifest your beliefs, dreams, and goals? For example, I need to know who the gatekeepers are to get into private members' clubs.

3. Where will you meet the people or networks that will assist you in manifesting your beliefs, dreams, and goals? For example, private members' clubs such as the Soho House; CORE: NYC, New York; Capital Club Dubai; Yacht Club de Monaco; The Battery, San Francisco; The Hurlingham Club, London; The Australian Club, Sydney; and 39 Monte Carlo, Monaco.

List where you will find the people and networks that will help and assist you on your path to your success.

4. How can you convince these people or networks to assist you on your mission to manifest your beliefs, dreams, and goals? Different people are motivated for different reasons. Some people want more money, some want more success, some want power, and some just want to be recognized or loved. Your job is to research and discover what the people you want help from need help with. Then you serve them first. Research and write down what they need, then put your plan in place to serve them.

Person/network 1's name is

Person/network 1's location or hangout is

Person/network 1 specializes in

Person/network 1 runs or owns

Person/network 1 needs this for them to win

____

____

____

I will provide person/network 1 with

____

____

____

for them to win____________________________

____

____

I need

____

____

____

from person/network 1 for me to win_______________

____

____

____

Person/network 2's name is

____

____

____

Person/network 2's location or hangout is

____

____

____

Person/network 2 specializes in

____

____

____

Person/network 2 runs or owns

____

____

____

Person/network 2 needs this for them to win

____

____

____

I will provide person/network 2 with____________________

for them to win

I need

from person/network 2 for me to win

Person/network 3's name is

Person/network 3's location or hangout is

Person/network 3 specializes in

____

____

____

Person/network 3 specializes in or owns

____

____

____

Person/network 3 needs this for them to win

____

____

____

I will provide person/network 3 with

____

____

____

for them to win________________________________

____

____

I need

____

____

____

from person/network 3 for me to win__________________

____

____

Person/network 4's name is

____

____

____

Person/network 4's location or hangout is

____

____

____

Person/network 4 specializes in

____

____

____

Person/network 4 runs or owns

____

____

____

Person/network 4 needs this for them to win

____

____

____

I will provide person/network 4 with

____

____

____

for them to win__________________________________

____

____

I need

____

____

____

from person/network 4 for me to win________________

____

____

Person/network 5's name is

____

____

____

Person/network 5's location or hangout is

____

____

____

Person/network 5 specializes in

____

____

____

Person/network 5 runs or owns

____

____

____

Person/network 5 needs this for them to win______________

____

____

____

I will provide person/network 5 with

for them to win

I need

from person/network 5 for me to win

Now you know what you want, who can help you, where to meet them, and what you are willing to exchange for their service or help. Let's now move on to Stage 4: Results.

Stage 4: Results

The more results you achieve, your beliefs will turn into facts. The more facts you accumulate, the more a belief will transform into knowledge. There is a big difference between believing something true and knowing something to be a fact. The difference between believing and knowledge (knowing) is the accumulated evidence. There is no proof or evidence when you are in a place of belief, but there is faith, trust, and acceptance. When you know, there is an experience, a journey, an adventure, and a destination with evidence that points toward the knowledge.

Hardship, near-misses of death, or a severe injury does something to most people that changes them into a mighty, unwavering, resilient powerhouse. This new character and energy they accumulate from cheating death give them a sense of stubbornness and invulnerability. Let me explain. When the rapper Tupac Shakur was shot in 1994, he believed he cheated death, and he became even more stubborn and sure of his invulnerability.

Yasser Arafat, a freedom fighter to some and a ruthless terrorist to others, had powerful enemies globally. In 1985, Israeli fighter planes bombed Arafat's headquarters in Tunis, killing many. But Arafat survived the bombing because he had stepped out for a morning jog moments before. That near-miss, alongside other near-misses, made Yasser Arafat resolute and gave him a sense of invulnerability.

Before John Wilkes Booth's assassination in 1865, the 16th US President Abraham Lincoln survived at least five other assassination plots.

Assassins tried to stab him and send him clothing infected with yellow fever. They also attempted to shoot him and even plotted to blow up the White House with him in it. On one occasion, while riding alone, a loud gunshot spooked Abraham Lincoln's horse. When his soldiers retrieved the hat that he lost when the horse spooked, they discovered a musket ball hole in his hat. The more attempts' assassins made on his life, the more resilient, steadfast, and sure of his invulnerability he became.

Pope John Paul II was the focus of many assassination attempts. In 1981, the Pope was shot four times and was critically wounded in St. Peters Square by a member of the Turkish nationalist organization, the Grey Wolves. The Pope survived. A year later, in 1982, another attempt was made when a former priest tried to stab him with a bayonet but was stopped by security guards. Then another attempt was made on his life in 1995 when Islamic terrorists tried to blow the Pope up, but the police foiled their plot before it could happen. Not only did the Pope become even more sure of his role and relationship with God, but his followers worldwide believed he had an even greater air of immortality. Near misses tend to make special people even more confident of their purpose in life and make their sense of invulnerability more accurate and valid to them.

Now it's your turn.

I have some questions for you.

What hardships or near-misses have you experienced that have cemented your knowledge? And when I say 'knowledge,' I mean God or some divine intervention wants you here for a more significant reason and purpose. That reason or purpose is why you are blessed and here to do something great. That reason or purpose is why you have a role on this Earth that you must see through and accomplish, regardless of the hardships and dangers you have faced and will continue to face. What events in your life have you experienced that are miracles and blessings? Do you believe you are protected by energy more superior and divine than yours?

Please share your experiences here:

Stage 5: Knowledge (Knowing)

Now you know for a fact that you are meant to be here on this Earth for a reason. You also understand that you are great, powerful, and unique, and no matter what happens to you, history and near-misses have proven that you are here to do something great and fulfilling.

Whatever the world and negative people have thrown at you, you will continue to survive and strive. As it says in Isaiah 54:17, "No weapon that is formed against thee shall prosper; and every tongue that shall rise against thee in judgment thou shalt condemn."

No matter what hardships and trials and tribulations you may have or will experience, you are here. You are strong, blessed, and capable enough to face all the tests that have and will come your way. Your greatness is undeniable, and anyone who dares to stand up against you will eventually fail miserably.

I want you to keep telling yourself this statement over and over again. "My greatness is undeniable, and anything, person, or energy that dares to come up against me will fail miserably." I want you to repeat this affirmation, but now out loud and with conviction.

"My greatness is undeniable, and anything, person, or energy that dares to come up against me will fail miserably."

Say it again, but louder.

"My greatness is undeniable, and anything, person, or energy that dares to come up against me will fail miserably."

One more time, but louder.

"My greatness is undeniable, and anything, person, or energy that dares to come up against me will fail miserably."

Now I want you to knowingly set your mission in place and be bold, powerful, and unapologetic.

So, what do you know to be true?

I could not have written this chapter or this book if I hadn't experienced some seriously dark times but also some beautiful and unforgettable times.

I am a gift from an even more potent source to help, build, and empower others. No matter how often I have been stabbed or cheated death, I am here for a reason. We all can survive our traumas and live beautiful lives after our traumatic experiences.

Let me share some of my traumas and experiences so you can understand more about my journey.

They shot and killed my brother, yet I am here.

One of my sons died, and the emotional pain was excruciating, yet I am here.

I've survived many assassination attempts, yet I am here.

I have been slandered and ridiculed by many, yet I am here.

Friends and family members have betrayed me, yet I am here.

I have been cheated on in relationships in the most heartless and callous ways, and though it broke my heart and my days were dark and the nights were even darker, I am here.

My appendix burst, poisoning my body and taking my life temporarily, but God—with the assistance of doctors—brought me back to life, and I am here.

I have been stabbed many different times, almost fatally, yet I am here.

I have experienced the deaths of a sister and another beloved brother, yet I am here.

I have nothing more to fear and every good feeling to experience, and so do you!

Demand and take what is yours. State emphatically what you want with certainty. You are here to be great, regardless of your near-misses. It is because of your near-misses that you are great.

I will see you at the top, my friend.

Kevin Bennett

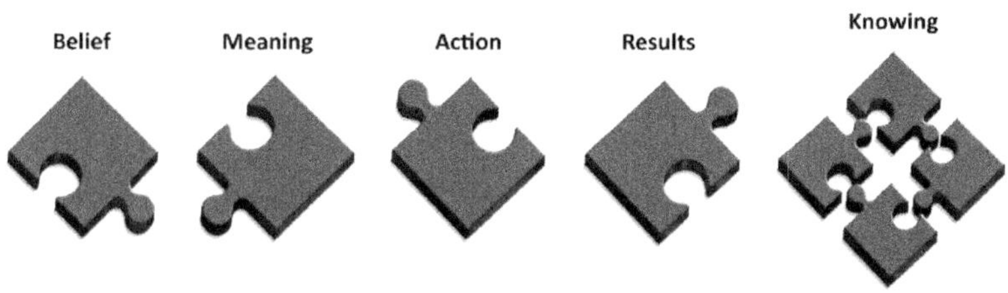

CHAPTER 8

WHY DO MOST PEOPLE FAIL WHILE OTHERS SUCCEED?

I have a question for you: what is success, and why is success so important?

Firstly, success is subjective; it's unique to us, it's beautiful, and it's carefully sculpted to reward our senses, beliefs, morals, and values when obtained. You will need some fundamentals—for your dreams, plans, and desires to bear fruit and succeed.

For example, to be successful, you must feel good about yourself and the people you serve.

To be successful, you must be of sound mind and health.

To be successful, you must feel some form of inner love and accomplishment.

To be successful, you must have a healthy relationship with God.

These are the fundamentals, but there are others that I believe must be in place to be inwardly and outwardly successful. Now, remember, I am aware that success is subjective, so please work with me here. Throughout societies globally, most—but not all—people tend to measure their success based on some primary factors. These factors include the job type, the letters after their name, the car and house they own, the amount of money they have in the bank, and the impeccable reputation they have built within their community and among their community peers.

People strive for these things to be successful, and one day with hard work and persistence, they achieve the title, the job, the house, the car, the admiration, and the money they want. They are seen and celebrated as being successful. But is this true? Perhaps we should ask Dr. Alex Hellman, the anesthetist who wanted to commit suicide due to his 'successful' well-paying job. Or how about Dr. Mitchell Hardison, who shot himself in the heart? Or the superstar comedian Robin Williams who made the world laugh, then put a belt around his neck? And let's not forget about the beautiful model Cheslie Kryst who inspired millions, then jumped to her death from her high-rise building.

There are many more moving parts to success than titles, accolades, money, cars, homes, and jobs. This chapter is all about the other moving parts. This chapter is about the KBenaire Life Board. By the end of this chapter, not only will you have more clarity, understanding, and focus about your success, but you will also accumulate tools to help you through the dark times and propel you forward with passion and vigor. I will give you a fully structured, ready-to-go system I have built and used globally with thousands of amazing people. From Bulgaria to China to India to the United States and throughout the United Kingdom, the Life Board has helped many.

I have used the KBenaire Life Board to help enhance the lives of top CEOs, politicians, aristocrats, and government entities. I have been asked countless times, "What is the difference between a vision board and a Life Board?" Well, a vision board represents your dreams, desires, and goals. Vision boards are intended to keep you focused and passionate about your goals while exercising the laws of attraction toward the desired outcome. As great as a vision board is, I have discovered over time that vision boards don't work well for most people. Here are some reasons:

1. Vision boards are great for motivation and desire but poor for planning and action. Suppose you know through your vision board that you want to visit the Taj Mahal, lose weight, and grow your family, but what do you do next? After meditating and visualizing with their vision boards, most people don't have a plan of action or a team to make their desires come to life. Most just climb under a rock and go back to their non-believing reality.

The KBenaire Life Board helps people recognize their dreams, believe in them, plan with certainty and accuracy to manifest their dreams, and act with action steps to achieve the once thought impossibilities.

2. Most people visualize what they believe will make them happy and successful. They spend most of their lives in the pursuit of their visual desires. After achieving them, they spend even more time wishing they never had them in the first place or wondering what went wrong when they felt unfulfilled. You see this with many lottery winners. They associate happiness with winning the lottery. But after they win and the fun and excitement die down, the problems and pre-lotto pains return to visit, but now even worse.

Now everyone—from the government to family members—wants that money, and the most charming gold diggers also want their unearned cut. Stress and paranoia become daily feelings. They can no longer blame their unfulfillment and unhappiness on poverty or the lack of finances. The lottery scratched that itch, but the itch still exists.

Most people seek happiness via cultural concepts and not from their inner sanctum. The KBenaire Life Board covers the inner person just as much as it covers the outer person—from your feelings to your business, from finances to family, and from friends to mentors. The KBenaire Life Board is simply life-changing. You must have one.

3. I have met many people who enjoyed achieving their goals individually on their vision boards. Still, I have also observed them feeling even more stressed and unhappy as they try to maintain the houses, cars, and boats they envisioned and work so hard to get. Vision boards don't have an aftercare system for feeling burned out or overwhelmed. The KBenaire Life Board has an aftercare system through its apps and a fantastic team that runs it.

Let's dig a bit deeper into the Life Board and the areas it covers.

Let's first start with the feelings assessment.

1. Feelings Assessment Branch

The feelings assessment branch of the Life Board assesses your feelings to discover if you are in a proton happy state or an electron negative state. Awareness of your happiness and emotional boundaries is vital to your growth, relationships, and mental health.

2. Core Values Branch

The core values branch of the Life Board is designed to get you to not only recognize your core values and add new relevant core values to help you move forward within your happiness, relationships with others, and just being a better person overall.

3. Legacy Branch

The legacy branch of the Life Board will help you in three main areas:

a) It will allow you to see that your behavior today will be your legacy of tomorrow.
b) It will help you map and implement your legacy.
c) The Life Board's legacy section will help you manage and structure your assets and liabilities.

4. Spirituality Branch

The spirituality branch of the Life Board is designed to help you understand your spiritual self. This will be accomplished through meditation, spiritual awareness, and a relationship with your creator.

5. Your Message to the World Branch

If you could change the world with a message, what would your words of wisdom be? This branch will help you establish your purpose and mission.

6. Lifestyle Branch

The Lifestyle branch is your vision board. With this branch, you will add pictures of your dreams, desires, and wants.

7. Investment Branch

The Investment branch of the Life Board focuses on your investments, wealth, and income.

8. Education Branch

For you to win, achieve your goals, and receive all your desires on the Life Board, you will need to be educated in each branch of your Life Board.

9. Social Branch

The social branch of the Life Board is as important as the blood in your veins. It focuses on the bonds you form with others, your relationships, and your social growth.

10. Mentors Branch

We all must have mentors to guide us through our life journey. The mentors' branch of the Life Board looks at the mentors we should have. For example, if you want to become a savvy investor, you must have mentors who are savvy investors. This section will help you on your path and journey to discover who your mentors are and who they should be.

11. Mastermind Group Branch

A mastermind group is a group of peers who meet to give each other advice, support, and inspiration to win, focus, and achieve. This branch will help you to build or join a team of your peers to win.

12. Circle of Confidence Branch

Everyone should have a Circle of Confidence to turn to. We all must have the following in our lives when in a dark or unconfident place. Here are the five we all must have to turn to:

a) God
b) Therapist
c) Spiritual and religious leaders
d) Family members
e) A friend

Get your pen and paper ready, and let's start your Life Board journey!

1. Feelings Branch

The feelings branch of the KBenaire Life Board is about your non-negotiable feelings. The feelings you want for yourself that you are not willing to sacrifice to please negative people. Even if you are not there yet regarding how you would love to feel, write them down and work toward them every moment, day, week, and month. Invite into your life feelings such as happiness, joy, love, enthusiasm, and greatness. Write them down on your KBenaire Life Board entitled 'Feelings,' then commit to them. Ask yourself, what feelings I want to invite into my life without compromise? To love others, you must first love yourself. You must know your feelings before sharing your love and positive feelings with others. Many people cannot be loved, and their happiness is currently out of service. These people find it hard to show love and receive feelings such as love, passion, fun, and romance. For others to love and value you, they must be taught and shown how to love you by observing how you love and value yourself.

I will start your list; then, you continue it.

Write these down, then commit to them:

1. No matter what, I will love myself no matter what.

2. I will always make an effort to feel good.

3.____

4.____

5.____

6.____

7.____

8.____

9.____

10.____

2. Core Values Branch

'Don't talk to strangers. Be kind and respectful to others. Work hard, and you will achieve your dreams.' These are some of the core values parents impart into their children during their early years. These core values are appropriate for infancy and childhood; however, some core values are age-specific and have a type of sell-by date attached to them. For example, for a person at age 30, 'Don't talk to strangers' is not an appropriate core value to maintain as an adult. You must talk to strangers in workplaces, meet new people, and socialize. Some core values should be kept, such as 'Be kind and respectful to others, and other core values need to be updated for you to survive and even thrive in your mature years.

Sometimes, we may have been taught only part of a core value but not the full value itself. The popular saying, 'a Jack of all trades is a master of none,' is only part of a full saying that some people are aware of. To be a 'jack-of-all-trades and a master of none' is commonly understood as it is better to have mastered a trade rather than trying to spread yourself thinly across many trades. But the full saying is more interesting and powerful. It is 'A jack-of-all-trades is a master of none, but oftentimes better than a master of one.' If you know the full saying, you will realize that the true meaning of this saying is the opposite of what is commonly understood. Its original meaning is a compliment. It says that a person who learns many skills instead of specializing in just one can be successful, useful, versatile, and an expert at doing many things.

This core values branch of the Life Board is designed to help you to discover new treasurable core values to help, build up, and empower you in the coming chapters of your life.

But before we continue, what are core values?

Core values are the fundamental beliefs that dictate your behavior, rights, wrongs, and relationship with the world you live in.

Let's divide your core values into three sections.

1. Your beliefs

2. Your principles

3. Your behaviors

Core values are your fundamental beliefs about who you are, what you are, and your relationship with God and the world you live in. To have core values, by default, you must have principles. Principles are the laws and the rules that govern you and your ruling truths. Your principles and rules then govern your behavior toward yourself and others.

When considering your principles, take the following into account:

A. What are your rights on this planet? What are the rights of your brothers and sisters that you share on this planet? Write down all that you believe are your rights (about 20, then consolidate them into 5).

For example:

"I have the right to be happy."

"I have the right to defend myself and my family."

"I have a right to my freedom."

"I have the right to feel safe and secure."

Add to or continue this list.

1.______________________________

2.______________________________

3.______________________________

4.______________________________

5.______________________________

6.______________________________

7.______________________________

8.______________________________

9.______________________________

10.______________________________

11.______________________________

12.______________________________

13.______________________________

14.______________________________

15.______________________________

16.______________________________

17.______________________________

18.______________________________

19.______________________________

20.______________________________

Now consolidate your 20 rights into 5 core rights you can recite, standby, die for, and most definitely live for.

1.______________________________

2.______________________________

3.______________________________

4.______________________________

5.______________________________

B. What motivates you internally to do good for yourself while serving others for their betterment?

Now write down 30 things you can do that will intrinsically motivate you. Once you have them all written, write next to each one how it may serve others while it also serves your happiness, purpose, or growth. This practice will help you to discover what you want and how it can serve and help others. You will discover your purpose in this exercise.

For example:

I love to cook / I can cook for food banks or open a restaurant

I love working on my mental and physical health / I am happy to try being a mental health support worker

Write your list and discover your purpose.

1.______________________________/______________________________

2.______________________________/______________________________

3.______________________________/______________________________

4.______________________________/______________________________

5.______________________________/______________________________

6.______________________________/______________________________

7.______________________________/______________________________

8.______________________________/______________________________

9.________________________/________________________

10.________________________/________________________

11.________________________/________________________

12.________________________/________________________

13.________________________/________________________

14.________________________/________________________

15.________________________/________________________

16.________________________/________________________

17.________________________/________________________

18.________________________/________________________

19.________________________/________________________

20.________________________/________________________

21.________________________/________________________

22.________________________/________________________

23.________________________/________________________

24.________________________/________________________

25.________________________/________________________

26.____________________/____________________

27.____________________/____________________

28.____________________/____________________

29.____________________/____________________

30.____________________/____________________

C. "Those who stand for nothing fall for anything." – Alexander Hamilton.

Next, what are your truths?

What do you stand for regardless of the punishments or penalties that may be imposed on you?

Good core values will help you through the most turbulent times and humble you when you are in a superior position to others. Your core values will teach you when there are no other teachers present at that moment. Spiritual core values will guide you when all the navigators are navigating elsewhere. Your spiritual core values will give you the strength to stand in the face of tyranny while fighting for your liberty.

The first-ever core value I made purposely and committed to it without the aid of my parents or guardians was when I was 14 years old. I remember attending Archbishop Michael Ramsey school in the south London region of the UK. An English teacher who looked like my mother had a Caribbean upbringing similar to my parents and matched my mother in age, height, and size; She always sternly told me that I would end up in prison or die by age 18.

Every day, she stated that I would never amount to anything. I remember her looks as though I had sickened her. Her words were not said with love or precaution. Her statements did not derive from care, concern, or hope. Her words and tonality were designed to attack with hate and venom. She was trying to conjure a spell of ill will or bad fortune on me. This happened daily for almost three months before I finally replied to her, saying, "You are not God." She replied, "I don't need to be God to see the facts, Kevin." "Your facts come from a hateful place," I responded.

On that day, I made my first-ever core value. "When your attitude is right, the facts don't count." That means other people's facts don't need to become your reality. The will of others can only manifest if you believe in their story, beliefs, and energy more than you believe in your own.

Rest in peace to my elder brother Andy. From a young age, he instilled in me that my bloodline came from kings and great leaders of the past. He taught me that I was of and from God. He encouraged me to read books about self-development and world leaders. I learned about the G7 and G8 from the age of 7. I was taught to play chess and was also taught leadership skills. Thank God I had enough self-belief to resist that teacher's belief system and energy.

Years later, reuniting with some of my school friends, I shared my story and journey with that teacher. Unsurprisingly, they all shared stories about her or had similar experiences with her. A classmate shared stories of the teacher's disrespectful, demeaning, disparaging behavior. But in her case, the teacher's statements affected her confidence in her later life.

Another former student shared her story about a classmate attending school before my time. She spoke about her friend who died from a stabbing incident at 18, just two years after he left the school.

She said, "All I could think about looking at his coffin at the funeral was that same teacher's words. She would tell him before us that he won't make it past his 19th birthday. 'I guess she was right with this one,' she remembered saying to herself as they lowered his coffin into the ground."

Now aged 44, all my core values derive from different experiences and journeys in my life. I will now take a moment to share all my core values with you. Then I want you to change them, add to them, or edit them into your core values.

Core Value 1: Feel Good Now

The most important of all my core values is to feel good now. Over many years, I have studied people, looked at my environment, and worked with thousands of people globally. Through that, I have discovered that most people only want to feel good about themselves when they have a particular aim or goal. Once they have concluded that their goal or achievement is accomplished, only then do they tend to want to celebrate themselves. Until that time, they seem to self-sabotage. They beat themselves up and purposely make their journey hard, to the point of not enjoying it anymore. They go to bed angry, wake up feeling anxious, and mostly live their lives frustrated and unfulfilled.

Feeling good—unlike feeling good **now**—for most people means that only when they achieve a goal will they make some kind of effort to feel good about themselves and their future. If you are one of those people, I want you to ponder this momentarily. For example—you want to buy a house, it will take you four years to fix your credit and get your deposit together. How long will it take for you to feel accomplished and good about yourself? Yep, four long years.

Here's another example: You are studying law at the university of your choice. The five-year course includes two years of qualifying legal work experience. If, once again, your core value is to feel good—unlike feeling good now—how long will it take to feel that you have achieved something special?

As simple as these examples may seem, truly dig deep and ask yourself at what points in your life journey are you hard on yourself? Then, at what point in your life journey will you celebrate yourself? You may discover that your celebratory moments are connected to your achievements, which have their terms and conditions.

For this reason, high depression and high suicide rates are rife among students, celebrities, and high achievers.

To Feel Good Now—unlike just feeling good—means that you are consciously aware of your presence at every moment. You must celebrate your moments with thankfulness, prayers, behaviors of gratitude, and moments of loving yourself.

This may be weird to some, but you must practice taking yourself out on a dinner date to remind yourself that you are awesome and worthy of a date.

Write down all your achievements, then read them out loud in front of a mirror. After reading each achievement, thank God, and tell yourself how strong, smart, powerful, and great you are. Wear bright colors of joy, hope, and happiness to raise vibrational frequencies. Read Psalms, or some form of belief, faith, or religious scripture that will empower you.

Contact your loved ones and tell them that you love them and that they mean the world to you; the distribution of vibrational love will always come back tenfold.

Enjoy your work or study but, most importantly, life's journey. Go for morning and evening walks and just live in the moment of gratitude.

Take time to observe the stars and the wind rustling through the trees, and have a romantic moment with the sun setting behind the picture frame of God's incredible artwork.

I want you to fall in love with the dawning of another day that God has blessed you with. To feel good now is to be present, to be present is to be aware, and to be aware is to be in the moment of being. Just try it. Anxiety, depression, and anger don't live there. You will discover peace, space, and awakening there.

Now I want you to write down your core value, even if the core value is not currently being practiced in your life. Introduce it into your life and work on it daily until it becomes your identity.

Write down your Core Value 1 here and live by it.

Core Value 2: Help, Build Up, and Empower

My second core value—Help, Build Up, and Empower—is probably one of the main reasons why I am not dead or in prison today.

Being young and living in Brixton in the '90s meant to some youths (like myself) that we had to run the gauntlet of a war zone. Stabbings, shootings, and brutal fights were regular occurrences in our lives. I had to deal with being stabbed on four different occasions and experiencing my brother and many of my friends being killed before the age of 25.

We were expected to suck it up and get on with life without therapy or counseling; yes, we exploded now and then. But why did we explode? When you know no better, you do no better. When you believe you have no options in life, you will use what's available to you.

At that time, we did not believe we had any other options but to fight to survive within our cultural street rules and codes. We had no second or third home in the countryside, or a villa in France to take a breather from the madness in Brixton, or any other communities to escape to. No social media existed to seek or discover external inspiration in the '90s. England had no Malcolm X, Marcus Garvey, or Nanny of the Maroons to guide us in the way the other young black people in America and the Caribbean had. We had no historical location we could be proud of like the Ethiopians, Nigerians, or Ghanaians had. They culturally had a dialect and a country they could call home. They also had a direct relationship with their historical leaders, such as Mansa Musa, who dominated the world in his time. And let's not forget about Haile Selassie, who had great influence and respect across the globe. We were limited and leaderless in the UK, so we had to make sense of our leaderless nonsense. We made up our laws and rules as we went along to lead us.

Going back to the 1950s, the Black British community had no choice but to find their way. Our elders had no choice but to fight back when the racist Teddy Boys ambushed black people and beat the living daylights out of them. Black youths had nowhere to turn to since the police were doing the same thing to young black men. The state of affairs was so bad that black men were beaten to paralysis or even death.

Over time and generations, the black community in the UK began to fight back and even resist police and racial brutality. The 1981 and 1985 riots galvanized the black community in Brixton, London, and across the UK to fight back and fight for equality and rights. Our relationship with the police were shattered going back to the 50s, 60s, 70s and 80s and even now in the 2000s.

Years of tension and resistance influenced and inspired our mindset and behavior for combat and warfare. We morphed from pure children to warlords. We became experts in reading body language and micro-expressions. If someone had a knife or a gun on them, their hands subconsciously molded to the type of weapon they were concealing. We were skilled in the art of surveillance and anti-surveillance measures. We wrapped ourselves up in cling film to not leave any DNA. We had photographic memories, remembering up to 20 car license plates at any one time just in case we were being followed. We could even remember the color of the socks people were wearing. We memorized the last 30 people we encountered when walking past them on the street. If cars or people tried to follow us, we could quickly lose them through back alleys, markets, and council housing estates.

Sometimes we went to the police station where the heart of their surveillance was located to mock them for their poor job of being incognito when trying to pursue us. “No comment” was our interview response. We trusted no one due to the years of generational abuse and lack of trust going back to the 1950s. Actually, some would disagree and say it goes back to ‘slavery.’

However, not everyone valued our codes and rules in our community. Friends would cut deals with the police for a better life by giving information about their friends. Many of our peers ended up in prison or dead because of jealousy and infiltration.

In the ’90s, the rise of the Yardies (Jamaican gangs) changed the temperature of violence on the streets of the UK. Fights, knife attacks, and fatal gun incidents started raising the temperature within the black community. We changed from a community of togetherness and quickly became estranged. Friends became traumatized foes, and the trauma was passed down through the generations. Eventually, the community of oneness turned into postcode wars. Around this time, traumatized people with no therapy or counselling immigrated into our community from war-torn countries. They previously witnessed beheadings and mass murders, some raped and abused and they had no outlet but anger to express themselves.

As a community, we needed help; we were traumatized and didn’t even know it. Boys and girls were raped or abused, but who could they turn to? Not the police—that was forbidden in the black and brown communities. Who could we share our deepest and darkest traumas with? Well, no one in our community—hurt people hurt others, so we kept our traumas to ourselves.

Traumatic events led to PTSD, which led to an inflammation on the brain and then all different types of depressions and mental illnesses occurred.

Over time, I discovered that we were all responsible for destroying our community somehow. Just by being in an electron zone and not self-developing, we were all causing more harm than good in our households and community. Negativity breeds negativity, regardless of whether you are the abuser or the one being abused. Victims and perpetrators live in the same electron frequency if there is no growth and change of vibrational frequency within themselves.

Electrons, neutrons, and protons do not care about gender, age, color, sexuality, or race. If you are in an electron zone, you will be rewarded accordingly, and if you are in a proton zone, both frequencies will try to gain your attention.

Just be sure which frequency to serve, the frequency of LOVE, the God frequency. Or the frequency of FEAR, the demon entity.

The more I started to read, educate, and love myself, the more I attracted educators, self-developers, and lovers. I fell in love with myself when I started to forgive myself. I fell even deeper in love with myself when I started to forgive others. My life improved when I discovered the amazing world and ~~journey~~ adventure of servitude. From when my awareness of servitude was born (my second core value): 'Help, build up, and empower people became my purpose.' Since the early to mid-2000s, up until this present day, I have helped, built up, and empowered millions of people globally. I have lectured in universities across the UK and given emotional, strategic workshops and talks to companies, government bodies, and organizations globally.

I sometimes appear on news networks such as *RT* (Russia Today news channel), and I have now launched a podcast called *Kevin Bennett's Trauma,* in which I help people suffering in silence. Helping, building up, and empowering people gives me a reason to live, build a legacy, and wake up another day to be proud of myself. This book was written solely because of this core value. Helping, building up, and empowering people is a three-dimensional process. *Help* means helping people who are in a dark place in their lives. To *build up* is to build up minds and communities globally so they will want and do better for themselves. To *empower* is to empower and inspire our future generations.

Here's my question: What is your second help, build up, and empower core value? Write it down and start serving the world by first serving and empowering yourself.

____

____

____

____

____

____

____

____

Core Value 3: Create Happy Memories

"I don't like people like her!" said Jada.

"Who?" I responded.

"Her!" she replied.

Now I'm looking around for the evil, horrible demon that Jada dislikes. Jada typically likes everyone. She's one of those happy-go-lucky people who lights up a party. She even gets the most boring, mundane, moody people, who tend to sit down at a party to stand up and shake a leg. So, to see Jada not liking someone was interesting to me.

"Who?" I asked again, looking up and down aisle 10. "

Her Kevin!" Jada said, now pointing with her nose, trying not to be rude by pointing with her finger.

"Ooooh, her," I said, looking over to aisle 12.

The woman I saw was cute and humble and had short, black bobbed hair. She had just come from the gym or a training session. She wore her gym clothes, a black Nike tracksuit with black, white, and orange Ascot trainers while carrying a black gym bag. She was picking fruit in the fruit and veg aisle.

“I could just strangle her!” Jada said, turning in the opposite direction to avoid meeting this woman face-to-face.

I looked over to this woman, who was minding her own business, not harming, or causing a problem to a single soul. But she was heavily disliked by Jada.

“Do you know her?” I asked.

“No!” Jada replied.

“Well, why don’t you like her?” I asked, now curious.

I would have let it go by now and moved on to another subject. But today, I was in a kind of provocative mood. I didn’t want to go food shopping with Jada that day, but Jada dragged me along for company. Plus, I didn’t want to let this conversation go. I had gone shopping with Jada primarily because of my boredom that day, but matching baked bean prices wasn’t my idea of a relaxing Saturday off. I could have been doing something fun such as watching paint dry or singing Christmas carols in the middle of summer.

“Why?” I asked again, now urging an explanation from Jada.

“Long story,” she said, trying to brush me off politely.

“How can a story be long about someone you’ve never met before?” I laughed.

Yep, I was being a bit sarcastic and an ass, but I was in one of my ‘Kevin Bennett moods’ as my ex-girlfriend would put it.

“Ok, Kevin, to be honest, she reminds me of the woman my ex-husband cheated on me with. She was the reason why we divorced, and my world crashed. Kevin, that woman looks exactly like the woman I caught my husband in bed with.

There! There's your long story shortened!" Jada said, then continued to walk down the aisle.

Whoops, I thought, I get it now. I replied, "Sorry to hear that hun."

Driving home that evening, I thought about it. Being hated for a crime you have never committed is brutal when you have done nothing wrong. I guess the good thing is that the woman wasn't aware of the directed hate from Jada.

It's funny how we can dislike someone we have never met before, or hate something we have never encountered. The dislike and negative feelings we can generate for another can majorly affect our health, happiness, legacy, and even relationships with our friends, partners, and families.

My question to you: Do you, or someone you know, hate a person, religion, thing, or location without ever previously encountering them or it? Yes [ ] No [ ]

If yes, do you believe it has an effect of your feelings and emotions for the worse? Yes [ ] No [ ]

Your memories of the past can serve you for good or be the cause of your suffering and pain. Creating forgiving, happy, respectful, and enjoyable memories—regardless of who is to blame—will either serve you for good in your future or cause massive emotional destruction because of your past. In the Feel Good Now part of the chapter, we will cover more about memories and feelings.

For your next core value, I want you to think about what mindset, behaviors, and values you can introduce into your life that will allow you to see previous negative experiences in more of a positive light. What can you do to change a negative narrative and memory into a happy, prosperous, triumphant one? For example, Jada could have looked at it differently to have a more peaceful mind. She could have changed her view and seen the woman in aisle 12 (who looks like the woman she caught in bed with her husband) as the woman she needed to thank. If it weren't for that day she caught them both in bed; she could have wasted years of her life in a treacherous and deceitful relationship. Sometimes what is deemed a curse is a blessing in disguise. What can you introduce into your core values to improve how you look at a negative experience and make it a positive outcome?

Core Value 4: Exude Fun, Passion, and Excellence

Let's break this core value up into three sections. We'll start with Fun.

Fun

I remember playing games such as tag, runouts, and dodgeball as a child.

Other children wanted to be a part of the fun we were experiencing. Even in moments of injury, such as when we were hit too hard in dodgeball, shoved to the ground during tag, or fell over in runouts, we still had fun. We cried for a bit, brushed ourselves off, and got back into the mix of the fun as if nothing ever happened.

Having fun makes you forget feelings of sadness, misery, and ill health. Every human being, at one point or another, desires fun and enjoyment. Fun is contagious, healing, and healthy for the soul, heightening our awareness of happiness. The problem is most people believe that childish fun is only for children and not for adults. Enjoying yourself and having childish fun, like playing tag, runouts, and dodgeball, heals the mind, body, and soul. Shamelessly tickling to the point of wetting oneself can be annoying but healthy for your energy. Karaoke singing or playing games like Twister with friends or strangers brings joy and fun. These are all healthy proton activities to do to promote happiness and joy.

Miserable electron people are avoided by people who are in a proton state, and people who are authentically in a proton state attract proton people. Fun is the builder of lifelong friendships and the killer of depression and anger. For this reason, I have made fun a part of my core values. Walking mountains is fun for me. Shamelessly being a childish kid playing pranks and acting like a fool around my loved ones also delivers me into a proton state. Plus, it reinforces bonding and connection with the people I love and care about the most.

Question: What fun core values and activities can you introduce into the childish part of your life? Dig deep into your childish self. Write down fun things you can do and get started now.

Fun Activity 1

____

____

____

Fun Activity 2

Fun Activity 3:

Fun Activity 4:

Fun Activity 5:

Fun Activity 6:

Fun Activity 7:

___

___

___

Fun Activity 8:

___

___

___

Fun Activity 9:

___

___

___

Fun Activity 10:

___

___

___

Passion

Over the years, I have personally discovered that passion will get you through the tough times while winning new friends, followers, and partnerships.

Humans thrive on passion and inspiration. The films we tend to love the most are those that are inspirational. We love the adventure of discovery, passion, and of the underdog who will fight, survive, and win. We admire people whose passion made them a success.

Passionate winners have a direct relationship with their beliefs, purpose, and values.

I want you to think about this question: What do you believe your purpose is? First, I want you to think about it, then write it down, then ask your friends and family members what they think your purpose is. Sometimes, the people closest to you can see things you can't.

Get started now.

Your Purpose 1:

Your Purpose 2:

Your Purpose 3:

Your Purpose 4:

Your Purpose 5:

____

____

____

Excellence

For almost 25 years, I suffered from being a perfectionist. I always wanted my projects, business ventures, and personal life to be perfect. It took me almost 20 years to truly discover that my desire to be perfect came from an underlying insecurity I didn't know I had. Not understanding successful people's journeys and just focusing on their destinations and achievements made me question myself and my abilities. I marveled at the success of people such as P Diddy, Mark Zuckerberg, and Frank Kern, but I failed to investigate and learn about the journeys that got them there.

I needed to learn and understand these people's ups, downs, lessons, advantages, and successes. One of my best friends, Richmond, unknowingly gave me advice that would change my outlook on life forever. He taught me about enjoying the journey more than just focusing on the destination.

It was 3:30 a.m., eyes slowly blinking to black; Richmond's sleep deprivation started to take its toll as his car crossed lanes on the dark, quiet motorway. Suddenly, a jolt startled Richmond back to consciousness. I think the cat eye studs (reflective pavement markers) on the motorway was what startled him.

"Kevin, I think you should take over the driving," Richmond said as he sat up straight, rapidly blinking his eyes and looking for a safe place to stop on the hard shoulder. I was happy; finally, I could drive Richmond's beautiful new Rolls-Royce Phantom! Only God and tiredness could convince

Richmond to hand over his beauty of a car to me. He found a safe place to stop, and we swapped seats. I buckled up, adjusted my mirrors, and put my foot down on the accelerator of what can only be called a Concorde of a car. I was moving at 30, 40, 60, 80, and even 100 miles per hour in seconds—it both surprised me and excited me. I was driving a bloody Concorde! "We will be in Bristol in no time," I said beaming from ear to ear while putting the car through its paces as Richmond faded to unconsciousness. My desire to go faster was my aspiration—I wanted to feel what a £300,000 (about $357,000 US) Rolls-Royce could do. Then Richmond said something that would change my outlook on life forever. Half asleep, Richmond opened one eye and said, "The faster you get to the destination, the less you will enjoy the journey. Kevin, this car is designed for you to enjoy the journey, not to speed to the destination. The quicker you get there, the sooner the ride will end, so just enjoy the journey and slow down!"

At that moment, everything became clear to me. My insecurities were all about my focus on the destination. I was unhappy because I always wanted the destination to be *now*. My sole focus was getting to the destination without appreciating the journey and the adventure.

I wanted to be perfect because I had been focusing on other people's successful destinations. My wanting to be perfect first manifested when I started to compare myself to other people's successes instead of comparing the current me to the me of yesterday. I'm not the only one to suffer the pain of other people's successes. I have seen people worldwide hating their journeys because they wanted their destination to be *now*. I have witnessed chefs overcook their rice because they wanted it perfect. I have also witnessed beautiful-looking people destroy their looks and bodies because of excessive cosmetic surgeries. Their desire to look like someone else became their mission, and looking like themselves was their greatest fear.

I have personally sabotaged great products and services within my own businesses because I wanted them to be perfect for the market. I then fell out of love with the product because I believed it was no longer good enough. It took me many years and great mentors to teach me to break my perfectionist mindset and behavior.

I have learned that the most successful companies understand the science of good enough, not perfection. When you purchase your new Android or Apple device, you quickly discover that they are just good enough for you to purchase. They have faults, bugs, and glitches before you take them out of the store. You power up your new device to discover that you must first update or install firmware and systems software. BMW, Mercedes, and Audi also understand that perfection doesn't exist. On average, their cars tend to be good enough to purchase but will also need system updates at some point post-purchase. In the world of gaming, I remember playing games such as *Command & Conquer* in 1995. It is a war-strategy game where you can create your army and go to war against the game itself or other gamers worldwide.

For the lack of great gameplay and technology in 1995, *Command & Conquer* wasn't perfect, but it was just good enough to be interesting. Until today, updates and spin-offs of *Command & Conquer* (such as *Art of War 3*) are still being played by millions of gamers, including myself, and there are still weekly updates to fix bugs and glitches.

We don't need to be perfect; we must focus on excellence.

I believe excellence is about being the superior you, striving for the best with the limited resources or knowledge you may have at the time. Excellence is a daily journey in which you work and strive toward greatness. Your goal is to be better than you were yesterday while giving your maximum effort, dedication, focus, and commitment today. Please never forget to enjoy the journey, not just the destination. I am now happily enjoying my journeys just as much as I enjoy my achievements and destinations.

I want you to write down everything that will make you a better person tomorrow. What are the bugs, glitches, and system updates that you need to improve on in your life? Get started now and push for excellence—not perfection.

What 10 things will make you a better person today than you were yesterday?

1.____

2.____

3.____

4.____

5.____

6.____

7.____

8.____

9.____

10.____

Core Value 5: Vulnerability Is Sexy

"Some of the greatest walls that have kept invaders out have also been some of the greatest walls that have kept good people in." — Kevin Bennett

Being guarded or protective of yourself is normal when you have experienced a previous breach of your trust, commitment, or love for another. I increasingly became more protective over myself as I was hurt in relationships with friends and my love life. The more I vowed that I would never be hurt again, the more the walls went up. The more I said "never again" to friends who breached my trust, the higher the walls became. "The invaders are finally at bay" I said to myself. I felt that I was safe from harm. The problem I then discovered was that the walls kept the lovers, the caregivers, the nurturers, and the protectors at bay. Being guarded stopped many good people from bonding with me on a personal level. They probably also didn't bond with me due to my distrust of them. I was radiating negativity, which defeated my goal of keeping the invaders out. I gradually became one of the invaders that I was running from.

You see, it wasn't bad intent from my side that caused my distrust, suspicion, and caution toward others. However, when an emotional trauma festers inside of you, it will inevitably affect you and your behavior. I struggled in friendships after Mark left me to die all those years ago, and when I also discovered that some of my brother's closest friends were connected to his death. That also made me struggle in relationships. When I discovered that my ex-girlfriend had cheated on me, that affected me. When I discovered that some of my closest family members were slandering my name due to jealousy, that affected me.

Being guarded is great when you never want to feel pain again, but being guarded will also keep you from feeling pleasure, love, protection, comfort, and celebration. Being guarded is a lonely place to live, and I don't recommend it.

Allowing yourself to feel will always come with terms and conditions. To love is to love. You cannot manipulate the ups and downs of love to suit you. How can you experience the ups of love if you close your heart to the downs of love? How can you enjoy the sun if you have never wanted to experience the moon? How can you enjoy friendships if you have never been a friend to the friendship itself?

Now don't get me wrong. Never allow yourself to be anyone's beating stick—physically or emotionally. Never allow people to experiment or express their negativities on you like you are a lab rat.

You must eradicate unnecessary negativity in your life and introduce and maintain positivity in your life. We cannot prevent what people did to us in the past.

However, we all have absolute control over how we want our story to continue.

'Vulnerability is Sexy' means you are relatable to others because you live and express your authentic self. Vulnerability is not a weakness but a vulnerable truth within your strength. We all loved Superman because of his cape and his relationship with Kryptonite, which made him vulnerable and relatable. Vulnerability is your large welcoming door in the middle of your large guarded wall with a welcome mat and a plaque saying, "Behind this door is love, comfort, peace, but also fear, doubt, and previous traumas." To be vulnerable is to be free from living a lie.

The sexy part about vulnerability is how attractive and freeing it is to allow yourself to be, and to have fun and enjoy yourself without fearing being judged and ridiculed. Because of this core value alone, I now have many good friends that I love and they love me in return. I have learned to trust; my reward is that others trust me in return. I am vulnerable around my friends and loved ones, and they allow me to express myself honestly. It is freeing to talk about my heartbreaks and insecurities, the things I would love to achieve, and how I may be unsure how to achieve them. It is sexy and extremely attractive to share the freeing of *you*,

the unsure you,

the trying you,

the scared you,

the experimental you,

the you who need help,

and the you who want to be loved.

My task for you now is to write down who you believe your authentic self is. What does that person (you) look like?

Who are you emotionally?

And are you living your truth?

Be honest and get started now.

Next, I want you to create a welcoming door within your guarded wall. What tools do you need to do to create that door with a welcoming mat? For example, seeking counseling or see a therapist. It may be forgiving yourself or someone else. Please write down all that needs to be in place to create your door.

Next, I have some very important questions for you. I want you to think about these questions and be completely honest with your discovery.

Question 1: With all your faults, character flaws, and personality, would you honestly marry yourself? Please highlight, or circle your answer.

[Yes, I would happily marry me] [No, I would need more work first]

Question 2: Knowing all the things you know about yourself, could you (if you were another person) spend the rest of your life with you?

[Yes, I am someone easy to be around and to live with] [No, I am very difficult to be around and to live with]

Question 3: Looking at your personality traits, values, and morals, would you be your best friend if you were someone else?

[Yes, I would be my best friend] [No, I need more work first]

Core Value 6: Be Teachable and Embrace the Moment

Would you rather be right or be happy?

We would all like to be both, but often we need to sacrifice one for the other. What I'm asking you is, what is more important to you? Being right is part of a fundamental driving force that pushes us to fight and even die for what we believe in.

Being right gives us confidence—a sense of righteousness and validity. In the name of religion, some people are suppressed and even killed if they question or challenge a God or a prophet.

In a debate, the need to be right can often stop a person from listening to the opposing party, regardless of how reasonable the opposing party's argument may be.

I was once one of those people who had to win—even if I knew deep down that I was wrong. More often than not, I couldn't accept another person being right, and my 'truths' being flawed. The 'who' of my personality was taught over time; that I was an uneducated black boy from Brixton who could only make music, sell drugs, play sports, or be a security guard.

For some time, I defended that premise against anyone who would dare to tell me that I am more than just sports, music, or drugs. I would fight or resist the positive people in my life, such as Mr. Jenkins (a teacher from secondary school) and my support workers, Michael Watson, and Hickey. They told me I could be so much more, such as an MP, a government official, or even a powerful businessman. It was as though I had Stockholm syndrome. I was defending and, at times, even fighting for the ones who were emotionally manipulating me into thinking and seeing myself as an uneducated black pleb with little to no prospects.

I was disobedient to the positive people in my life who were trying to charge my batteries. I wasn't disobedient because I wanted to be but because I didn't know who else to be. Being right doesn't always mean it is good for you or that it is the actual truth. Being right simply means it is the current view of your reality.

"Be teachable and embrace the moment" means, whether you are wrong or right, by just listening to another person's views, you will more than likely discover a new truth that will elevate you to a better, happier, and more successful place.

Embracing the moment means, even in the middle of a heated exchange, you can control your emotions and be open to listening to another person's opinions and beliefs.

Many world leaders hate each other; however, for the most part, they know how to communicate perfectly. In the name of the bigger picture, they are brilliant listeners when they meet to discuss world affairs.

Mediators go into negotiations knowing the outcome they would like to achieve. However, they spend much of their time discovering how to serve the opposing side and come to an agreement or arrangement by learning what the opposing side needs, wants, and desires.

Being teachable and embracing the moment also means being present and open to new things and ideas. My life drastically changed when I discovered this core value; I now spend more time being a listener and readily accepting different viewpoints. I am now officially teachable.

I want you to write down all the areas in your life where you believe you need to be more teachable and where you also need to accept change in your life.

Let's start with Question 1.

1. How can you become more teachable in your life? For example, I can listen more when disagreeing with my wife, husband, or clients. Get started now.

____

____

____

____

____

There's a saying, 'If you want to make God laugh, tell him your plans.' We all want, desire, and plan for the perfect outcome. However, what we wish to do will rarely work out how we want it to. Embracing the moment is to accept the good, the bad, and the indifferent that we didn't plan for. We need to make our bad, good, and indifferent moments ours. We must have the mindset and values of 'either we win, or we learn.' To embrace the moment is to accept whatever comes our way. We all want to be nimble in a fast-paced world. Embracing the moment is a brilliant value to have. I want to you to embrace this value and allow it to work for you.

Good luck.

Core Value 7: Kaizen

I have a few questions I want you to consider, even though I will answer them for you.

Question 1: Where does happiness live? Not where does it come from, but where does it *live* inside of you?

The answer: In your environment of continuous improvement.

Question 2: Where does your growth live? Once again, not where does it come from but where does it live?

The answer: In the environment of your continuous improvement.

Question 3: Where does your success live? As I mentioned before, not where does your success come from but where does it grow, sleep, and manifest?

The answer: In the environment of your continuous improvement.

I can 100% state that your happiness, personal growth, and successful results you've had in your life have all been connected in one form or another to Core Value 7: Kaizen.

Kaizen is a Japanese word meaning 'continuous improvement.' *Kai* means "change," and *Zen* means "for the better." But I don't believe the Japanese translation of Kaizen into English does it justice. To truly understand Kaizen, you must first understand what tremendous discipline and commitment look like. To me (inspired by Masaaki Imai), Kaizen is an everyday improvement, everybody improvement, everywhere improvement—and one that I've added to it—every behavior improvement.

I wanted to talk to successful people who used the science of Kaizen. So I met up with two of my friends to ask about their Kaizen.

One of them was Kye Whyte, who is the Tokyo 2020 Olympic BMX silver medalist. The other, Michael Pusey MBE, who is Kye Whyte's manager, trainer, and the owner of a highly successful BMX club. We decided to meet in Brixton's Satay Bar. We ordered rounds of drinks and food and settled in to have a catch-up after the success of Kye's win in the Olympics. I pressed the record button on my phone, and we got started. Here's how it went:

I asked my first question of Whyte: "What do you do that makes you improve daily?"

Whyte replied, "I make sure I improve by working harder the next day than I did the day before. If I am training my legs on Monday, I will do 5 sets of 5 squats, with or without weights. Then on Tuesday, I would do 6 sets of 6 squats. If I do another 5 sets of 5 on Tuesday, the same as Monday," Kye continued, "I will add more weights to my weight bar when doing squats. My goal is always continuous improvement."

I asked Michael Pusey the same question.

Pusey responded, "Discipline, discipline, discipline, and more discipline. Everyone who knows me knows I get up at 5 a.m. every morning. First, I drink water, eat the right foods, and focus on positivity and affirmations. My goal daily is to improve by at least 1% every day. No matter what happens, improve by 1% daily in your professional and personal life."

What Kye Whyte and Michael Pusey epitomize is Kaizen—continuous improvement with discipline. In the BMX racing world, to make it to the Olympics, you must qualify through many stages and many, many competitions. You must compete against hundreds of elite riders worldwide. You first have the regionals, then nationals, British championships, European championships, world championships, then the Olympics. Whyte and Pusey won or made it into the top three in all competitions at some point in their career as rider and coach.

Excited and inspired by both, I wanted to ask them more about their achievements and successes.

My second question: "What do you say to yourself before a race and when focusing on the moment to win?"

Whyte first replied, "Peckham BMX, 1 way up!"

Pusey echoed Whyte, "Peckham BMX, 1 way up!"

Now, even more inspired, I asked, "What does that mean?"

Whyte answered, "First, I visualize myself winning. I see what starter gate I will start in and how the race will play out. Sometimes I tell my team what will happen before the race starts; other times, I tell myself. I then seal it with 'Peckham BMX, 1 way up!' I did it in the Olympics and came second, receiving silver. Next time it will be gold!"

"Where did the 'Peckham BMX 1 way up!' mantra come from?" I asked.

"Me!" Michael said. "It first came about when we made a movie for MTV and Netflix. But before then, my whole belief was that everything I do must only go in one direction: that's up. When I started the BMX track in Peckham, it was a dusty, broken-down, unusable track. I worked hard and, over time, raised 1.2 million pounds [about $1.4 million US] and built the amazing BMX track we have today. See, I had no choice but one way—that was up. When I created my children's care home, I had no children referred to us for one year because we were new in that sector. Again, I said there is only one way this project will go, and that's up. Now the care home, Safe House, is doing very well. Peckham BMX started with only two children; now, we have over one hundred members. Kevin, the secret is to improve by 1% every day," Pusey concluded.

Now I will set your Kaizen '1 way up' tasks:

1. What can you do in your personal and professional life that will improve your life by 1% every day—from Monday to Sunday? Write down one thing for each day that will improve your life by at least 1%.

Monday____

Tuesday____

Wednesday____

Thursday____

Friday____

Saturday____

Sunday____

3. Legacy Branch

Your legacy of tomorrow will be a direct result of your behavior today. How you act and interact with the world on a day-to-day and moment-to-moment basis will not only be an amalgamation of how you are remembered many years from now and how your children and grandchildren will be treated after you are long gone. For example, would you like to be the son or daughter of Adolf Hitler, Joseph Stalin, or Ted Bundy? How would you feel if you were the beneficiary of their legacy?

On the flip side, how would you feel if you were the son or daughter of Mother Teresa, Leonardo da Vinci, Martin Luther King Jr., or the Dalai? Your legacy of tomorrow all depends on your intent, actions, and results of today.

I want you to now write down on your Life Board what you want your legacy to be on your Life Board. Then I want you to identify if you are living your legacy today. Your goals and mission are to be the person today that your children, grandchildren, and world will be proud of tomorrow.

Question 1: What would you want your legacy to be?

____

____

____

____

____

Question 2: Are your daily actions, behaviors, and results aligning with your legacy?

[Yes] [Not sure] [No]

4. Spirituality Branch

What is spirituality, you may ask? Well, let's start with what spirituality is not. You cannot touch, taste, or smell spirituality. It's not a religion or a culture. It's not faith or a cause. Spirituality is not the mind or the body. Spirituality is a relationship with the *I AM* that's within and around you—you are the *I AM*—you were spirit before you were body, and you will be spirit after your body is gone. Spirituality suppresses all restrictions and boundaries. It cannot be detained or understood in any certain terms.

People tend to be depressed, anxious, and unsatisfied with their lives when they are not in alignment with their spiritual selves. Being in alignment allows you to be in harmony with yourself and the world around you. People who are spiritually in tune are less fearful and reactive to turbulent situations and events. The mind will declare war on your spiritual side because the spiritual side doesn't need the mind. But the mind doesn't like to be ignored or excluded when you are connecting with the *I AM*, your spiritual self.

You will discover that, when meditating or doing yoga, your mind will send waves of distractive information when it realizes it's not needed or required. It does this when the other side of you is connecting with the *I AM* within, or when you are in a state of meditation.

Most people who want to be in alignment with self would normally now ask, 'Where do I start to have this inner relationship I have been yearning for?' Well, your relationship with self has already started - it's not linear; it doesn't wait for you to start or catch up. You are self, and self is you. You want a better relationship with yourself.

Money doesn't bring you closer to self, nor does poverty. There is no A, and there is no Z; you can't measure it as it is immeasurable.

But you can get on the conveyor belt to a better relationship by just first being aware—being conscious. I am not talking about mental awareness but awareness itself. The more conscious you become, the more plugged in you will be. Don't focus on the future or dwell on the past. Just be in the now.

Yes, you must be interested in your future and past but don't live there. People who tend to live in the future live anxious lives, and people who live in the past tend to live regretful, angry, depressed lives. Be aware of what was and what will be, but live here and live now!

I have daily and moment-to-moment exercises to heighten and strengthen your awareness and relationship with self:

1. Meditate daily.
2. Take time out just to focus on your breathing. Take deep breaths and focus on them. Then breathe normally and focus on that. This exercise will take you away from unwanted thoughts.
3. Practice yoga on a daily or weekly basis.
4. Be aware when your ego tries to make decisions on your behalf. Try to stop it in its tracks through self-inquiry by investigating your self-conversations. Investigate your 'whys' before you make any crucial decisions. Investigate where your decisions are coming from. Are they coming from pain or pleasure, anger, or lust? The more you investigate, the more you will discover about yourself.
5. Keep your positive energy up. Be aware of your conversations with yourself and others. Manage your energy intake just like you would manage your sugar or salt intake. Energy flows like a current, so it can't

be stopped. But it can be transformed from positive to negative and negative to positive. That part is up to you.

6. To be aware is to accept the reality of your circumstances—you can then choose to change your relationship with your circumstances.

I want you to now add more to your spiritual list here. Get started:

5. Your Message to the World Branch

If you could change the world with a message, what would your words of wisdom be? This branch of your Life Board will help you with your purpose and mission in life. However, to be passionate, you must explore what makes you want to change.

For example, are you passionate about climate change or equality? Animal rights or modern-day slavery?

Greta Thunberg at The World Climate Summit in 2019 spoke to world leaders. Her hook was, "How dare you!" Her message to these leaders was that they needed to take climate change more seriously and not put the burden on future generations.

In 2019, Sir David Attenborough, at the WWF International conference, warned, "What we do in the next few years will determine the next few thousand years." That was again a stark warning to world leaders about their behavior and obligations for a cleaner, greener planet before it's too late.

You may not believe you have the platform or the power to make a change. If that is your belief, please think again. People's messages are going viral daily for trivial and irrelevant reasons. Your commitment to change will influence listeners and viewers, one person at a time. Please try to answer the following questions.

Question 1: What makes you emotional or angry about wanting change in the world?

____

____

____

____

Question 2: What makes you tearful and breaks your heart about what's currently happening in the world?

Question 3: What is your message to the world?

6. Lifestyle Branch

Just like the traditional vision boards, it's time to be unapologetic and say what you want, own it, and mean it. More than 50% of my clients have felt shy or even embarrassed when talking unapologetically about what they want, then truly owning it. They tell me how greedy they feel or don't want to come across to others as too materialistic. It normally takes me about twenty minutes to readjust their belief systems and get them to accept what they want deep down, and receive it openly and happily.

This Life Board is about serving others while serving yourself to be the best you. The KBenaire Life Board urges you to be good to your neighbor and respect the Earth you walk on while aligning with God or your creator. Each branch on this Life Board is designed for your betterment. The Lifestyle Branch of the Life Board is about you, your desires, and your lifestyle.

Let's break down your Vision Board, a.k.a. Lifestyle Branch into five areas. But before we start, let me clarify this—what some may call a *Vision Board*, I call the *Lifestyle Branch of my KBenaire Life board*. This process requires you to look for pictures online or in magazines, cut them out, or print them off. They can be pictures of anything that represents what you want in your life, such as your ideal car, ideal home, dream holidays, future spouse, or how you would like to look physically. I want you to fall in love with this process. I want you to go to bed with it at night, dream about it as you sleep, wake up with it in the morning, romanticize about it on your daily travels, and talk about it to anyone willing to listen to you talk on and on about it. I want you to pray and meditate over it. I want every personal and professional lifestyle decision you make to be with your ideal lifestyle in mind.

Now let's get you started.

Questions for you to think about:

Question 1: What is the ideal car(s) you want? Find pictures of it (them), and add them to the lifestyle part of your Life Board.

Question 2: Do you want a boat, helicopter, or plane? Once again, add them to the Lifestyle branch of your Life Board, even if you don't believe you can achieve it, or them. Add them anyway. We will address achieving them later in this chapter.

Question 3: What does your ideal home look like? Is it a mansion or a maisonette? Is it a villa or a boat house? What do the interior and furniture look like? White and gold? Or grand oak wood? How about your backyard? Is there an endless forest at the back of your yard? Or just a nice, conservative backyard with some beautiful tropical flowers? Your ideal home is your choice. Add the pictures and get started desiring your dreams.

Next, how about your clothing? Dig into fashion magazines and discover what works for you. Have you found your husband or wife yet? Cut pictures out of how you want your family to look and the vacations you will go on together in the future. Do you want to go to the gym? Brilliant! Add the pictures. Get started now! I strongly suggest you purchase the KBenaire LIFE BOARD and start your adventure toward manifesting your dreams and goals. The KBenaire LIFE BOARD app will also serve you daily in the same way a friend or a life coach will hold you to account as an on-the-go tool to success.

7. Investment Branch

To have the lifestyle you desire and a financially secure future for you and your family, I can't stress enough how important it is to become financially literate and financially free as soon as possible. That said, I believe everybody's life should have an investment and business branch in their life and Life Board. I understand that many of us just want to focus on our jobs and rely on our pension plan after retirement. As good as the old model was for the baby boomers, I don't think the pension model and government welfare can sustain themselves much longer.

According to ons.gov.uk, life expectancy for people born in the UK in 1960 was 74.2 years for females and 68.2 years for males. Life expectancy, if you were born between 2017 and 2019, was 83.1 years of age for females and 79.4 years of age for males. With modern-day medicine and healthier lifestyles, people live up to 13 years longer than the 60s babies. If you were born in 1960, your pension age in the UK would be 66. If you were born in 2017 in the UK, your pension age would be 68 years—2 years more than the pension age of people born in the 1960s. This is expected to rise as modern-day medicines, healthier lifestyles, and technology sustain and prolongs life.

People dying in their mid-'70s to mid-'80s are breaking the system. Governments and pension companies did not anticipate people living longer today; some experts say that the planet is becoming overpopulated, partly because of modern-day medicine, healthier lifestyles, and technology! The UK NHS is also bursting at the seams, and taxes are expected to rise to unrealistic heights due to COVID-19, Brexit, companies relocating from the UK, immigration, and world wars.

Relying on broken governments and unsustainable pension companies is enough to make the toughest of us anxious and have sleepless nights. Just saving money in the bank alone isn't enough to sustain you in retirement. The UK's inflation rate for August 2017, 2018, and 2019 was 0.5%. In August

2021, the consumer prices index rose by 0.7% from the previous month, compared with a fall of 0.4% in the same month the previous year. In this book's writing, if you were to rely on your bank savings in the UK, you can expect to receive anything from 0.45% to 1.75% in interest.

What I'm saying is with the rise of inflation, while relying on your savings in a bank alone, you will feel more pain than pleasure in saving money. Relying on banks and governments is not a great financial strategy. It's not all doom and gloom, though. I must state that I am far from a financial expert, but it doesn't take a financial expert to see that the system cannot continue this way or sustain itself. A change is about to come, whether we like it or not, are ready for it, or want it.

Your tasks for this Investment branch of the Life Board are the following:

1. Research and seek out investments and financial experts to educate you and point you in the right direction regarding what is working in general and what is good for you to invest in.

2. Seek financial planners who will help you create a financial road map.

3. Take action—"Faith without works is dead." To score, you must first take a shot. The sooner you get started, the better off you will be in the long term. Good luck with this set of tasks and your mission toward financial freedom.

List financial experts who can help you on your journey to financial freedom here:

____

____

____

List your financial goals here:

Once you have received advice, list the investments you are considering here:

8. Education Branch

Education is the key to your success.

"But what do I need to be educated in?" you may ask. Let me put it this way; you need to be educated in all of the previous branches of your Life Board to achieve all the things you desire and require in your life.

So, let's quickly recap your Life Board so far.

We have covered the following:

Your Feelings

Your Core Values

Your Legacy

Your Spirituality

Your Message to the World

Your Lifestyle

Your Investments

If there is any time to be more educated to further your growth, happiness, and success, it's now. I want you to go out now and learn what investments you need to be financially free. I want you to educate yourself about your spirituality and who you are intrinsically. I want you to explore everything you need to learn to achieve your desired lifestyle. I want you to meet the rich, the wealthy, the happy, and the healthy and become friends with beautiful souls and great minds so they can educate you.

You may have heard this statement before: "Your network is your net worth." This statement is very true. The successful people you can call upon, talk with, hang out with, invest in, and have them invest in you, will elevate your successes to unbelievable heights. You need to be educated within the sectors we discussed and take courses to further your educational growth in your fields of interest. I also think it is a good idea to create a list for your Wealth 100.

The Wealth 100

The best gift you can give yourself is a powerful network of people. By surrounding yourself with inspirational people, they will emit positive energy, invaluable knowledge, resources, and wealth into your life. You will, at some level, share their resources.

They will build you up when you're in a place of self-doubt.

They will protect you when the world is against you.

They will elevate you when you believe you can no longer climb.

They will pray over you when your faith is dwindling. They will teach you to enjoy life when life feels unenjoyable.

They will help you to be financially free and self-abundant when all you can think about is paying your next bill and surviving.

They will introduce you to their networks, who will then introduce you to their networks, where you will eventually become a desired network yourself.

I have added 'The Wealth 100' to this Life Board because, after many years of research, I have discovered that the most successful people in the world tend to have a network of more than 100 people to call upon for assistance in winning. Within this branch, I recommend that you build your network of 100 people who will help you with your growth, positivity, and prosperity.

I know it may sound like a lot. I mean, what 'normal' person can call upon 100 people for growth, positivity, health, and prosperity? First, let's start with the fact that you are not 'normal.' You are special and here to achieve things 'normal' people can only dream about.

Let's break down The Wealth 100.

The Wealth 100—#1: We must first start with spirituality. I suggest you have at least three spiritual advisers who can guide you and help you to navigate closer to yourself and your creator. They can also help you to be shielded from evil intent and demonic and sinister behaviors toward you.

We can all see and sense the growing negativity sweeping across the world and throughout our communities. We need spiritual protection for this spiritual entity of FEAR. Having people praying with you and over you should be a practice to consider.

With that said, I suggest you must have seven more people you can trust to pray with and over you. You can discover these people in your church, mosque, synagogue, or any other place of worship. Having faith and spiritual practitioners on your side is needed in today's world. Go out and start connecting. Please NOTE: Make sure your spiritual team is praying and following the right proton spiritual energy, not something evil and demonic.

Wealth 100—#2: You need to have people in the legal sector in your corner. Having solicitors, barristers, lawyers, and even a judge in your Wealth 100 is imperative in today's world.

Legal practitioners within your network will reduce stress, save you money, and can even save your life. Connect with these people by joining VIP members' clubs and attending lawyers' and barristers' conventions. The Lawyers Conference in the US is the Judicial Division's home for legal students and professionals interested in working closely with judges. Connect with these groups who can help you expand your legal network.

Wealth 100—#3: Accountants in your Wealth 100 are like blood in your body—you need to have accountants as you climb your wealth ladder. I believe you must have a minimum of two accountants within your team. Good accountants will minimize your tax bills, show you how to take full advantage of the ever-changing laws and give you financial advice on the incomings and outgoings you need to grow your wealth.

Wealth 100—#4: You need a younger and more mature network. Your younger network must consist of people between 18 to 35, whereas your mature network must consist of people aged 50 and up. You will lose touch with modern-day trends, opportunities, and cultures if you do not have young, trendy, and vibrant people in your network. Your younger network will push you to be and do more. They will give you the energy you once thought you had lost. They will keep you updated, fresh, and on-trend. Your mature, wiser network will keep you grounded and pensive. They will educate you on their past wins and woes. They will remind you not to neglect your family and to look at the bigger picture, as time is not promised to us all.

Wealth 100—#5: You need well-being networks. I don't need to tell you how important it is to be fit and healthy in mind and body. Having partners for brisk walking, gym buddies, nutritionists, and even joining a yoga class will help you to eradicate stress, depression, and anger problems. Having a well-being network will undoubtedly maintain your health and fitness. Don't be surprised if you discover up to 20 people in your well-being network once you have connected with your gyms, yoga classes, etc.

Wealth 100—#6: You need CEOs and many different types of leaders apart of your network. CEOs, community leaders, domestic leaders, leaders in the world of finance, and policy-makers are crucial to be connected to. I cannot stress enough how important having a powerful network within your network actually is. Nowadays, it's not what you know but who you know—then what you know becomes relevant. You must be connected to policy-makers and community leaders.

We all have had injustices happen to us at some point in our lives, and we all need to get in the door through the back at some point too.

That said, we need leaders of all types in the network we can call upon. However, we must also bring something to the table. You must render your services to these people who are game-changers. I believe everyone in life needs aid and servitude from another. You must know what you bring to their table and what you want in return. Servitude is good, but being another person's slave is bad. There is a fine line between serving people and being a slave to another person's demands. Become relevant in your networks' lives, then negotiate what you need.

Wealth 100—#7: You must have hobbies. Hobbies create happiness, joy, bonding, business, and friendships. Friendships are typically discovered when you are sharing interests and hobbies with others. Many CEOs and powerful leaders tend to meet, bond, and talk business while playing golf, hiking, and mountain climbing.

Hobbies are significant for finding lifelong friends because they take trust in vulnerable times such as hiking and mountain climbing. Football, ice hockey, tennis, rugby, and soccer are all sports that require cooperation and teamwork. Those sports will allow you to meet new people who can introduce happiness, friendships, and stress relief into your life. The theater, museum, and art galleries are good places to meet like-minded people with unique interests and gifts. I am sure you will have 40 to 50 new people that you will connect with across the above hobbies. I am sure that some people you will meet will eventually become lifelong friends.

The Wealth 100 may seem like a mammoth task, but it's not—it's just an adjustment to your lifestyle and intent. Being purposeful will eventually give you the life and lifestyle you require and desire for yourself and your family to win. I can guarantee that you have or will have people who talk and introduce negativity into your mindset and belief system. The Wealth 100 is designed to introduce positivity and prosperity into your life on every level. Come out of your comfort zone and get started with your Wealth 100 now.

Who is in your Wealth 100?

Who are the three spiritual advisers you can call upon?

1. ______________________________

2. ______________________________

3. ______________________________

Which 7 to 10 people can you spiritually trust to pray with you and over you in times of pain, pleasure, and gratitude?

1. ______________________________

2. ______________________________

3. ______________________________

4. ______________________________

5. ______________________________

6. ______________________________

7. ______________________________

8. ____

9. ____

10. ____

What legal members' clubs and conventions are you going to join or attend where you will meet lawyers, barristers, judges, legal students, and other legal professionals etc., to join your Wealth 100? Write down the clubs and conventions you will attend here.

1. ____

2. ____

3. ____

4. ____

5. ____

6. ____

7. ____

8. ____

9. ____

10. ____

Write down at least two accountants and three advisers you will need for your financial growth and advice. Research them and what they do, then add them to your Wealth 100 list here.

1. ______________________________

2. ______________________________

3. ______________________________

4. ______________________________

5. ______________________________

Write down the people within your younger network between the ages of 18 to 35. Remember, they will keep you on-trend, young-minded, and vibrant. List their names here and ask them to keep you on-trend and in the know (culturally and in the world of technology).

1. ______________________________

2. ______________________________

3. ______________________________

4. ______________________________

5. ______________________________

6. ______________________________

7. ______________________________

8. ______________________________

9. ______________________________

10. ______________________________

Now list your aged 50+ more mature and wiser network of people who will keep you grounded, reflective, and educated with their past wins and woes and will teach you not to neglect family and the bigger picture.

1. ______________________________

2. ______________________________

3. ______________________________

4. ______________________________

5. ______________________________

6. ______________________________

7. ______________________________

8. ______________________________

9. ______________________________

10. ______________________________

Now create your well-being network. I now want you to list your brisk walking partners, the gym you will join, or attend, and your gym buddies you will train with. I want you also to list your nutritionists, yoga class, and all the other well-being activities you will add to your Wealth 100 here.

1. ______________________________

2. ______________________________

3. ______________________________

4. ______________________________

5. ______________________________

6. ______________________________

7. ______________________________

8. ______________________________

9. ______________________________

10. ______________________________

11. ______________________________

12. ______________________________

13. ______________________________

14. ______________________________

15. ______________________________

16. ______________________________

17. ____

18. ____

19. ____

20. ____

CEOs, community leaders, domestic leaders, leaders in the world of finance, and policy-makers need to be a part of your Wealth 100. I am not saying it will be easy to add these people to your list, but it's imperative to have them as part of your network is imperative. I suggest you go to town and city meetings, charity events, protests, dinner galas, and all the other places where you will meet leaders and policy-makers. Research and list the leaders you want to add to your Wealth 100

1. ____

2. ____

3. ____

4. ____

5. ____

6. ____

7. ____

8. ____

9. ____

10. ____

Your happiness, joy, bonding, business, and friendships will all be discovered in your hobbies. I want you to list the hobbies that you are either going to start or are currently doing.

1. ____
2. ____
3. ____
4. ____
5. ____
6. ____
7. ____
8. ____
9. ____
10. ____

Mentors Branch

It's that time for another quick recap. We keep recapping as we progress through each branch of the Life Board because each branch complements the previous branch. Let me explain. How you should feel must always come first. You cannot progress if you are sad, broken, or depressed. To know what your legacy should be, you must first know what your core values are. Your message to the world comes from your values. Your spirituality must be in tune, or you will lose yourself and have a dangerous and destructive lifestyle. We all would love to have the lifestyle of our dreams.

However, you cannot live the lifestyle you desire without an income and investments. You will need guidance and great minds for all the branches of your Life Board to manifest. With that said, you need mentors and masterminds in your life.

A mentor offers you their wisdom and advice to help you reach your goals and dreams. Just like a car satellite navigation system, mentors will provide you with the best routes to travel and the ideal time to get there. They will show you where the traffic and roadblocks are and help you to avoid being caught up in the noise and the road rage of life. You will need mentors with unique expertise for each branch of your KBenaire Life Board. I strongly recommend it.

Before I continue, I must state that you must—and I repeat—must first learn who your mentors are morally and spiritually. You cannot be a person of God and then connect with a mentor who is demonic with dark energy. You should seek a mentor who has spiritually good energy, a person with good intent and has integrity. With that said, here are 11 more reasons why I believe you must have a mentor starting today.

1. Mentors have been there and done what you aim to do. They have already achieved your dreams and the goals you desire. They understand your struggles and your self-doubt, they know what your self-conversations are saying, they will

also know how to help you get out of your way when you are your biggest obstacle.

2. Good mentors make you dream bigger than you are currently dreaming. They will push your mind and abilities further than you currently push yourself.

3. Mentors are not emotionally attached to you, or your dreams like your friends and family are. They are unbiased, straight-talking fact-speakers. If you have a bad idea, they will say it's a bad idea; if it's good, they will say it's good. Your friends and family may lie to you or not be truthful with you to not hurt your feelings.

4. Your mentors have the networks and contacts you need. They are bigger players who hang with even bigger players. If your mentor believes in you, they will introduce you to other players who will further your growth and success.

5. Your mentor will spot your branches' flaws and the benefits. They will give you deeper insights into your field of interest or journey. They will connect dots that are almost impossible for you to see or connect yourself. A brilliant mentor will ask you a crucial question: "What is your existing strategy?"

6. A really good mentor will help you to have discipline. Your mentor will hold you to account and make sure you take positive action on the tasks you normally avoid and categorically refuse to do. Your mentor will help you with your timing, speed to market, priorities, and focus is off. Your mentor will kick your ass to prevent you from procrastinating. They will teach you that you can't do everything and to trust outsourcing and other teams for help.

7. Mentors with proton morals, energy, and spirit will put you in your place if you start to move into an electron-dark place. Sometimes we can become too greedy, selfish, arrogant, or uncaring. Proton mentors will tell us the truth about our arrogance.

8. Most mentors will urge you to be an avid reader. Readers are leaders, and leaders tend to be avid readers. If you struggle with reading, listen to educational audiobooks, and watch videos, documentaries, and podcasts. Be prepared for your mentors to tell you to read, read, and read again.

9. A mentor could save you a lot of time and money on the things you may think are assets, which may turn out to be liabilities.

For example,

Is your car liability or an asset?

Is your home your biggest investment or your biggest liability?

Do you pay for your flights and holidays?

Are all the above, good ways to spend your hard-earned money?

The right mentor could save you tens of thousands through a single conversation.

10. If you and your ideas are worth the investment, your mentor could be your first investor. They will become more invested in you and help your dreams become a successful reality.

My advice, present yourself well and become the inspiration your mentor would love to be around. You will surely be invited to networking parties and VIP members' clubs where you can shake hands with your future. Before you approach your potential mentors, I urge you to do some things first.

1. Learn about your potential mentor. What do they like?

2. What do they need?

3. How can you best serve your potential mentor for them to want to serve you in return?

4. What makes them happy?

5. What do they fear the most?

6. What are their beliefs about bettering themselves and the world?

7. Why do they do what they do?

You must learn about your potential mentor before you ask them to mentor you. Watch videos, read blogs, and listen to podcasts about them.

Learn about their interests and their children and partner. Learn other details, such as whether they are married or divorced. If it's a 'yes' to either one, investigate why.

The more you know about your potential mentor, the more you will know how to serve them best and persuade them to serve you. Be thick-skinned and accept rejection, but do not accept being rejected. Keep pushing and keep persisting until they eventually say 'yes.' However, if your potential mentor has a genuine reason why they cannot mentor you, let go and move on to the next potential mentor on your list.

I now want you to list 13 mentors for each branch of your Life Board below.

Good luck!

Name of mentor 1: ______________________________

____

Mentor 1 specializes in: __________________________

____

Contact details for mentor 1: ______________________

____

What you need from mentor 1: ______________________

____

In return, you will offer mentor 1:___________________

____

Name of mentor 2: ______________________________

____

Mentor 2 specializes in: __________________________

____

Contact details for mentor 2: ______________________

____

What you need from mentor 2: ______________________

____

In return, you will offer mentor 2:____________________

____

Name of mentor 3: ______________________________

____

Mentor 3 specializes in: __________________________

____

Contact details for mentor 3: ______________________

____

What you need from mentor 3: ____________________

____

In return, you will offer mentor 3: __________________

____

Name of mentor 4: ______________________________

____

Mentor 4 specializes in: __________________________

____

Contact details for mentor 4: ______________________

____

What you need from mentor 4: ____________________

____

In return, you will offer mentor 4: ______________________

____

Name of mentor 5: ___________________________________

____

Mentor 5 specializes in: ______________________________

____

Contact details for mentor 5: __________________________

____

What you need from mentor 5: _________________________

____

In return, you will offer mentor 5: ______________________

____

Name of mentor 6: ___________________________________

____

Mentor 6 specializes in: ______________________________

____

Contact details for mentor 6: __________________________

____

What you need from mentor 6: _________________________

____

In return, you will offer mentor 6: ______________________

____

Name of mentor 7: ____________________________________

____

Mentor 7 specializes in: ______________________________

____

Contact details for mentor 7: __________________________

____

What you need from mentor 7: __________________________

____

In return, you will offer mentor 7: ______________________

____

Name of mentor 8: ____________________________________

____

Mentor 8 specializes in: ______________________________

____

Contact details for mentor 8: __________________________

____

What you need from mentor 8: __________________________

____

In return, you will offer mentor 8: ______________________

____

Name of mentor 9: _____________________________________

____

Mentor 9 specializes in: ________________________________

____

Contact details for mentor 9: ___________________________

____

What you need from mentor 9: __________________________

____

In return, you will offer mentor 9: ______________________

____

Name of mentor 10: ___________________________________

____

Mentor 10 specializes in: _______________________________

____

Contact details for mentor 10: __________________________

____

What you need from mentor 10: _________________________

____

In return, you will offer mentor 10: ______________________

____

Name of mentor 11: ________________________________

____

Mentor 11 specializes in: ____________________________

____

Contact details for mentor 11: _________________________

____

What you need from mentor 11: ________________________

____

In return, you will offer mentor 11: ______________________

____

Name of mentor 12: ________________________________

____

Mentor 12 specializes in: ____________________________

____

Contact details for mentor 12: _________________________

____

What you need from mentor 12: ________________________

____

In return, you will offer mentor 12________________________

____

Name of mentor 13: __________________________________

____

Mentor 13 specializes in: _____________________________

____

Contact details for mentor 13: _________________________

____

What you need from mentor 13: ________________________

____

In return, you will offer mentor 13: ______________________

____

Mastermind Group Branch

So first, what is a mastermind group? A mastermind group is when two or more minds come together in spiritual, emotional, and psychological harmony to attain a definite purpose. This mastermind group could be a husband and wife, friends or neighbors, work colleagues, or networking members. The rules and science of the mastermind principle must be of a perfectly harmonious union among all parties. You cannot obtain a spiritual command and dominance if the members of the mastermind group are not all vibrating on the same frequency.

Before inviting members into your mastermind group, you must set rules and boundaries.

Here are the rules:

1. All mastermind members must be within the same proton frequency. The wrong frequencies can work against you instead of for you.
2. Your mastermind meetings must be within the correct quarters of the moon. As mastermind practitioners, the new moon and the first quarter are the only quarters during which to exercise your energies together. If it's not within the time of the full moon or last quarter, please refrain from your positive mastermind practices.
3. Before you start your mastermind alliance, the room or environment must be clean and cleared of all unwanted clutter, negative items, and energies. You do not want undesirables affecting your work.
4. At the start of each mastermind session, all members must pray together and focus on the positive aim, goal, and intention. You don't want different mastermind group members to introduce their daily or weekly woes into your positive space. Your prayers and meditations must bless the energy and mood of the individuals and the environment.
5. Have your mastermind meetings weekly, outside the days of the full moon and the last quarter.
6. Have a precise set time, rules, and structure for each meeting. You don't want people turning up 10 minutes late or multitasking on their phones or other devices. Tell them to turn their phones off and focus until the meeting has ended.
7. Have each member share their weekly successes and setbacks within the first 5 to 10 minutes of your mastermind meetup (either before or after your prayers and meditation). This is a good time for people

to express their feelings, break the ice, and get things off their minds.

8. Once the members' successes and setbacks are discussed, ask them the following questions:
   a) What is the next major goal you must achieve? Have you set a timeframe for the achievement?
   b) What have you committed to that is still pending?
   c) What are the clear challenges that need to be resolved now?
9. Once all the mastermind group members have answered all the above questions, ask the members to focus with positive thoughts and enthusiasm to find solutions to each goal and challenge.
10. Everyone in the mastermind group must have an accountability partner. An accountability partner will hold the other member to account for what needs to be done and the timelines within which it needs to be achieved.
11. End your mastermind sessions with a prayer and affirmations.

Now I want you to list all your mastermind group members

____

____

____

____

____

____

____

____

____

____

____

Circle of Confidence Branch

There is a famous saying about the three faces we have. The saying goes something like this:

There is one face that we show to the world.

There is another face we show to our friends and family.

There is a third face that we never want to show to anyone at all.

The first face we show is designed to make ourselves look perfect to the world. This mask we present is designed to protect us from shame, ridicule, embarrassment, abandonment, and rejection. It is a facade. It is well rehearsed and beautifully scripted, ready to perform to whoever is willing to accept the distortion of our public reality.

Our second face is designed and less strategically presented to friends and family. This face is carefully masked and delivered to suit our parents, friends, and extended family members. Unlike the first mask, our second mask is more authentic and honest to our loved ones – but much is still held back with this mask to protect ourselves from being judged, rejected, or even abandoned by our nearest and dearest.

Then you have our third face. This face is the face we never show or want to show anyone. This face scares us. It's our authentic face—no mask, no makeup, just raw truths. This is our self-conversational face that never lies to us but tells us our ugly truths.

We become petrified of being judged, abandoned, rejected, and ridiculed about our deepest, darkest insecurities and traumas when this face looks into the mirror. This face is the face that only you can see in the mirror, and only you know that no moisturizer or makeup can conceal how we truly feel about ourselves.

All three faces tend to cause massive pain and disconnection from people who could more than likely introduce joy, love, romance, acceptance, and belonging into our lives.

I believe we all should have a circle of confidence. This circle of confidence will serve and protect all three faces.

So, what is the circle of confidence? It is a small network of trusted advisers you can share your traumas and dark thoughts with. Most people who suffer from depression and often fantasize about committing suicide tend to either bottle up their pain or self-conversate about not wanting to be on this planet anymore. I suggest your circle of confidence should start with the following members to prevent all the above pains from happening.

1. God

Get two chairs and set them up facing each other as though you are having a face-to-face conversation with someone. Next, sit on one of the chairs and talk to God as though God is your therapist sitting in the other chair. Talk to God, be vulnerable with God, release your traumas, and be you. You will be surprised how your talk with God will help traumas and solve problems and pain.

2. Therapists

Talk to a trained, qualified, and certified professional to help you deal with your stresses and traumas. You need a professional who understands your head, heart, and behavior. Every moving part on this planet needs a mechanic, and so do you.

3. Spiritual and Religious Practitioners

Spiritual and religious practitioners tend to be good listeners. They can also help give a religious or spiritual perspective on how to deal with your woes. There's comfort and warmth involved in talking with spiritual and religious practitioners. Pray with them, talk with them, bond with them.

4. Family Members

Family members can be a bit tricky as it all depends on the trauma you have or the trouble you are facing. Only you can gauge what you can and cannot share with your family, or specific family members. I must say, if you have members of your family you can go to and be vulnerable with, then be honest, be true, and let them help you.

5. A friend

I hope, in your case, a friend actually means a real friend—someone you can trust with your deepest and darkest secrets. Only you know what qualifies your friend to be called your *friend*. Once again, gauge whether your friend can be trusted with your traumas. Your friend should be the type of person with whom you can be tearful and honest with about how you feel. Too many good people have died because they felt like they had no one to talk to or listen to when they actually did. They had good people happy and ready to serve them.

I want you first to assess your family, friends, and spiritual practitioners to see if you can share with them what is extremely personal and important to you.

Questions to ask yourself:

A) Can the people you invite into your circle of confidence keep and value other people's secrets? Or do they tell you and others what shouldn't be shared? If they share other people's secrets, maybe they are not a good choice for your circle of confidence.

B) When angry, do your potential circle of confidence members become vindictive with you or others? If yes, they are not ideal to introduce into your circle of confidence. You don't want your world and secrets stored in the mind of a vindictive soul.

Once you have assessed them all, start building your circle of confidence today. Call therapists and interview them to see if they are the right fit for you. Approach your friends, family members, and spiritual and religious practitioners and ask them if you can confide in them in the future. Express yourself clearly regarding all that concerns you and investigate if they are willing to take on the role of your trusted adviser and confidant.

Suppose they say 'yes,' set rules and boundaries with them. Set up a WhatsApp or Telegram group. If a situation is code red (a dire straits problem), only then should you use the group messenger with all of your circle of confidence members in it. A dire straits problem could be you feeling suicidal or deeply depressed.

You do not want to burn out your circle of confidence members with easily solvable challenges. You can talk to a particular member for a code green situation (talk to clear your thoughts) or a code amber situation (you have some concerns and need to discuss them). I repeat, **only** use your group messenger for a code red situation, such as suicidal thoughts and behavior.

Get started now.

Who are the people you are going to select for your circle of confidence?

You don't need to write down God for obvious reasons. So start where you please, but fill out all the areas below.

God bless.

Name and list the therapists you selected for your circle of confidence.

Name and list the spiritual and religious practitioners whom you have selected to include in your circle of confidence.

Name and list family members that you have selected to include into your circle of confidence.

Name and list friends that you have selected to include into your circle of confidence.

____

____

____

____

____

Time to take action.

You now have a plan. You have a defined reason to be focused and committed to being, doing, and having all you desire and all that you want to achieve in your life. It would be a great idea to now make an investment into purchasing the KBenaire Life Board. Your life will change forever. It's worth the investment!

CHAPTER 9

WHERE YOUR FOCUS GOES, YOUR ENERGY FLOWS

Marlo said, "It's nice," as he looked down at Andre's big, sparkling gold ring.

"What?" Andre replied, following Marlo's nod toward the ring on his finger. "Oh, you like that?" Andre said uncomfortably rubbing and twisting his ring from side to side. He hoped the conversation with Marlo would somehow disappear. "I've had it for a long time now," Andre said, trying his best to look and sound as confident as possible.

"It's got some sentimental value." Andre continued, trying to downplay the value of his prized possession.

Marlo menacingly stared at the ring, then moved his eyes up into Andre's fearful face. "What's the real value?" Marlo asked.

"Huh?" Andre uttered, hearing every word that Marlo said but trying to stall for time. He needed to think of a plausible answer that would save him and the precious gold ring that he worshiped. But before he could say anything else, Marlo interrupted him. "**Real value**?" he said, demanding the ring with a hand gesture: Season 4, Episode 4, the cult series, *The Wire.*

As I watched the episodes throughout season 4, I noticed that this ring had the tendency to pop up whenever something bad was happening. It wasn't that this ring was special, nor was it worth thousands, but it held a power that would lead people to fight and even kill over it. From one negative sadistic killer to another, the ring would somehow seek out new owners to curse.

In watching *The Wire*, it is easy to get caught up in the surface messages of violence, drug dealing, and the thuggery lifestyle that is perpetuated throughout the series. But I noticed that there was a deeper message in the cult TV series. It's a message about negative and positive energy and the negative energy that was centered around a ring. In the film series *The Lord of the Rings*, there are also deeper-rooted underlying messages that should not be ignored.

The Lord of the Rings is a novel written by J. R. R. Tolkien. With more than 150 million books sold, it is a story about the fate of the One Ring, which has been lost for centuries. Powerful forces are unrelenting in their search for the ring. But fate has placed it in the hands of a young Hobbit named Frodo Baggins who inherited the Ring. His life changed forever when he came into possession of it. Even in the world of science and fantasy fiction, there are real facts and truths laid out within both *The Lord of the Rings* and *The Wire.*

I have a question for you: Do your rings and other jewelry carry a curse or a blessing into your life?

In the documentary *How the Earth Was Made: America's Gold*, we learn that "gold has mesmerized man for thousands of years, it is the oldest-known precious metal, and it plays a powerful role in almost every culture on Earth." In the same documentary, geologist Richard Goldfarb says, "Since humans have been on this planet, gold has been prized. It is such a unique mineral. It is beautiful. You can take an ounce of gold and stretch it into a thin string, and it will go for 35 miles."

So why is gold so precious?

"Gold doesn't get used up; it gets recycled. The ring you're wearing may be the same gold that was in some of the gold the pharaohs wore centuries ago with all the same properties; it's no wonder gold has been treasured by man down through history," Richard Goldfarb affirmed.

In *The Lord of the Rings*, the cursed ring was passed down through the centuries. It even was lost in a riverbed for more than 2,000 years and was rediscovered again.

So, do you think I am a fictional fantasist by using *The Wire* and *The Lord of the Rings* to show examples of reality? By the end of this book and this chapter, I plan to either reinvent your belief system or confirm your beliefs about the negative and positive energies we can purposely or mistakenly bring into our lives.

In *The Lord of the Rings*, we learn that 19 powerful rings were forged: three were given to the elves' kings, seven to the dwarf lords, and nine to humans. The purpose of these rings was to govern and have control over the Earth and each race.

As the story continues to depict, there was one more ring that the elves, dwarf lords, and men did not know about. That ring, made by Sauron, the dark lord of Mount Doom, was made to have total dominion over all the other rings. It was said that, in this one ring, he poured his negative electron energy of cruelty, malice, and ill will to dominate over all life.

A question for you, can negative or positive energy be poured into a ring to manipulate the frequencies of all who wear it?

Let's explore to see if it's possible.

First, where does gold come from, and what is gold made from?

Gold is extraterrestrial in contrast to what some people may think. Gold didn't just appear in some mountains or washed up from a stream or seabed. Gold came from the stars. It was derived and first cooked up in space through a cataclysmic supernova. An explosion in space that was so intense that it fused atoms into gold. The gold particles then mixed with rocks and dust, which in turn formed our planet. Other heavy elements, such as iron and nickel, also formed our planet. Everything is made up of atoms. We are atoms. We are also made up of the same elements as our planet and the stars, including hydrogen, oxygen, carbon, nitrogen, and yes, even gold.

God is an atom, and we are all created by God. We have protons in an atom (positive energy). We have electrons in an atom (negative energy). We have neutrons in an atom (neither negative nor positive, but they stabilize its nucleus). We are made up of the same atoms that gold is made of. We are all interconnected in some way. When we are in a proton state, we vibrate in the frequency of LOVE and all the emotions and feelings within it. When we are in an electron state, we vibrate FEAR and all the negative emotions and feelings that vibrate within it.

Back to the TV series, *The Wire*.

"Full house!" Marlo said while pulling his lollipop out of his mouth and dropping it into the ashtray. Marlo had a thing for gambling; that was his leisure time when he wasn't running his multimillion-dollar criminal empire. As he collected his winnings of thousands of dollars, a man with a long, dark-brown trench coat holding two silver semi-automatic handguns rushed into the room. One gun pointed at Marlo, and the other scoped the room, ready to shoot any card player who thought they were brave enough to make a move. This man was Omar, the local robber who got off on robbing all the drug kingpins in Baltimore. As Omar stripped the gamblers of their money and belongings, it was as if something called to Omar to grab his attention. It was the same ring Marlo had taken from Andre.

"I like that ring too," Omar said. Marlo looked away, calm and silent but extremely furious.

Marlo knew he was in a losing situation, so he slowly took off the ring and placed it on the table. Omar then picked it up, and the ring's curse transferred to its new owner.

I have three questions for you to think about.

Question 1: Do you believe Andre's negative drug dealing lifestyle attracted the low-vibrational negative ring into his life?

[Yes] [Maybe] [No]

Question 2: Do you believe the ring could have sought out Andre, Marlo, and Omar?

[Yes] [Maybe] [No]

Question 3: Do you believe that everybody in the room was vibrating the same negative frequency (FEAR) as Marlo and Omar?

[Yes] [Maybe] [No]

Back to *The Wire*—this time, to season 4, episode 6.

One evening, Omar buys a drink and exits the store. Officer Walker, one of the most corrupt police officers, sees Omar walking down the dark unlit street and decides to stop and search him. While patting him down, something catches his attention, as if something has summoned him. It was the ring.

With no restraint, Officer Walker confiscates the ring and keeps it for himself—another ~~owner~~ victim of the ring.

Humans are electric, magnetic beings. We are energy beings that have electricity flowing through our brains and bodies. Scientists and alchemists have discovered that gold is a superconductor connecting and attracting positive and negative frequencies from the universe.

Gold within and on our body can attract frequencies from across the globe. Wearing a chain or a ring heightens your spiritual connections to other forces, depending on the purity and how much gold you wear at a particular time. But it doesn't just stop with gold. Other metals and materials you wear will also attract different types of wanted or unwanted energies into your life.

Andre lived a miserable life because of the energy and frequency he entertained until he was killed.

Marlo opened himself up to all sorts of negative frequencies. He spent his life in and out of prison, yearning to be loved, feared, and respected.

Everybody whom Omar cared for, loved, and connected with, died a miserable death, or suffered a lifetime of unbearable misery. So said, so done! It was also the fate of electrons that turned out to be the demise of Omar. He was eventually murdered by a single gunshot to the head by a kid he had terrorized on the Baltimore streets.

The corrupt cop, Officer Walker, was attacked by the local kids because of his corruption. One of those kids, Michael, felt the energy of the ring and took it from Officer Walker. The same ring that Walker, Omar, Marlo, and Andre attracted, now had a new owner, Michael. Michael's life and fate relived the rings previous owners.

These examples are not just about the negative streets of Baltimore or any other ghetto around the world. The karma of positivity and negativity rules are the same for us all.

You could be rich or poor, black or white, male or female. We are all made from the same atom constituents.

So now I pose a question to you: What negative or positive metals and materials are there in your life or home which are governing your moods, emotions, frequencies, and energy for both good and bad?

Let's discover them together and find a positive way to move you one step closer to your success and happiness.

CHAPTER 10

REDISCOVER YOUR POWER AND HAPPINESS

We are all governed by laws. Some laws we choose to recognize, and others we choose to ignore. Some laws we know, and others we are oblivious to. Laws are laws, and all laws must be understood, respected, and obeyed, if you want a happy, prosperous life. Ignorance of the law is no excuse.

When I talk about laws, you may think I'm talking about government legislations, statutes, constitutions, ordinances, regulations, codes, and other human-made laws. However, human-made laws are different from God's laws, universal laws, and the planetary laws. Let me explain in greater depth.

God made humans with divine laws; humans then made human-made laws to rule over humankind. Human-made laws can never, should never, and will never, trump God's laws, universal laws, and the planetary laws. For example, humans made laws for taxes, travel, dress codes, and even speech based on the democracy of the people or the tyranny of a ruler. If no one is looking, these human-made laws can be broken, and there will be no consequences for the law-breaker. Human-made laws will always change as time and people change. God's laws, universal laws, and planetary laws will never change and have never changed throughout human history.

With these laws, whether everybody is looking, or nobody is looking at you, if you obey or break these laws, you will not escape the associated rewards or punishments. With God's laws, planetary laws, and universal laws, you will reap what you sow.

So, what laws must we learn, obey, and use to benefit ourselves and our planet?

Firstly, what are universal laws?

They are:

1. The Law of Energy
2. The Law of Rhythm
3. The Law of Inspired Action
4. The Law of Oneness
5. The Law of Gender
6. The Law of Polarity
7. The Law of Relativity
8. The Law of Transmutation
9. The Law of Compensation
10. The Law of Cause and Effect
11. The Law of Attraction
12. The Law of Correspondence

Let's start from the top of the list.

The Law of Energy

The Law of Energy states that energy can neither be created nor destroyed—only converted from one form of energy to another.

If the electron energy of stress, anger, and trauma does not convert positively, it will cause pain, inflammation, mental disorders, or even diseases in the mind and body. When a trauma has occurred, the electron energy of the trauma must be released as soon as possible.

For example, a child being bitten or attacked by a dog can cause a lifetime of fear and phobias about dogs. Traumas must be dealt with immediately after the negative traumatic event. They must be approached first, allowing the person to release negative energy by crying, screaming, or even hitting a punching bag. Once the negative electron energy is released, proton energy must be reintroduced into the person's mind and body as soon as possible. Don't allow the trauma to linger. The energy of LOVE, care, security, reassurance, and compassion must then be reintroduced.

What fears or phobias are currently controlling your life?

For example, the fear of being attacked or bitten by a dog.

Fear/phobia 1:______________________________________

Fear/phobia 2:______________________________________

Fear/phobia 3:______________________________________

Fear/phobia 4:______________________________________

Fear/phobia 5:______________________________________

Here are four questions for you:

Fear/phobia 1: Question 1

What is your account of what happened that caused fear/phobia 1 to exist in your mind and body up until this current day?

For example, a large dog jumped on me when I was six, and I believed I would be bitten or killed.

____

____

Fear/phobia 1: Question 2

How has fear/phobia 1 negatively affected your life?

For example, I now experience anxiety and panic attacks when seeing large dogs.

____

____

Fear/phobia 1: Question 3

How will your life improve when you get fear/phobia 1 out of your life forever?

For example, I will be more confident and feel happier in the presence of dogs. Parks will be an amazing and enjoyable experience because I enjoy nature and camping.

Fear/phobia 1: Question 4

What will you do today to address fear/phobia 1?

For example, I will contact a professional today to help me deal with my fear/phobia.

Fear/phobia 2: Question 1

What is your account of what happened that caused fear/phobia 2 to exist in your mind and body up until this current day?

Fear/phobia 2: Question 2

How has fear/phobia 2 negatively affected your life?

Fear/phobia 2: Question 3

How will your life improve when you get fear phobia 2 out of your life forever?

____

____

Fear/phobia 2: Question 4

What will you do today to address fear/phobia 2?

____

____

Fear/phobia 3: Question 1

What is your account of what happened that caused fear/phobia 3 to exist in your mind and body up until this current day?

____

____

Fear/phobia 3: Question 2

How has fear/phobia 3 negatively affected your life?

____

____

Fear/phobia 3: Question 3

How will your life improve when you get fear/phobia 3 out of your life forever?

____

____

Fear/phobia 3: Question 4

What will you do today to address fear/phobia 3?

____

____

Fear/phobia 4: Question 1

What is your account of what happened that caused fear/phobia 4 to exist in your mind and body up until this current day?

____

____

Fear/phobia 4: Question 2

How has fear/phobia 4 negatively affected your life?

____

____

Fear/phobia 4: Question 3

How will your life improve when you get fear/phobia 4 out of your life forever?

____

____

Fear/phobia 4: Question 4

What will you do today to address fear/phobia 4?

____

____

The Law of Rhythm

I want you to close your eyes for a moment and picture a tall grandfather clock with a long pendulum swinging from left to right in an infinite motion. This is the Law of Rhythm. The Law of Rhythm states that everything in nature has a rhythm, flow, and pattern. If you pay close attention, you will discover that everything in nature constantly swings and sways in a rhythmic dance.

Everything that goes one way must come back the opposite way. The tide in the ocean comes in and goes out, and the pattern repeats over and over again. Flowers open, then they close, and the pattern continues. When you breathe, you inhale, then you exhale. Not understanding the science of the Law of Rhythm can cause you to inhale when you should be exhaling in water, which can be the catalyst to drowning. To be alive is to obey the Law of Rhythm.

The moon's rotation transitions from the new moon to the first quarter, then to the full moon, then to the last quarter, then back to the new moon again. Not understanding the different vibrations and frequencies of the moon's quarters can cause you massive frustration, anguish, and even failure in your personal and professional lives.

Sometimes in your life, you feel as though everything is falling out of rhythm and nothing is working for you. The truth is, nature hasn't fallen out of rhythm with you—you have fallen out of rhythm with nature. Nature is consistent.

We cause ourselves pain when we want the law of rhythm to break its own rules and laws to suit our needs and wants. We want the emotion of happiness to be constant, to stay with us for days, nights, weeks, and years with no break. But the pendulum of rhythm disagrees. Happiness is not designed to stay, and neither is sadness and rage. The pendulum of emotions can work for you if you respect every emotion it sends your way, or it can work against you if you try to break or fight against the Law of Rhythm. You will discover that each feeling and emotion you experience is perfectly designed to teach you a valuable lesson about what has been, what is, and what will be.

Your feelings and emotions are not your enemies, but they are also not your friends. They are there to serve, warn, guide, command, and remind you. Some people never want to feel love again because of the disappointments and pains of the past. They sabotage any potential love in relationships even from friends and relatives. Love is seen as an inconvenience to them.

Many people hate love for leaving, but they reward pain for staying by giving it much attention and energy.

Going with the flow, being attentive to nature, being present in the moment, and showing gratitude are the key components to complement the Law of Rhythm. Take time to experience the pendulum of nature. Don't fight the flow. Don't rush or deny your current season. Not every season is yours to do as you please; respect and accept the results, and your time will come around again.

"Everything must change, nothing stays the same, everyone will change. No one stays the same, the young become the old, and mysteries do unfold." These lyrics comes from the 1974 Quincy Jones song, 'Everything Must Change'. Sometimes this song brings tears to my eyes and humbles me when I think about the friends and loved ones that I've lost over the years to stress, depression, and trauma. In hindsight, they were all fighting against the tide of the Law of Rhythm. And rhythm won!

Question:

What can you do to be more in sync with the Law of Rhythm?

Could you be more aware of your current feelings and learn from them to understand what the universe is telling you?

Start to learn how to use the different phases and energies of the moon to benefit and serve yourself and others.

The Law of Inspired Action

We must take effective, positive action over our lives to see inspired changes happen. Every action we take creates a result and a new reality. The Law of Inspired Action is the supreme level of creation. Without this law, no creation, manifestation, or true progress will exist.

Don't get me wrong, let me clarify that there are many different types of actions. Thoughts and imagery are actions, but they are not physical actions. Meditation and prayers are actions, but faith without works is dead. We need all the above before we step out of our homes to win and actively create a legacy our creator will be proud of.

So why is the Law of Inspired Action so relevant and extremely important for your journey?

We all take action in one form or another, but why do we take the actions we do? I had to ask myself this question many times over the years after feeling an overwhelming unfulfillment and emptiness despite achieving goals others would deem successful.

At the age of 18, I owned a beautiful red convertible Porsche 911 with cream leather seats and limited-edition wheels. I had purchased my dream car. People stopped and took pictures, friends would celebrate my achievement, and women looked, smiled, and flirted. The world saw success, but my feelings of short-term success quickly turned to unfulfillment and frustration, and I couldn't understand why.

From the age of 12 to 23, I had an overwhelming amount of success in the music industry. I started as a 12-year-old DJ, playing reggae, dancehall, R&B, and hip-hop music at any outdoor location where people would listen to me. With thousands of hours of learning how to mix and match reggae artists such as Beenie Man and Chaka Demus and Pliers on my Technics turntables, I started to master the art of entertaining crowds. The size of the crowd was sometimes in the hundreds, then eventually in the thousands. As the demand and my success grew, so did my frustration and unfulfillment. "But why?" I seriously felt as though I was committing a crime against my gratitude. At the height of my success at being a DJ, I quit. It didn't feel right. I wasn't being genuine and authentic to my inner self.

I went on to study music engineering at Norwood College, located in the south of London. I then furthered my studies at Morley College, learning the science of sounds and instruments. Now educated and confident, I was ready for my next venture.

After a lot of networking and handshaking, I eventually skipped the long queue of junior producers and engineers to become an apprentice at one of the leading production companies in the UK. For almost a year, I was a runner and an assistant working with pop stars and R&B groups such as Eternal and Honeyz. With more experience and even more confidence, I took even more action and opened my own recording studio and production company, called Sound City Entertainment.

Located in the back of a timber yard, Sound City Entertainment was open for business. With long nights and even longer days, we auditioned young talent. After six months of recording, we finally found a song that would kick our company into the spotlight. UK radio stations and nightclubs played the tracks we produced. Some called what Sound City Entertainment achieved in the early to mid-2000s a success. But I didn't. Once again, I felt massive career emptiness and personal unfulfillment. I also felt ungrateful and started to become frustrated with life itself. Not just with my career but also having to come to terms with the murder of my brother around that time.

Once again, I heard that voice, 'It's time to move on Kevin!' I felt like a runaway groom dashing out of the church, leaving another career at the altar before I could say, "I do."

My name and reputation were now firmly cemented within the UK music community. I was then presented with another opportunity that my longing and emptiness couldn't refuse. The owner of the Fridge Bar in Brixton approached me and said, "We have a name and brand that was very successful back in the day for great parties and events. How do you feel Kevin, about helping me to relaunch it for a new, fun and vibrant under-18s audience?" I said 'yes' quicker than he could finish his sentence.

Within one year of our agreement, we created the most successful under-18 events the UK had ever seen. We built relationships with mainstream and pirate (bootleg) radio stations. Back then, no social media existed, so we had to get in with the movers and shakers. We needed friends on the inside of record companies and radio stations. We studied DJs' needs, wants, and desires, then approached them with offers they could not refuse.

On a shoestring budget, we convinced radio stations and DJs to promote our events. But we wanted more than promotion. We wanted to have some of the biggest artists of the early to mid-2000s perform at our events—for free!

We returned to the drawing board and asked ourselves, "How can we get for free what other promoters are paying thousands of pounds for?" After days of brainstorming, we came up with a genius idea. We decided to change how we would usually ask the artists and record companies to perform at our events.

If we made our events sound like big business with big profits then they would have charged us accordingly, so we hatched our plan. We convinced our DJs to tell us when the biggest and most popular artists were in town and on their promo tours. We then got the DJs to convince the tour managers to add our events to their rosters as one of the best ways to promote the artist and their new single or album. We ensured that the DJs emphasized that the artists would be performing to teens, not working professionals or executives. Just barely in my 20s, we were about to do what no one my age in the UK had ever done before. We found a way not to be charged by some of the world's biggest artists to perform at our events.

For almost two years, every month (give or take), we had the best chart-topping hip-hop, R&B, and dancehall artists performing at our events called Chillin. The name 'Chillin' was on the lips of excited teens from across the UK. One month, Puff Daddy and 112 performed, then the next month Dru Hill; another month Jay-Z, then K-Ci and Jo Jo, Another Level, Brandy, Kelly Price, and the list went on. Queues of screaming teens went around the block, waiting in line to enter the Fridge Night Club. Once again, another success; and once again, more unfulfillment; and the strong feeling of unhappiness was again introduced into my life. The runaway groom was about to leave yet another bride at the altar.

I went on to launch fashion companies, salons, online beauty stores, and dance companies among many other business ventures. I was unstoppable but unhappy and unfulfilled.

From the age of eight, I was appointed different mentors by my elder brother Andy to help me to get to a place of excellence and success in my life. By the age of 12, I had mentors for business, motivation, finances, and then there were the ones from the streets. I had more mentors and teachers than I could even count on the hands and fingers of three people. But there was one particular mentor who was special. He had gifts, abilities, and knowledge that could only have come directly from either God, angels, or aliens—he was my spiritual mentor, Dr. Watkis.

Dr. Watkis could see and read things in people that would send chills down their spine. He told me about events in my life that only I knew about. He also predicted events and situations with absolute accuracy—and when I say 'accuracy,' I mean they were dead on. He was accurate down to the date that events were going to happen. He had a 98% manifestation rate.

Over four years, my spiritual mentor Dr. Watkis taught me about astrology, angels, colors, planets, stars, frequencies, vibrations, and prayers. At age 22, I lost contact with him. He went on a spiritual journey, and I returned to my daily life without my mentor.

After years of deep unfulfillment and losing contact with Dr. Watkis, one day, I received a call from him—almost five years after we'd last contacted each other. I was both happy and relieved. I could finally share my deep unfulfillment with someone who understood me, and who I knew I could get my long-awaited answers from.

I was excited, anxious, and thirsty for his knowledge. We arranged to meet a week later, and I was on time—no, I was early. I had an A4 notepad full of questions I needed to address. We hugged and greeted each other, then we sat and spoke in a warmly-lit feng shui room with only two chairs facing each other. We talked about life, dreams, and goals for over an hour. Then I reached into my backpack and pulled out my notepad. He gently smiled and said, "Put your notepad back into your bag. I have all the information I need from you Kevin."

"You do?" I responded.

"Yes," he replied. "For the last hour, I have been extracting all I need from you."

“So, what is my unfulfillment?” I asked.

“Your reasons and your actions,” he replied.

“What?” I said, befuddled. “My reasons and my actions?”

“Yes, let’s talk about your reasons,” he said, looking into my eyes sternly with a lower baritone voice of seriousness.

“Question: Why did you become a DJ all those years ago?” he asked. “I want you to close your eyes and place yourself back to when you were 7, 8, 9, 10 years old, up until you were 12. Take your time and relax. Furthermore, there is no time,” he said slowly and calmly. “Just relax. There is no time,” he repeated. “This is about you, your thoughts, feelings, memories, and moments. Relax your hands.”

My hands loosened, then eased.

“Relax your shoulders.”

My shoulders slumped.

“Your eyelids will become heavy and relaxed.”

They did.

“I now want you to have a conversation with the God in you, with your inner voice.”

I felt like I was sinking into my chair like Daniel Kaluuya in the film *Get Out*. I also felt free and away from my worldly stresses. I could now look into myself and observe without ego, judgment, or influence. Then something amazing happened—my A4 notepad of questions all became answers within me. *I AM* the answers to my questions; I *AM* the answers before my questions, *I AM* the *I AM* of my universe.

I had become a product of my environment. I believed I solely made my decisions. But they weren't. My ego demanded any experience—good, bad, treacherous, or dangerous. It didn't care about the consequences as long as it had entertainment. My inner soul whispered and used monosyllabic words and feelings to explain what was, what is, and what will be. That was completely unlike the dissertations my ego gave me to justify the next unfulfilling action and subsequent happenings in my life. The more I listened to my ego, the less I heard the whispers and the gut feelings from my soul. The ego, followed by my actions, chased the next high. Then my soul and inner conversations had to pick up the pieces of the resulting unhappiness and unfulfillment I felt.

But where did all my decisions originate?

Firstly, all five of my brothers were in the music industry. Even my father played music in the 1960s up until some point in the 1980s. We boasted and said that music was in our bones. Some of my brothers were event and concert promoters, some were DJs and artists, and three produced records. Everywhere I turned, from friends to family, 90% of them were in the music industry. Music provided a means of easing the intense trauma and poverty that was prevalent within our Caribbean culture and community.

Bob Marley sang about oppression and redemption, whereas Bounty Killer Deejayed about resorting to violence if our people continued to be oppressed, abused, and ignored. There were also songs about love, romance, and growth, but we only really resonated with songs about struggle and war.

As far back as the 1960s my parents had to fight racism and discrimination. Shops, restaurants, and homes had signs that read, "No blacks, no dogs, and no Irish." Racist teddy boys (white gangs) chased and beat any black and brown people they could corner. The police did the same, and the politicians of the time spewed hate speech. As fresh immigrants coming from the fresh deep-rooted colonization of Jamaica, my parents weren't too focused on excellence; they were focused on survival.

What they had back then to keep them sane were music and community. From one generation to another, the community fought for survival and equality, not excellence and opulence. The only black success we saw over the years, as far back as the 70s, right through to the 2000s, was in the music industry and in sports.

Now looking inward, I never wanted to be in the music industry—I can't even bloody dance. I tried playing football (soccer) for a while and discovered very quickly that I had two left feet. My inner self wanted to travel the world and learn about different cultures and people. I realized I wanted to help people in some way, but that was shouted down and voted out by ~~my~~ the ego, my friends, and my environment. Looking back, the universal laws were trying to help me fulfill what my inner spirit was radiating, but I, the student, wasn't ready to listen or take inspired action. What I saw in my environment and culture had more power and control over me than the monosyllabic whispers of my soul.

Looking back, I can see that the universe didn't care about racial injustices. It didn't care about my lack of world knowledge or opportunities. It was there to serve what I was yearning for. The first time this emerged was when I was 11 years old and was looking for my secondary school after graduating from primary school.

When you graduated from primary school in the UK back in the 80s, you had three options of secondary schools (high schools) to choose from. The best schools had strict entry conditions, criteria, and regulations. The best schools were usually located in affluent areas. We lived in the undesirable part of south London where the crime rates were high, and the schools and educational system were, at best, dismal.

I had to choose from one of three not-so-great schools back then. They were Dick Sheppard School, Stockwell Park School, and Lilian Baylis School. We had to take what we were given. Then one day, out of the blue, before I was about to choose one of the dismal three, I received a letter through the mail that didn't make any logical sense. It was from a school called London Nautical.

London Nautical School was one of the leading schools in London. It was located only 1.8 miles away from Buckingham Palace. If you were driving from London Nautical School to Buckingham Palace, it took about 10 minutes to get from door to door. The school was out of my school district, and there were already more than a thousand qualified, prioritized pupils on the list to get in.

You could count on one hand the number of black children who attended that school. If you made it to the top of the waiting list, you then had an entry exam to see if you even qualified to join such a prestigious school. Nothing on paper said that I qualified for this school, but somehow, I did. The letter I received stated that they would like me to be a pupil at a school I didn't even apply for. Joining the school was way beyond the scope of my reality but well within the radar of my desired energy. My inner self wanted to travel the world; London Nautical School would have allowed me to meet people from all around the globe, and travel the world.

The London Nautical School was formed in 1915 as a direct consequence of the sinking of the RMS *Titanic* in 1912. The Board of Trade Enquiry recommended introducing several nautical training schools to improve seamanship. The London Nautical School is the only one of those training schools that maintains its nautical and maritime history.

Until this current day no one within the education system can explain how it happened, but it did.

I visited the school and was at the top of the list, they were waiting for my approval to join.

Within the soft and subtle advice, the blessings of the universe were waiting to hand me what my soul was asking for. I didn't take inspired action that day. My spirit simply said, "Take it. It's a gift for you!" But my mind and environment declared war on it.

Friends said, "Why go to that stupid school? It's a boys' school with no girls and no black people. You may even end up gay or drown at sea." My mind then taunted me at night, telling me that all my friends and relationships would be gone forever if I chose London Nautical. At age 11, and not being spiritually in tune with myself and not understanding the laws of the universe, I caved to the threats from ~~my~~ the ego instead of submitting to the gifts of the universe. After turning down London Nautical School, I chose the school my friends were going to, that school was Dick Sheppard School. The democracy of my spiritual voice became quieter, and the tyranny of the voice in my mind took charge.

I was stabbed for the first time within a year of attending Dick Sheppard School. The school was so dangerous that parents nervously waited for their teens at the school gates after school. Violence and rapes were reported, and when enough was enough, the government closed the school down. Shortly after, the headmaster of Dick Sheppard School was stabbed to death, and many of the pupils were also either killed, sent to prison, or detained under the mental health act.

The Law of Inspired Action comes from within. This is when the spiritual you and the universe align in harmony to work together for you to take action and achieve. Your mind is different. It wants an experience and doesn't care much for harmony and self-preservation.

This is where suicidal thoughts, base-jumping, cave diving, free solo climbing, and other activities of extreme danger appease the mind's need for short-term entertainment.

I spent many years listening to the tyranny of my mind, which was influenced by limitations, lack of foresight, bias, and ignorance of my environment. I discovered that my friends were only my friends when my success suited them. I also discovered that your family and culture would happily give you the cold shoulder when your new path stops benefiting them.

You will see this within many cultures and communities worldwide, where the son or the daughter is not living up to the family's expectations to become a lawyer or a doctor, so they are branded as absolute failures. Or how about the suicidal farmers who hate farming but have to live up to their family's 100-year farming legacy, suffering in silence until the end of a rope is the only way to eternal peace?

I want you to be honest with yourself. I want you to write down what actions you have taken or are currently taking that are negatively influencing your life. Think about the following:

a) Actions negatively influenced by family.
b) Actions negatively influenced by friends.
c) Actions negatively influenced by culture.
d) Actions negatively influenced by the community.
e) Actions negatively influenced by your ego.

Action 1:______________________________________

Action 2:______________________________________

Action 3:______________________________________

Action 4:______________________________________

The Law of Gender

Before we start to talk about The Law of Gender, I want to approach this universal law from a slightly different perspective than how others would usually speak about it. I also want to address this law, not just from the occurrence of trauma, but the energy, traits, and rules we set for ourselves, our families, and our love lives if we have trauma.

Please have your pens or pencils ready, as I will ask you some powerful questions that will make you think about how you look at yourself, the reasons for your relationships, and how you may—or have—brought up your children. Furthermore, this may be a good time to include your spouse, family, and children in this chapter to get different perspectives and opinions.

Ok, are you ready? Let's go.

The Law of Gender is based on the interconnectedness of male and female energy. It is not necessarily about men and women but about how masculine and feminine energy works together in nature.

To live a fulfilled life, you must balance the divine masculine and divine feminine energies—the yin (feminine energy) and the yang (masculine energy).

Feminine traits include operating from the heart space, intuition, compassion, acceptance, forgiveness, sensuality, gentleness, kindness, patience, and tenderness. Whereas masculine traits include logic, reasoning, objectivity, assertiveness, action, risk-taking, discipline, dominance, and control, to name a few.

The two energies have a delicate symbiosis. The masculine needs the feminine, and the feminine needs the masculine—one can't survive without the other. The masculine trait of dominance and control can be destructive if it isn't tempered with the feminine traits of gentleness, love, and acceptance.

At the same time, relying on the feminine traits of gentleness and acceptance would only end in failure if you intended to run any society, as it would allow for inactivity, lack of progression, and insurrection.

In nature, there is no such thing as a gender-neutral state. Everything in nature is either masculine or feminine, and the masculine and feminine must work together for each to exist. For example, how would you know what is hot if there is no cold? How do you recognize what is dry if you have never experienced wetness? We need both the feminine and the masculine in all things.

In the same way that there is a balance of gender in nature, we also need the same balance of the Law of Gender in our lives. Below is a list of nature's yin (feminine) and yang (masculine) that governs life and existence.

Yin	**Yang**
Feminine	Masculine
Negative charge -	Positive charge +
Black	White
Shade	Light
Night	Day
Moon	Sun
Water	Fire
Cold	Heat
Wetness	Dryness
Fall/Winter	Summer/Spring
Faded	Vibrant
Discreet	Obvious
Indirect	Direct
Rounded	Straight
Softness	Hardness
Flexibility	Solidity
Inactivity	Activity

Stillness	Movement
Calm	Energetic
Slow	Fast
Tired	Lively
Front side	Back side
Left side	Right side
Internal	External
Interior	Exterior
Closed spaces	Open spaces
Mental	Physical
Even numbers	Odd numbers
Intuition	Logicality
Storage	Usage
Quiet	Loud
Receptive	Giving
Death	Life
Higher pitches	Lower pitches

Now that you have an understanding of what masculine and feminine energies are and the fact that they need each other for all of us to exist, let's now take a look at your own life. What masculine and feminine traits are required in your life for it to be prosperous, abundant, and balanced?

Let's start with children. Every child needs a mother and a father in their life. Mothers can give their children so much masculine energy, and fathers can only provide so much feminine energy. If there is an imbalance of masculine and feminine energy in the home, it will affect how the child thinks, feels, and behaves.

Lion cubs rarely survive in nature without a dominant male to protect their pride, and female lions collaborate to nurture and feed their young. Children struggle in life without protection, discipline, boundaries, confidence, and logic— all of which are masculine traits. They also struggle without nurturing, being in touch with their emotions, operating from their heart space, and forgiveness, compassion, and acceptance—all of which are feminine traits.

If a child is raised in a home that once had a balance of feminine and masculine energy, and one of the parents or guardians' leaves, it is likely to upset the balance of energy. Just like with the effects of global warming on our planet, what was once balanced can turn into a turbulent imbalanced environment.

From toddler to teen and teen to adulthood, an imbalance of feminine and masculine energy could lead to several negative feelings and behaviors, including abandonment, anxiety, and a lifetime of disorders. These disorders include borderline personality disorder, dependent personality disorder, and anxious attachments.

If a person hasn't been nurtured with a balance of masculine and feminine energies, they can start to develop a wounded, traumatized energy. This wounded energy can be both feminine and masculine.

Here is a list of mindsets and behaviors of both traumatized feminine and masculine energies:

Traumatized Feminine Energy	Traumatized Masculine Energy
Vindictiveness	Abusiveness
Powerlessness	Dominance
Weakness	Aggressiveness
Manipulation	Controlling
Passive-aggressiveness	Confrontational
Neediness	Avoidance
Codependency	Unsupportiveness
Over-sensitivity	Criticism
Overly-emotional	Instability
Victim-minded	Perpetrator

The most successful people, are those who can transition between their feminine and masculine energies effortlessly, and maintain a healthy balance between the two. They're able to be logical, assertive, empathetic, understanding, and nurturing. In a relationship it is essential to have a healthy balance of feminine and masculine energies between you and your partner. Having two equally masculine or feminine energies in a relationship is likely to end up in tears. Here is a list to help you understand what to look for when searching for feminine and masculine energy in a relationship:

What Makes It Feminine?	What Makes It Masculine?
Unconditional love	Confidence
Understanding	Protection
Nurturing	Clarity
Flow	Inner strength
Radiance	Responsibility
Collaborative	Boundary-setting
Surrender	Focus
Kindness	Courage
Sensitivity	Discipline
Intuitiveness	Capability
Emotionality	Logicality
Creativity	Decisiveness
At ease	Stability
Feeling	Certainty
Allowing	Direction
Tenderness	Assertiveness

When a relationship becomes toxic, and the intimacy is pretty much non-existent, here are some energies, mindsets, and behaviors that may occur:

Feminine	Masculine
Intimacy Killers	Intimacy Killers
Feeling unseen	Being criticized
Feeling misunderstood	Feeling disrespected and put down
Feeling unsafe	Feeling controlled
Feeling hurt	Name-calling

When the feminine energy in a relationship is feeling unsafe, unloved, and hurt, that energy will go into an electron zone of insecurity, passive-aggressiveness, lack of trust, depression, and frustration.

When the masculine energy is feeling criticized, disrespected, controlled, and put down in a relationship, that energy will also go into an electron zone, and the relationship and intimacy will suffer. Feminine energy in a relationship needs to feel understood, safe, loved, and secure. Masculine energy in a relationship needs to feel supported, trusted, important, and believed in. These needs and wants from the feminine and masculine energy in a relationship cannot be served by each other until they are both in a proton-positive state.

You cannot truly love others until you can LOVE yourself, and you cannot make anyone feel secure until you can feel secure within yourself. This is why men, women, boys, and girls need to LOVE themselves, trust themselves, and have self-esteem.

The helpline must have a healthy balance of yin and yang in their personal and professional relationships. People tend to want to receive love and be served the same way they love and serve others. You cannot accomplish this if, on the one hand, you are not in touch with your emotions or, on the other hand, you are not logical, responsible, or decisive.

All these mindsets and behaviors are generally desired within the five love languages. Here's the list of the five love languages:

- Love language #1: Words of affirmation
- Love language #2: Acts of service
- Love language #3: Receiving gifts
- Love language #4: Quality time
- Love language #5: Physical touch

So how do they work?

If you want to help our helplines, love them with words of affirmation, create acts of service for them, and give them gifts to make them feel seen, understood, and appreciated. Spend quality time with a lonely, broken, or suffering heart. Hug and comfort them with physical touch, allowing the helpline to feel secure, wanted, and loved. Helplines are both masculine and feminine energies. Love and care for them accordingly.

By becoming better, you can make all you encounter better—from your children to your relationships, from your work life to your home life, but most importantly, you, you, and you! You must make yourself better, happier, stronger, and more fulfilled before you can help and be there for others.

Let's get you started.

What energy do you need to work on more to progress and grow in your life?

Please select the energies you need to work on for your personal development. Mark it with a [x] on your selected energies listed below.

Feminine Energies	**Masculine Energies**
Unconditional love [ ]	Confidence [ ]
Understanding [ ]	Protection [ ]
Nurturing [ ]	Clarity [ ]
Flow [ ]	Inner Strength [ ]
Radiance [ ]	Responsibility [ ]
Collaborative [ ]	Boundaries [ ]
Surrender [ ]	Focus [ ]
Kindness [ ]	Courage [ ]
Sensitivity [ ]	Discipline [ ]
Intuitiveness [ ]	Capability [ ]
Emotionality [ ]	Logicality [ ]

Creativity [ ]	Decisiveness [ ]
Ease [ ]	Stability [ ]
Feelings [ ]	Certainty [ ]
Allowing [ ]	Direction [ ]
Tenderness [ ]	Assertiveness [ ]

Now let's take a look at your relationships.

Women with excessive masculine energy find maintaining relationships with feminine-energy men hard. Excessive masculine-energy women tend to dominate their partners and then gradually lose respect for them.

Those excessively masculine-energy women struggle to submit to their masculine partners overall, which leads to a lifetime of broken and unfulfilled relationships.

Let's dig even deeper. Excessively masculine people— men and women who, by default, dominate their partners— annoyingly become uninspired by their partner's so-called 'weakness.' Then the stages of disrespect and stonewalling will start to manifest.

On the other hand, excessively emotional feminine energy can lead to massive problems in all relationships and in life in general. Being too emotional can lead to making poor, impulsive decisions. These emotional decisions tend to lead to future outcomes they will massively regret. Without the masculine balance of logic, discipline, and reasoning, emotional people in relationships tend to cause more impulsive harm than good. Overspending, emotional manipulation, and impulsive behavior will eventually end in someone's tears.

Masculine overconfidence, excessive domination, or being too emotional will always result in abuse of power, position, and trust. We, as a society, have seen this repeatedly over the years. Do you remember what happened in the 2008 crash that jolted the global financial system? No? Well, in September 2008, Lehman Brothers, one of the world's biggest financial institutions, went bankrupt. Ninety billion pounds (approximately US$107 billion) was wiped off Britain's biggest companies' value in a single day. Other companies also suffered. Merrill Lynch, AIG, Freddie Mac, Fannie Mae, HBOS, Royal Bank of Scotland, Bradford & Bingley, Fortis, Hypo, and Alliance & Leicester all were close to crashing.

The *Financial Times* reported that 47 bankers were sentenced to jail for their role in the financial crisis and were held personally accountable for the financial sector's crash. I believe the excessive yang of masculine energy in the financial sector had led to overconfidence, lack of empathy, arrogance, and grandiosity, which was the underlying reason for the initial stages of the crash. A masculine-yang environment needs feminine-yin energy to complement it.

Bad decisions are made when there are too many yin, or yang energies on either side having too much free rein. Many people committed suicide due to the 2008 financial crisis. Some people never recovered financially. There are world wars now pending due to excessive masculine-yang energy coupled with evil intent. Don't make the mistakes of the past, instead choose to be the blessings in our future.

I want you to look at the energy scales below and discover what you need more and less of. Is it masculine energy or feminine energy?

I want you to now rate your energy on a scale from 1 to 12, 1 being too much feminine energy, and 12 being excessive masculine energy. 6 being a healthy balance.

Feminine energy Healthy balance Masculine energy

Energy [1] [2] [3] [4] [5] [6] [7] [8] [9] [10] [11] [12]

Do you believe you need to work on the above? [Yes] [No]

If yes, what do you believe you need to work on?

Let's now dig even deeper into your traits. How would you rate yourself on the following traits?

Draw a circle around the ones that best suit you.

Accepting or Not Accepting

Q1: Are you an accepting person?

In this case, accepting means you are someone who (or not) practices the energy of acceptance. This means you recognize a situation for what it is, accept it, and perhaps think it's fate or destiny. Or you are not an accepting person, you deny, or reject all that comes your way.

Too accepting Healthy balance Deny/reject

Accepting Energy [1] [2] [3] [4] [5] [6] [7] [8] [9] [10] [11] [12]

Do you believe you need to work on the above? [Yes] [No]

If yes, what do you believe you need to work on?

Action-oriented or State-oriented

Q2: An action-oriented person will take swift action to deal with a situation, no matter how scary, disturbing, or troubling the situation is.

A state-oriented person is a person who is unable to regulate their emotions, feelings, and behaviors to take action or effective action.

Are you more action-oriented or state-oriented?

Action-oriented State-oriented

Action-oriented [1] [2] [3] [4] [5] [6] [7] [8] [9] [10] [11] [12]

Do you believe you need to work on the above? [Yes] [No]

If yes, what do you believe you need to work on?

Assertiveness

Q3: Are you an assertive person?

Are you a) a forceful person who dominates in your communication and relationships with others, or are you b) more shy, submissive, and restrained?

Shy\submissive\ restrained	Healthy balance	Forcefully aggressive
⟷	⟷	⟷

Assertiveness [1] [2] [3] [4] [5] [6] [7] [8] [9] [10] [11] [12]

Do you believe you need to work on the above? [Yes] [No]

If yes, what do you believe you need to work on?

____

____

Boundaries

Q4: What are your boundaries?

Are you a person with rigid boundaries? Do you emotionally or physically keep others at a distance, perhaps because you never want to be hurt again?

Or, are you a person with poor boundaries? Do you need to learn about the person or people you are opening yourself up to before you get too close, too quickly? People with poor boundaries may fall in love or give their body up too quickly. These people tend to share their intimate secrets without taking time to know the person or people they share with.

Poor boundaries	Healthy boundaries	Rigid boundaries
⟷	⟷	⟷

Boundaries [1] [2] [3] [4] [5] [6] [7] [8] [9] [10] [11] [12]

Do you believe you need to work on the above? [Yes] [No]

If yes, what do you believe you need to work on?

____

____

Collaboration

Q5: Are you an effective collaborator?

Dennis Brown, one of the most celebrated Jamaican artists of all time, once sang a song with the words, "No man is an island, No man stands alone." Collaboration is vital in all relationships, from personal to professional. Collaborating means looking outside of yourself, actively listening to others, sharing, and knowing when it is time to follow and when it is time to lead. It means to know when it is time to go to the aid of a partner and when it is time to ask your partner to come to your aid. To collaborate, ask yourself first, "How can I serve or help the person or people I want to collaborate with?"

To be an effective collaborator, you must first know who you are, what you stand for (core values, beliefs, morals), and what you are willing to give up or sacrifice.

To be a successful collaborator, you need to do the following:

1. Have strong leadership skills.

2. Have clearly defined goals and roles with your partner.

3. Be consistent and enthusiastic, and try to make an effort, even when you don't want to.

4. Be effective and frequent in your communication with your partner.

5. Be fair and share resources.

6. Put all ego aside and listen and learn.

7. Always thank, celebrate, and go the extra mile for those who are serving your goals and successes.

8. Let go and delegate tasks.

So, are you successfully collaborating in your personal or professional life, or both?

Not collaborating enough	Healthy collaboration	Yes, collaborating well
⟷	⟷	⟷

Collaboration [1] [2] [3] [4] [5] [6] [7] [8] [9] [10] [11] [12]

Do you believe you need to work on the above? [Yes] [No]

If yes, what do you believe you need to work on?

____

____

Compassion

Q6: Are you compassionate?

To be compassionate is to feel deeply for other people as they experience their ups and downs. You will know your compassion when you feel genuinely for others.

Compassionate people have the following traits:

A) Honest and caring toward others.

B) Emotionally connected to other people's plights.

C) Mindful, kind, and encouraging with acts of service.

On the other side, to be indifferent is to lack interest, concern, or empathy.

Where are you on the scale of indifference and compassion?

Indifferent	Healthy balance	Compassionate
⟷	⟷	⟷

Compassion [1] [2] [3] [4] [5] [6] [7] [8] [9] [10] [11] [12]

Do you believe you need to work on the above? [Yes] [No]

If yes, what do you believe you need to work on?

____

____

Confidence

Q7: Are you a confident person?

To be confident is to be sure of yourself and your abilities. To be confident is to feel secure rather than insecure.

Here are the traits of confident people:

1) They have happiness from within. Do you?
[Yes] [No]

2) They don't pass judgment on others. Do you?
[Yes] [No]

3) They don't say yes unless they really want to. Do you?

[Yes] [No]

4) They listen more than they speak. Do you?

[Yes] [No]

5) They seek out small victories. Do you?

[Yes] [No]

6) They don't seek or need attention. Do you?

[Yes] [No]

7) They are not afraid to be wrong. Are you?

[Yes] [No]

8) They celebrate other people. Do you?

[Yes] [No]

9) They are not afraid to ask for help. Are you?

[Yes] [No]

10) They are comfortable with how they look and feel. Are you?

[Yes] [No]

Now you know the components of a confident person. What are the root causes of an insecure person? First, the controlling emotion of all insecurities is FEAR. FEAR controls behavior toward oneself and others.

FEAR will cause a person to self-harm and cause harm to others.

The entity of FEAR will make a person self-sabotage and not want others to win.

Here are some of the mindsets and behaviors of insecure people:

1. They feel jealous of others' success. Do you?
   [Yes] [No]

2. They try to find fault in everyone and everything. Do you?
   [Yes] [No]

3. They believe in "fake it till you make it." Do you?
   [Yes] [No]

4. They always blame others for their failings. Do you?
   [Yes] [No]

5. They never admit to their mistakes. Do you?
   [Yes] [No]

6. They feel bad when they see other people's successful lifestyles. Do you?
   [Yes] [No]

7. They boast about their expensive items to feel good about themselves. Do you?
   [Yes] [No]

8. They (passively) want to take revenge. Do you?
   [Yes] [No]

9. They try to build a life or career or both just to prove to others that they are worthy. Do you?
   [Yes] [No]

10. They interrupt and don't listen to others' views and opinions. Do you?
    [Yes] [No]

11. They actively make fun of others and talk behind other people's backs. Do you?
    [Yes] [No]

12. They judge anyone and everyone. Do you?

[Yes] [No]

13. They chase perfection. Do you?

[Yes] [No]

Where are you on the scale of insecurity and confidence?

Insecure Confident

Confidence [1] [2] [3] [4] [5] [6] [7] [8] [9] [10] [11] [12]

Do you believe you need to work on the above? [Yes] [No]

If yes, what do you believe you need to work on?

Courage

Q8: Do you have courage?

'But what is courage?' you may ask. To have courage is to have the ability to push through your FEARS and all that frightens you to overcome the challenges and troubles that face you. To have courage is to be brave. To be brave is to be actively strong in the face of pain, difficulty, danger, and grief.

To have courage and bravery is to take action regardless of your electron feelings and emotions.

But I must add that there are different types of courage. There are:

- Physical courage
- Social courage
- Moral courage
- Emotional courage
- Intellectual courage
- Spiritual courage

Now let's look deeper into what makes a person have courage.

1) Self-confidence. Courageous people may not feel confident about a situation. It may even scare the living daylights out of them. But, regardless of how much the situation may scare them, they believe in themselves enough to take action. Do you have self-confidence? [Yes] [No]

2) Strength in Adversity. Courageous people stare in the face of adversity and say, "Do what you must. I will keep persevering." Courageous people run toward the problem rather than away from it. They prefer to be in control

rather than be controlled. Do you have strength in adversity? [Yes] [No]

3) Conviction. Courageous people stand for what they believe in. They are extremely passionate about their beliefs and their core values. They are consistent and never blindly follow the crowd. What they say goes. Do you have conviction? [Yes] [No]

4) Integrity. Courageous people are honorable and trustworthy, with solid morals and principles. They speak up against injustices and fight for emancipation. They don't just talk—they also back it up. Would you say you are a person with integrity? [Yes] [No]

5) Leadership. Courageous people take charge of controlling what is bad, dangerous, or difficult. Courageous leaders know if they don't take charge and lead, things will get worse and out of control. These leaders motivate others to help themselves and grow to be courageous in their own lives. Would you say you are a courageous leader? [Yes] [No]

6) Compassion. Courageous people put other people's needs above their own. Courageous, compassionate people observe what happens to others and sympathize with them. They also make decisions to help, build up, and empower others. Would you say you have compassion? [Yes] [No]

7) Embrace the Unknown. Courageous people follow their intuition. They feel what is about to happen; they follow that vibe and prepare for the worst. You will hear these courageous people say things like, "What will be, will be,"

and other statements like, “It is what it is!” Whether they like it or not, courageous people embrace the unknown and deal with what comes, whether good, bad, or difficult. They will always be prepared. Would you say that you embrace the unknown? [Yes] [No]

Now you know what it takes to have courage. Where are you on the scale of courage?

Not enough courage   Lots of courage

Courage [1] [2] [3] [4] [5] [6] [7] [8] [9] [10] [11] [12]

Do you believe you need to work on the above? [Yes] [No]

If yes, what do you believe you need to work on?

Creativity

Q9: Are you a creative person?

To be creative is to have curiosity, playfulness, open-mindedness, flexibility, independence, risk-taking, intuitiveness, thoroughness, ambition, and energy.

Let’s start with curiosity.

Are you a curious person? Creative people are extremely curious, almost to the point of coming across as nosey at times. Curious people will investigate, constantly building their knowledge and understanding of the world. Curious people are “How?” “Why?” and “What?” people. These people are great leaders, very supportive, and extremely fascinating to be around. They also tend to be better love makers than the average Joe. Their minds investigate instead of wanting the world to investigate them. They will learn your blind spots and things about you and your environment that you may not be able to see.

"How does it taste? How do you feel?" and "How does it work?" To be curious is to be interested instead of trying to be interesting. "How?" alongside 'Why?' and 'What?' are the foundational questions that will lead you to understand all of creation, from life, to love, from friendships, to our creator.

'Why?' questions are the foundation for self-discovery; such questions can extend into exploring all things and people. "Why do we feel what we feel?" "Why are we here? "Why is there a God?" "Why is there a leap year?" To be curious is to ask "Why?" questions.

Next, How?

How can I help you?

How can I be a better person?

How can we grow together?

How will I know?

"How?" questions seek solutions.

To ask "How?" questions is to want to be better, do better, and become better for yourself and others. To ask "How?" is to tell yourself and others that you are curious and you care. I must add, "How?" questions can have a positive or negative effect on yourself and others. It all depends on the root of the "How" energy.

Some people ask "How?" questions with the energy of sarcasm or apprehension. The best "How?" questions come from a proton zone, not an electron zone. Think and be positive when using these powerful questions with yourself and others. Your universe depends on it.

Next.

What do you want?

What do you need?

What excites you?

What are your core values?

What motivates you?

What can I do to serve you better?

What can I do to be a better person?

"What?" questions demand an answer. "What?" questions are connected to action steps—either internal action steps that must be taken, or external action steps that must be taken.

To be successful with your curiosity is to explore the world of "What" questions. The more you explore, the more inquisitive you will become. The more inquisitive you become, the more likely you are to care, and to care is to be kind, and to be kind is to be gentle to both yourself and others. You will discover forgiveness within the adventure of your curiosity. What we investigate can sometimes be fragile, such as a person's feelings, or the premature opening of a petal. Our curiosity should never be so important that it causes us to destroy ourselves or others. I believe that curiosity is a beautiful feminine energy that should be embraced and accepted into our lives and our relationships.

Here is my question to you: Are you a curious person?

[Yes] [No]

Not a curious person	So-so	Very curious
⟷	⟷	⟷

Curiosity [1] [2] [3] [4] [5] [6] [7] [8] [9] [10] [11] [12]

Do you believe you need to work on the above? [Yes] [No]

If yes, what do you believe you need to work on?

____

____

Playfulness

Creative people play with various ideas until they find what feels good and works for them. Creative playfulness means you have fun with your creativity and do not take what you do too seriously, to the point where joy becomes painful, unimaginative, and unproductive.

Being playful helps with stress, depression, and trauma. Playful people like to socialize, and socializing helps with depression. But what other traits are there for playful, creative people?

1. Playful, creative people are energetic but also like to have quiet downtime.

   [Yes, that's me] [No, not me]

2. Playful, creative people are smart yet naive at the same time.

   [Yes, that's me] [No, not me]

3. Playful, creative people alternate between imagination and fantasy to allow for fun and playfulness.

   [Yes, that's me] [No, not me]

4. Playful, creative people are both extroverted and introverted in their own unique way.

   [Yes, that's me] [No, not me]

5. Playful, creative people are rebellious but also conservative.

   [Yes, that's me] [No, not me]

6. Playful, creative people are passionate about their work, yet they can also be extremely objective about it.

   [Yes, that's me] [No, not me]

7. Playful, creative people struggle with being bored and being around boring people.

   [Yes, that's me] [No, not me]

8. Playful, creative people are open-minded and willing to try new things and ideas.

   [Yes, that's me] [No, not me]

9. Playful, creative people are spontaneous.

   [Yes, that's me] [No, not me]

10. Playful, creative people are both cheerful and unpredictable.

    [Yes, that's me] [No, not me]

How creatively playful do you believe you are?

Not playful at all   Healthy balance   Too playful

Playfulness [1] [2] [3] [4] [5] [6] [7] [8] [9] [10] [11] [12]

Do you believe you need to work on the above? [Yes] [No]

If yes, what do you believe you need to work on?

____

____

Open-mindedness

Creative people tend to be very open-minded. They are willing to hear others out and are also willing to try new things.

Being open-minded means not judging others or believing that the only way is your way. Let's look at even more traits of open-minded, creative people.

1) Open-minded, creative people are curious to hear what other people think.

[Yes, that's me] [No, not me]

2) Open-minded, creative people welcome being challenged.

[Yes, that's me] [No, not me]

3) Open-minded, creative people are less likely to get angry when they are proven to be wrong.

[Yes, that's me] [No, not me]

4) Open-minded, creative people are very empathetic toward other people's plights.

[Yes, that's me] [No, not me]

5) Open-minded, creative people care what other people think and feel.

[Yes, that's me] [No, not me]

6) Open-minded, creative people seek knowledge and experiences.

[Yes, that's me] [No, not me]

7) Open-minded, creative people seek mentors and teachers beyond their scope.

[Yes, that's me] [No, not me]

How open-minded do you believe you are?

Closed-minded ⟷ Healthy balance ⟷ Very open-minded ⟷

Open-mindedness [1] [2] [3] [4] [5] [6] [7] [8] [9] [10] [11] [12]

Do you believe you need to work on the above? [Yes] [No]

If yes, what do you believe you need to work on?

____

____

Flexibility

You cannot be creative without being flexible. To be flexible is to be readily adaptable to new, different, or changing circumstances or conditions in your life.

Not every circumstance in life can be controlled by you, and not being in control can sometimes make you feel like you are losing control.

Flexibility as a creative personality trait is to be able to change easily and adapt to different situations and circumstances in very short periods.

To be flexible is to do the following:

1. I challenge myself when my circumstances change.

   [Yes, that's me] [No, not me]

2. I am willing to try new ideas and experiences.

   [Yes, that's me] [No, not me]

3. I am willing to live out of my comfort zone.

   [Yes, that's me] [No, not me]

4. I don't allow bad situations to take control; instead, I take the wheel quickly to do whatever is necessary to turn bad situations into good life lessons.

   [Yes, that's me] [No, not me]

How flexible or rigid do you believe you are?

Too flexible ⟷ Healthy balance ⟷ Very rigid ⟷

Flexibility [1] [2] [3] [4] [5] [6] [7] [8] [9] [10] [11] [12]

Do you believe you need to work on the above? [Yes] [No]

If yes, what do you believe you need to work on?

____

____

Independence

Creative, independent people happily work with others but are just as comfortable and happy to work alone.

Working independently allows creative people to be free to express their gifts, fantasies, and desires, without small-mindedness people second-guessing their creations.

The traits and behaviors of independent, creative people include the following:

1) They want the freedom to express their creativity without judgment.

   [Yes, that's me] [No, not me]

2) They despise the thought of being micromanaged.

   [Yes, that's me] [No, not me]

3) They want their own space to be left alone to create.

   [Yes, that's me] [No, not me]

4) They can be prone to depression when in isolation for too long and when their projects are not going to plan.

   [Yes, that's me] [No, not me]

5) They cannot be controlled or categorized.

   [Yes, that's me] [No, not me]

Do you believe you are independent to the point where you don't need anyone? Or do you believe you are very dependent on others?

Very dependent | Healthy balance | Very independent

Independence [1] [2] [3] [4] [5] [6] [7] [8] [9] [10] [11] [12]

Do you believe you need to work on the above? [Yes] [No]

If yes, what do you believe you need to work on?

Risk-taking

You are not a creative person if you don't take some form of risk. However, there is a fine line between why you take risks and whose detriment the risk is on. We have all read, watched, or experienced reckless and negligent behavior across many professions because of overzealous risk-taking.

A very important question to ask yourself is, "Am I taking risks because I can't feel anything (I am emotionally numb)?" Or "Am I taking risks because I feel too much (emotionally hurting)?"

Another good question to ask yourself is, "how far am I willing to go to take risks to be creative?"

Creative risk-takers are willing to take risks to discover and achieve what others would never usually try or even consider. Risk-takers get excited by the thrill of the forbidden. Where the forbidden lives, is where the adventure is found for the creative risk-taker.

The pros of the creative risk-taker are that they will push their creativity to the limits to expand humankind's consciousness.

The cons of the creative risk-taker are that they can break and destroy all that was once good. Overzealous risk-takers don't know when to stop. I believe some creative risk-takers take risks to discover and feel; I also believe other risk-takers take risks because they are hurting and in pain.

So, what about you?

1. To what degree are you a risk-taker?

Low risk [1] [2] [3] [4] [5] [6] [7] [8] [9] [10] [11] [12] High risk

2. Are you a "better safe than sorry" person? [ ]

Or

"You only live once so I will try anything" person? [ ]

3. Do you tend to take more or fewer risks when you're bored or depressed?

[More] [Less]

4. Do you believe you feel more alive when you take risks, or less alive when you don't?

I feel less alive ⟷ Healthy balance ⟷ I feel more alive ⟷

Risk-taking [1] [2] [3] [4] [5] [6] [7] [8] [9] [10] [11] [12]

Do you believe you need to work on the above? [Yes] [No]

If yes, what do you believe you need to work on?

____

____

Intuitiveness

Creative people are very intuitive. They tend to follow their hearts instead of following the money. They feel their way to their success instead of following the rule books that are made by others. They cannot be controlled, boxed in, or categorized.

1) Intuitive, creative people listen to their Inner voices.

[Yes, that's me] [No, not me]

2) Intuitive, creative people have an amazing awareness of their environment and surroundings.

[Yes, that's me] [No, not me]

3) Intuitive, creative people's dreams play a massive role in their decision-making.

[Yes, that's me] [No, not me]

4) Intuitive, creative people's feelings govern whether they should take action or walk away—no matter how big the prize or reward is.

[Yes, that's me] [No, not me]

5) Intuitive, creative people tend to be more optimistic than pessimistic in general.

[Yes, that's me] [No, not me]

6) Intuitive, creative people have a strong sense of purpose in their lives.

[Yes, that's me] [No, not me]

7) Intuitive, creative people are extremely deep thinkers.

[Yes, that's me] [No, not me]

8) Intuitive, creative people need time for peace and relaxation.

[Yes, that's me] [No, not me]

9) Intuitive, creative people tend to believe in a creator.

[Yes, that's me] [No, not me]

How intuitive do you believe you are?

Not very intuitive — Healthy balance — Very intuitive

Intuition [1] [2] [3] [4] [5] [6] [7] [8] [9] [10] [11] [12]

Do you believe you need to work on the above? [Yes] [No]

If yes, what do you believe you need to work on?

Thoroughness

Creative people are extremely thorough, and they pay intricate attention to detail in everything they do. All the luxuries we enjoy in our society, from luxury homes to art, cars, and entertainment, all come from the following: creative thoroughness, hard work, dedication, risk-taking, thoughtfulness, consideration, and an absolute attitude of servitude to others.

Would you say that you have thoroughness in all the work you do or the service you provide to others?

Let's explore thoroughness together:

1) Do you work hard on your projects?

[Yes, that's me] [No, not me]

2) Do you dedicate your life to your craft?

[Yes, that's me] [No, not me]

3) Are you thoughtful?

[Yes, that's me] [No, not me]

4) Are you considerate of others?

[Yes, that's me] [No, not me]

5) Is your love language acts of service?

[Yes, that's me] [No, not me]

6) Do you pay massive attention to detail?

[Yes, that's me] [No, not me]

7) Do you finish what you start?

[Yes, that's me] [No, not me]

8) Do you clean up along the way?

[Yes, that's me] [No, not me]

9) Do you have a very high-quality control?

[Yes, that's me] [No, not me]

10) Do you plan your projects before you start them?

[Yes, that's me] [No, not me]

11) Do you seek feedback from your clients or customers?

[Yes, that's me] [No, not me]

How thorough do you believe you are?

Not very thorough	Healthy balance	Over the top with thoroughness
⟷	⟷	⟷

Thoroughness [1] [2] [3] [4] [5] [6] [7] [8] [9] [10] [11] [12]

Do you believe you need to work on the above? [Yes] [No]

If yes, what do you believe you need to work on?

____

____

Ambition

Creative, ambitious people rarely have safety nets. They also understand that they must "eat what they kill". That simply means they are responsible for every part of their success. These people respect time, they also hold people to account for their hourly rates, wages, and they focus on building their income streams. The same free-thinking, risk-taking, and independence traits that constitute a creative person are the same components and reasons why creatives don't have safety nets.

Creative, ambitious people cannot be free-thinking, risk-taking, and independent under another person's control. Because of this, creatives tend to either be freelancers or entrepreneurs, and the creatives, under the employment of others, tend to feel painfully restricted and miserable working for them.

So, are you a creative, ambitious person?

1) Do you sacrifice job security for creative freedom and control?

    [Yes, that's me] [No, not me]

2) Are you curious and eager to win?

    [Yes, that's me] [No, not me]

3) Do you go out and build solid relationships at networking events?

    [Yes, that's me] [No, not me]

4) Are you passionate about your growth?

    [Yes, that's me] [No, not me]

5) Are you self-sufficient and responsible?

[Yes, that's me] [No, not me]

6) Do you keep a perspective on all that is going on in your life?

[Yes, that's me] [No, not me]

7) Do you never quit, no matter what setbacks or tragedies may happen in your life?

[Yes, that's me] [No, not me]

8) Are you willing to take risks that could bankrupt you but will give you overwhelming success and joy regardless?

[Yes] [No]

9) Do you surround yourself with other ambitious people?

[Yes] [No]

10) Do you seek freedom or security?

[Freedom] [Security]

How ambitious do you believe you are?

Unambitious ⟷ Healthy balance ⟷ Overambitious ⟷

Ambition [1] [2] [3] [4] [5] [6] [7] [8] [9] [10] [11] [12]

Do you believe you need to work on the above? [Yes] [No]

If yes, what do you believe you need to work on?

____

____

Energy

When you're young, energy is your currency. When you become older, resources are your currency. Creative people tend to be energetic and resourceful. However, energy will always come first, and resources will always follow.

But what is a creative, energetic person?

Creative, energetic people tend to be highly active, always on the move, always networking, putting systems together, perfecting their craft, and maintaining their psychological and physical well-being. They also tend to have busy schedules alongside daily routines. As the entrepreneur and rapper Sean Combs, also known as P. Diddy, once said, "We can't stop, we won't stop". Energetic creatives are obsessed with the mission and goal.

Question: Do you still have the energy of a 4-year-old child? This childlike energy is almost the same as highly active entrepreneurs and creatives.

1. Are you an energetic person? [Yes] [No]
2. What age range would you place yourself energy-wise? It could be as young as a 4-year-old or as old as a 90-year-old. What age do you feel? ____________________
3. Are you enthusiastic about your life and your work?

   [Yes] [No]
4. Would you describe yourself as fun, loving, and sociable?

[Yes] [No]

5. Do you enjoy new experiences?

[Yes] [No]

6. Are you comfortable around new, and different types of people?

[Yes] [No]

7. Would you say you are a competitive person?

[Yes] [No]

8. Are you actively using the gym and/or exercising?

[Yes] [No]

9. Are you a high achiever?

[Yes] [No]

10. Do you have busy, productive routines and schedules?

[Yes] [No]

How energetic do you believe you are overall?

	Fatigued	Healthy balance	Hyperactive
	⟷	⟷	⟷

Energy [1] [2] [3] [4] [5] [6] [7] [8] [9] [10] [11] [12]

Do you believe you need to work on the above? [Yes] [No]

If yes, what do you believe you need to work on?

____

____

Now that we have looked at your characteristics, personality, and energy traits, such as; curiosity, playfulness, open-mindedness, flexibility, independence, risk-taking, intuition, thoroughness, and ambition. How would you rate your creativity overall?

Creativeness [1] [2] [3] [4] [5] [6] [7] [8] [9] [10] [11] [12]

Do you believe you need to work on the above? [Yes] [No]

If yes, what do you believe you need to work on?

____

____

Decisiveness

Q10: Are you a decisive person?

Some of the characteristics of a decisive person is their ability to make decisions quickly and not procrastinate, stress, or even ponder too much over the decision-making process.

Let's investigate together and see how decisive you are.

1. Decisive people are very confident when making decisions.

[Yes, that's me] [No, not me]

2. Decisive people are comfortable with risks, especially if it's an informed or educated risk.

[Yes, that's me] [No, not me]

3. Decisive people can be resistant to change once they have made their decision.

[Yes, that's me] [No, not me]

4. Decisive people do not procrastinate.

[Yes, that's me] [No, not me]

Now you have answered the questions, how decisive do you believe you are?

Indecisive ⟷ Healthy balance ⟷ Very decisive ⟷

Decisiveness [1] [2] [3] [4] [5] [6] [7] [8] [9] [10] [11] [12]

Do you believe you need to work on the above? [Yes] [No]

If yes, what do you believe you need to work on?

____

____

Positive Direction

Q11: Do you have a positive direction for your life?

[Yes] [No]

People with a positive direction for their lives tend to be more successful, fulfilled, and happier than others from their peer group.

Positive people tend to have loving characteristics—they express themselves with positive words, loving gestures, and appreciative actions. They warm their environment with their smile, making others feel loved, wanted, and understood. Are you one of those loving, positive people?

[Yes] [Not really] [No]

Positive people are very optimistic. They use words like "*adventure*" instead of "*journey*". The glass is realistically half full for them, but their eyes are always fixated on purchasing the glass and water factory. The optimistic mind is confident about the future regardless of the woes of the past. They tend to see the positivity and growth in all things, which others cannot see. The goals and missions of the optimistic mind tend to be bigger than them; they thrive when serving people and God.

They take positive, decisive actions, knowing that a higher purpose goes beyond them and their current situation. The key to their success is their optimism. You will repeatedly them say, "No matter what, all will work out. All will be okay".

Here's my question: Would you say you have a positive, optimistic mind?

[Yes] [No]

Positive people focus with optimism and direction: "Where your focus goes, your energy will flow". They love and care for others but will never allow people or situations to stand in their way. They do not see failure as failure but as an educational moment to do better and be better. They believe that "whoever fails to plan plans to fail". My question for you is, have you planned for this year and the next five years with optimism and certainty?

[Yes] [No]

Now you have answered the questions, do you believe you have optimism and a positive direction in your life?

Not positive ⟷ Somewhat positive ⟷ Very positive ⟷

Positive Direction [1] [2] [3] [4] [5] [6] [7] [8] [9] [10] [11] [12]

Do you believe you need to work on the above?

[Yes] [No]

If yes, what do you believe you need to work on?

____

____

____

With love, care, and attention, I wrote this book to provide you with valuable information, tools, and techniques that you need to combat chronic stress, depression, trauma, and suicidal ideation. You may have noticed throughout the reading of this book I have repeatedly asked you some questions, over, and over again. Some of the questions are personality-based, some are based on your emotions and feelings, others are focused on your relationships with yourself, God, and others. The same questions, but different reasons.

This book is designed to help you, build you, and empower you and your loved ones. I really want the best for you. You deserve to be happy and successful. I would now like us to explore your resilience.

Resilience

How resilient are you?

Resilient people can recover quickly from their difficulties. They also have the personality and energy to bounce back from negative experiences.

Your resilience, or the lack of resilience, can be strengthened by the following:

1. Resting and Relaxing

The more sleep and rest time you get, the more your mind and body can focus and recoup to deal with problem-solving and stressful events. The less time you sleep, the more likely you are going to experience a low sex drive, a weaker immune system, cognitive problems, weight gain, heart problems, and increased risks for diabetes and cancer. For a better healthier life, you should aim for 7 to 9 hours of sleep time per night.

2. Thinking Positively

Positive thinkers don't allow negative thoughts, feelings, and subjects to derail their progress or linger inside of them. They address the problem quickly, find a solution, then deal with it. The positive thinkers I am talking about prefer to shake hands and find a solution rather than harbor animosity and carry resentment toward others. These same positive thinkers are optimistic about life and the luxury of life. They also live life with abundance and gratitude.

I want you to name five abundances in your life and five things you are grateful for.

Five Abundances

1.____

2.____

3.____

4.____

5.____

Five Things You Are Grateful For

1.____

2.____

3.____

4.____

5.____

3. Editing Your Outlook on Life

Where your focus goes, your energy flows. Two armies go to war. One soldier turns to his comrade and says, "The sooner I die, the sooner I will be with my God. God is great, and I will be at his side in paradise." He turns with a smile and continues firing at the enemy. The other soldier replies, "If I die, my wife will marry another man, and my children will find another father. My parents will die of a broken heart. All that I own and have worked hard for will be sold or left to rot. I can't afford to die today." He then turned around and started to run away. The enemy saw the soldier running and shot him in his back. That soldier died. With the energy of God and Paradise, the other soldier pushed the enemy back to the point of retreating. That soldier lived for another 60 years, well into his 90s. He eventually died happily with his children, grandchildren, and wife at his bedside.

What you focus on from an energy perspective will serve you accordingly. One soldier focused on loss and pain, and he was rewarded accordingly. The other soldier focused on pleasure and Paradise and was rewarded accordingly.

4. Learning from Your Mistakes and Failures

If you shoot, you must intend to score. But to not shoot, is to fail 100% of the time. Shooting for your goals and dreams will always provide feedback.

Feedback will always allow you to readjust your aim to take the next shot.

To not try is the true failure. If we don't take active steps to improve our lives, we cannot fix our personalities, relationships with others, and all that we did in the past to make a better future.

Yes, there are some things in our past that we are ashamed of. And yes, other things in our past scare the living daylights out of us. But we have bounced back before, and we will do it again, and again, and again, and again. We cannot build a successful, resilient future if we are not learning from the past. Life is about lessons, growth, learning, mistakes, and failures.

What mistakes and failures in your past do you need to address or work on?

Let's get started.

1.____

2.____

3.____

4.____

5.____

6.____

7.____

8.____

9.____

10._______________________________________

5. Noticing What Makes You Happy.

Question, "What makes you happy?" In answering the question, we have set some rules for you: You cannot include friends, family, children, and partners. You also cannot say anything that will cause harm to your mind or body, such as, drugs or alcohol.

Following the prior rules of "What makes you happy?", you must choose activities, moments in time, and memories that have given you great joy, happiness, excitement, fun, and feelings of being loved; these feelings and memories must go back as far as your memory can take you.

There's another catch to this task. For each and every year that you have been alive (except for your first five years, 0-5 years old), you must write down a happy memory you have experienced. For example, if you are 40 years old, your list should comprise of a minimum of 35 things, experiences, or activities; a minimum of one experience for each year.

Why is this task relevant? We tend to make good and bad future decisions based upon pivotal moments and feelings in our past. Your list of happy feelings and moments will generate feelings of gratitude, happiness, joy, abundance, and optimism moving forward. You will use this list as your reflective happy moments whenever you need to rebut your negative thoughts, and feelings.

Let's get started.

1. ______________________________

2. ______________________________

3. ______________________________

4. ______________________________

5. ______________________________

6. ______________________________

7. ______________________________

8. ______________________________

9. ______________________________

10. ______________________________

11. ______________________________

12. ______________________________

13. ______________________________

14. ______________________________

15. ______________________________

16. ______________________________

17. ______________________________

18. ______________________________

19. ______________________________

20. ______________________________

21. ______________________________

22. ______________________________

23. ______________________________

24. ______________________________

25. ______________________________

26. ______________________________

27. ______________________________

28. ______________________________

29. ______________________________

30. ______________________________

31. ______________________________

32. ______________________________

33. ______________________________

34. ______________________________

35. ______________________________

36. ____________________

37. ____________________

38. ____________________

39. ____________________

40. ____________________

41. ____________________

42. ____________________

43. ____________________

44. ____________________

45. ____________________

46. ____________________

47. ____________________

48. ____________________

49. ____________________

50. ____________________

51. ____________________

52. ________________________________

53. ________________________________

54. ________________________________

55. ________________________________

56. ________________________________

57. ________________________________

58. ________________________________

59. ________________________________

60. ________________________________

61. ________________________________

62. ________________________________

63. ________________________________

64. ________________________________

65. ________________________________

66. ________________________________

67. ________________________________

68. ____

69. ____

70. ____

71. ____

72. ____

73. ____

74. ____

75. ____

76. ____

77. ____

78. ____

79. ____

80. ____

81. ____

82. ____

83. ____

84. ______________________________

85. ______________________________

86. ______________________________

87. ______________________________

88. ______________________________

89. ______________________________

90. ______________________________

91. ______________________________

92. ______________________________

93. ______________________________

94. ______________________________

95. ______________________________

96. ______________________________

97. ______________________________

98. ______________________________

99. ______________________________

100. ____

Question: How would you rate yourself from 1 to 10 on the following? 1 (not so positive) 10 (very positive).

Resting and relaxing [ ]

Thinking positively [ ]

Editing your outlook on life [ ]

Learning from your mistakes and failures [ ]

Noticing what makes you happy [ ]

Now rate your overall positive direction.

Negative direction   Positive direction

Direction [1] [2] [3] [4] [5] [6] [7] [8] [9] [10] [11] [12]

Do you believe you need to work on the above? [Yes] [No]

If yes, what do you believe you need to work on?

____

____

Masculine Vs Feminine Energy

Now let's dig even deeper into your feminine and masculine energies. Let us now look at your career, and work environment concerning your femininity and masculinity.

When you work with others, what five energy traits do you believe you exude toward your colleagues or customers, or both? Be honest with your answers, or ask your colleagues or customers for their opinions.

Feminine Energy	Masculine Energy
Unconditional love [ ]	Confidence [ ]
Understanding [ ]	Protection [ ]
Nurturing [ ]	Clarity [ ]
Flow [ ]	Inner strength [ ]
Radiance [ ]	Responsibility [ ]
Collaborative [ ]	Boundary-setting [ ]
Surrender [ ]	Focus [ ]
Kindness [ ]	Courage [ ]
Sensitivity [ ]	Discipline [ ]
Intuitiveness [ ]	Capability [ ]
Emotionality [ ]	Logicality [ ]
Creativity [ ]	Decisiveness [ ]
Ease [ ]	Stability [ ]
Feeling [ ]	Certainty [ ]
Allowing [ ]	Direction [ ]

Tenderness [ ]	Assertiveness [ ]

Now that you have selected the five energy traits you believe you exude toward your colleagues or customers, what five energy traits do you believe you need in addition to those you wrote down?

Feminine Energy	**Masculine Energy**
Unconditional love [ ]	Confidence [ ]
Understanding [ ]	Protection [ ]
Nurturing [ ]	Clarity [ ]
Flow [ ]	Inner strength [ ]
Radiance [ ]	Responsibility [ ]
Collaborative [ ]	Boundary-setting[ ]
Surrender [ ]	Focus [ ]
Kindness [ ]	Courage [ ]
Sensitivity [ ]	Discipline [ ]
Intuitiveness [ ]	Capability [ ]
Emotionality [ ]	Logicality [ ]
Creativity [ ]	Decisiveness [ ]
Ease [ ]	Stability [ ]
Feeling [ ]	Certainty [ ]
Allowing [ ]	Direction [ ]
Tenderness [ ]	Assertiveness [ ]

Your Loving Relationships

What five energy traits do you believe you exude in your loving relationships?

Feminine Energy	Masculine Energy
Unconditional love [ ]	Confidence [ ]
Understanding [ ]	Protection [ ]
Nurturing [ ]	Clarity [ ]
Flow [ ]	Inner strength [ ]
Radiance [ ]	Responsibility [ ]
Collaborative [ ]	Boundary-setting [ ]
Surrender [ ]	Focus [ ]
Kindness [ ]	Courage [ ]
Sensitivity [ ]	Discipline [ ]
Intuitiveness [ ]	Capability [ ]
Emotionality [ ]	Logicality [ ]
Creativity [ ]	Decisiveness [ ]
Ease [ ]	Stability [ ]
Feeling [ ]	Certainty [ ]
Allowing [ ]	Direction [ ]
Tenderness [ ]	Assertiveness [ ]

Now you have selected the five energy traits that you believe you exude in your loving relationships, what five energy traits do you believe you now need in addition to your previous five to be a better partner? Please open this conversation with your partner and ask them what five traits they believe are needed in your relationship.

Feminine Energy	**Masculine Energy**
Unconditional love [ ]	Confidence [ ]
Understanding [ ]	Protection [ ]
Nurturing [ ]	Clarity [ ]
Flow [ ]	Inner strength [ ]
Radiance [ ]	Responsibility [ ]
Collaborative [ ]	Boundary-setting [ ]
Surrender [ ]	Focus [ ]
Kindness [ ]	Courage [ ]
Sensitivity [ ]	Discipline [ ]
Intuitiveness [ ]	Capability [ ]
Emotionality [ ]	Logicality [ ]
Creativity [ ]	Decisiveness [ ]
Ease [ ]	Stability [ ]
Feeling [ ]	Certainty [ ]
Allowing [ ]	Direction [ ]
Tenderness [ ]	Assertiveness [ ]

Now you have looked at what you exude energy-wise in your relationships, what do you believe you need, energy-wise, from your partner in your relationship?

What are the top-five energy traits you are looking for in your partner?

Feminine Energy	**Masculine Energy**
Unconditional love [ ]	Confidence [ ]
Understanding [ ]	Protection [ ]
Nurturing [ ]	Clarity [ ]
Flow [ ]	Inner strength [ ]
Radiance [ ]	Responsibility [ ]
Collaborative [ ]	Boundary-setting [ ]
Surrender [ ]	Focus [ ]
Kindness [ ]	Courage [ ]
Sensitivity [ ]	Discipline [ ]
Intuitiveness [ ]	Capability [ ]
Emotionality [ ]	Logicality [ ]
Creativity [ ]	Decisiveness [ ]
Ease [ ]	Stability [ ]
Feeling [ ]	Certainty [ ]
Allowing [ ]	Direction [ ]
Tenderness [ ]	Assertiveness [ ]

Your Children

Now let's look at your child or children. If you don't have any children, maybe you can look at your nephew, niece, godchildren, or cousin.

Question: What are the top-five energy traits you believe your male child or nephew currently exudes?

Feminine Energy	**Masculine Energy**
Unconditional love [ ]	Confidence [ ]
Understanding [ ]	Protection [ ]
Nurturing [ ]	Clarity [ ]
Flow [ ]	Inner strength [ ]
Radiance [ ]	Responsibility [ ]
Collaborative [ ]	Boundary-setting [ ]
Surrender [ ]	Focus [ ]
Kindness [ ]	Courage [ ]
Sensitivity [ ]	Discipline [ ]
Intuitiveness [ ]	Capability [ ]
Emotionality [ ]	Logicality [ ]
Creativity [ ]	Decisiveness [ ]
Ease [ ]	Stability [ ]
Feeling [ ]	Certainty [ ]
Allowing [ ]	Direction [ ]
Tenderness [ ]	Assertiveness [ ]

Now you have looked at what you believe your male child or nephew exudes in the world, what are the top-five energy traits you want your male child or nephew to take into the world?

Feminine Energy	Masculine Energy
Unconditional Love [ ]	Confidence [ ]
Understanding [ ]	Protection [ ]
Nurturing [ ]	Clarity [ ]
Flow [ ]	Inner Strength [ ]
Radiance [ ]	Responsibility [ ]
Collaborative [ ]	Boundary-Setting [ ]
Surrender [ ]	Focus [ ]
Kindness [ ]	Courage [ ]
Sensitivity [ ]	Discipline [ ]
Intuitiveness [ ]	Capability [ ]
Emotionality [ ]	Logicality [ ]
Creativity [ ]	Decisiveness [ ]
Ease [ ]	Stability [ ]
Feeling [ ]	Certainty [ ]
Allowing [ ]	Direction [ ]
Tenderness [ ]	Assertiveness [ ]

Daughters, Nieces, or Maybe a Female Cousin

Question: What are the top-five energy traits you believe your female child or niece currently exudes?

Feminine Energy	Masculine Energy
Unconditional love [ ]	Confidence [ ]
Understanding [ ]	Protection [ ]
Nurturing [ ]	Clarity [ ]
Flow [ ]	Inner strength [ ]
Radiance [ ]	Responsibility [ ]
Collaborative [ ]	Boundary-setting [ ]
Surrender [ ]	Focus [ ]
Kindness [ ]	Courage [ ]
Sensitivity [ ]	Discipline [ ]
Intuitiveness [ ]	Capability [ ]
Emotionality [ ]	Logicality [ ]
Creativity [ ]	Decisiveness [ ]
Ease [ ]	Stability [ ]
Feeling [ ]	Certainty [ ]
Allowing [ ]	Direction [ ]
Tenderness [ ]	Assertiveness [ ]

Now you have looked at what you believe your female child or niece currently exudes into the world, what additional top-five energy traits do you want your female child or niece to take into the world?

Feminine Energy	**Masculine Energy**
Unconditional love [ ]	Confidence [ ]
Understanding [ ]	Protection [ ]
Nurturing [ ]	Clarity [ ]
Flow [ ]	Inner Strength [ ]
Radiance [ ]	Responsibility [ ]
Collaborative [ ]	Boundary-setting [ ]
Surrender [ ]	Focus [ ]
Kindness [ ]	Courage [ ]
Sensitivity [ ]	Discipline [ ]
Intuitiveness [ ]	Capability[ ]
Emotionality [ ]	Logicality [ ]
Creativity [ ]	Decisiveness [ ]
Ease [ ]	Stability [ ]
Feeling [ ]	Certainty [ ]
Allowing [ ]	Direction [ ]
Tenderness [ ]	Assertiveness [ ]

Now that you have looked at the feminine energy traits and the masculine energy traits of your child or children, I want you to answer the following questions.

1. Will the energy traits you selected make your child/children a good wife or husband?

   [Yes] [No]

2. Will your selected energy traits make your child/children loving and caring?

   [Yes] [No]

3. Will the energy traits you selected make your child/children strong and fair leaders to others?

   [Yes] [No]

4. Will the energy traits you selected make your child/children responsible adults?

   [Yes] [No]

5. Will your selected energy traits make your child/children honest and loyal to others?

   [Yes] [No]

6. Will the energy traits you selected make your child/children kind and empathetic to others?

   [Yes] [No]

7. Will the energy traits you selected make your child/children giving and generous people?

   [Yes] [No]

8. Will your selected energy traits allow your child/children to be happy people?

   [Yes] [No]

9. Will the energy traits you selected enable your child/children to create their own families with morals and values that you would be proud of?

   [Yes] [No]

10. Will your selected energy traits give your child/children drive and ambition?

    [Yes] [No]

Now I want you to conclude all your findings.

Let's start with what you discovered about yourself.

1. What energy traits do you need to work on within yourself?

   I need to work on______________________________

   ____

2. What energy traits do you need to work on within your relationships with others?

   To be a better person for my partner, I need to work on____

   ____

3. What energy traits does your family need to work on to make you all grow together as a better, stronger family?

   We need to work on our__________________________

   ____

4. What have you discovered about the person you are within your work environment?________________________

____

The Law of Polarity

The Law of Polarity is the principle that everything in the universe has an opposite. To have a North Pole there must be a South Pole. In order to have good, there has to be evil. There must be a negative terminal (which comes first on a battery) to have an active, positive terminal on a battery. I believe the depth of our relationship with God is based on how much we repel the devil. For the universe to exist, it must remain balanced through its dual poles.

Everything in our universe comes from one, which is then divided into two. For example, if we refer to temperature, the temperature is the one; that one (temperature) then divides itself into two, hot and cold.

The same principle applies to the oneness of volume. The oneness of volume divides itself into two, positive (loud) and negative (soft or quiet).

To go back into the, *I AM* within you is to return to oneness.

The *"I AM"* sees all. It sees the duality of the negative and positive thoughts battling against each other, but it is not the thoughts. It only observes the thoughts. The *I AM* within you also observes love and fear, but it is not those emotions. It observes it all like a CCTV camera, watching the order and disorder internally and externally. If a couple disconnected from each other for whatever reason, they were once connected and attracted to each other for some reason.

To succeed through the Law of Polarity, you first have to recognize that there is a oneness before the duality—like the oneness of the temperature before the hot and cold and the oneness of the volume before the loud and the quiet. To be successful, you have to recognize the oneness of gratitude before success and failure.

When you are winning, you must practice gratitude; when you are losing, you must practice gratitude. When you exercise the power of gratitude first, you will never live in a dark place or feel like you are a failure. When water runs, it starts negative cold and then becomes positive hot. The same with quiet, then loud, and struggle, then freedom. To accept oneness is to accept duality, and to accept duality is to accept oneness. People who do not accept the negative and just want the positive in life will always end up either depressed, envious of others, or suicidal.

Now I want you to write down 10 things you are grateful for, regardless of your good and bad times. Then I want you to read them out daily—in the night before bedtime and again in the morning before you start your day.

Let's get started:

1.____

2.____

3.____

4.____

5.______________________________________

6.______________________________________

7.______________________________________

8.______________________________________

9.______________________________________

10.______________________________________

The Law of Relativity

My friend, may I ask you a question? How do you feel about your life, lifestyle, finances, and current circumstances? Please be as honest as possible and write them down here.

____

____

____

____

____

OK, thank you.

Your answers will be concluded on how you have positioned yourself in the world according to other factors, such as your friends, age, neighbors, previous circumstances, health, and what you see others do and 'achieve' on social media and real life.

OK, let me explain: You are happy, frustrated, angry, jealous, or sad based on the comparisons you've made between yourself and something or someone else. For example;

Two women are in a nightclub—Emily, 26, and Jen 25 years old. Emily is 5'7" in height, and Jen is 5'4". They both have strict rules about what they look for in dating men. Their number-one rule is that they do not want to date men shorter than they are. Their second rule is that they do not date men under 25 years old or men over 40 years old. Michael is 28 years old and is 5'6" in height. He sees these beautiful women standing by the bar. He approaches them.

Which woman will consider Michael for a date?

More men see these beautiful women at the bar. Jake is 41 years old and 6'2" tall, and Ron is 24 and 5'8". Who qualifies for these women? I will get back to them in just a bit.

Robert, who is 52 years old, has two children—Shaleen, 7 years old, and Otto, 3. After 20 years of marriage, his now-estranged wife Rachel—who is 45 years old— filed for divorce after she felt that Robert was not progressive enough for her and their children moving forward.

How did Rachel come to this conclusion?

Robert's hourly wage for working in a supermarket was £9.85 ($11.70 US). Rachel's hourly wage working as a dental hygienist was £29.50 ($35.04 US). They were both once very happy with their income and 3-bedroom apartment in Peckham. Their friends and neighbors in Peckham were all making around the same hourly wage as Robert and Rachel—between £9.50 and £32.00 ($11.28 US to $38.00 US). Robert and Rachel jointly split their mortgage, utilities and all other costs relating to their children. Rachel was happy living in Peckham and happy with their wages until she went to visit her best friend, Miah, who moved into her new 6-bedroom house in West Brompton with her husband Alex.

Rachel's best friend Miah earned £43.75 ($51.96 US) per hour as an events manager. Miah's husband Alex was a tax specialist barrister who earned up to £600 ($712.58 US) per hour. For the first time in their 40-year friendship, Rachel inquisitively asked Miah and Alex, "How much do you both make to afford this beautiful house?" As she glided from beautiful room to beautiful room. As Miah rolled up her sleeves, she warmly looked at her husband with love and admiration. She said, "Between the both of us, we can make anything up to about £5000 ($5,938.15 US) per day. Excluding taxes."

That evening, when Rachel returned to her Peckham home, something inside of her changed and would never be the same again. For the next eight months after her first visit to Miah's mansion, Rachel no longer wanted to live in Peckham. She now despised her husband's £9.85 ($11.70 US) hourly wage and demanded he becomes more ambitious and find a better-paying job. Robert loved his job and lifestyle. He loved his neighbors and community. He also didn't mind his hourly wage.

It wasn't that Robert was unambitious. Two years before Robert met his wife, Rachel, he suffered his final nervous breakdown working for a hedge fund company at age 28. At that time, Robert was making more money as a hedge fund manager than Alex and Miah were earning collectively. His desire to win and be successful led him to have multiple mental health breakdowns and burnouts. At age 29, Robert tried to commit suicide. He failed the attempt and sought help. Robert decided that the pressure of the rat race wasn't worth his health or his life. He decided to work at a job that would suit his stress levels and depression. Working in the supermarket saved Robert's life.

Question: What made Rachel despise Robert and want a divorce after 20 years of happiness and fulfillment as a couple and family?

The Law of Relativity, pertaining to us human beings, is all about perspective and perception. For perspective and perception to exist, people need a reference point. For example, how do you know affluence if you don't know what poverty looks like? How do you know what tall is if you don't have a reference point for short?

Let's return to Emily and Jen at the nightclub. Both women used the Law of Relativity to measure their relationship requirements. Emily, at 26 years old and 5'7" in height, only wanted a partner who was taller than her and was aged between 25 to 40 years old.

The three men in the bar approached Emily and Jen throughout the evening. Michael was the first to approach the girls at 28 years old and 5'6" in height. He had eyes only for Emily. He is a good-hearted and attractive man, but Emily refused him because he wasn't tall enough for her. Jake, 41 years old and 6'2" in height; and Ron, 24 years old and 5' 8" in height, approached Jen that evening. Jen also refused them both due to their ages. One was too young, the other too old. Jake is a successful property developer who attended Oxford University. He is a good man who believes in love, romance, and marriage. Ron is a DIY specialist, who works as a carpenter, frequently featured on DIY TV shows. Ron is fun to be around, and loved karaoke. The truth is, Ron, Jake, and Michael are neither too short, tall, old, or young. Emily and Jen were only unhappy with them when they compared them to their "ideal" man's age and height; oddly enough, they had no other requirements.

Similarly, Rachel despised her and her husband Robert's lifestyle only when she compared it to Miah and Alex's lifestyle and income. Robert's wage is neither too little nor too much, and Miah and Alex's lifestyle is neither too affluent nor too impoverished. Everything in life just is, until we compare it to something else.

The Law of Relativity suggests that we are inclined to compare everything in our minds to make sense of our reality. We make sense of things in our minds by giving them a meaning, a story, feelings, and emotions to validate them. But, in reality, everything is neutral. It is, what it is!

It is us, you, and I, who cause ourselves massive heartache, pain, unhappiness, and jealousy when we compare ourselves to others. Our biases also come from previous hurts, traumas, and pain from comparing. Emily and Jen dramatically cut their chances of love when they concluded that the height and age of the men in the bar somehow wouldn't give them happiness, love, and security. Rachel threw away her family and a loving long-term relationship for her concept of success and affluence elsewhere. She used her best friend and her best friend's husband as reference points for her new-found happiness and success. She also used Miah and Alex's lifestyle to measure her husband as a failure.

Here's my question for you. What biases do you have that you believe are causing you unnecessary pain in your life? What comparisons are you making in your life that are causing you more pain and heartache than happiness and pleasure?

Jealousy, greed, unhappiness, and dissatisfaction all need reference points.

What five comparisons in your life are causing you heartache and pain?

1.____

2.____

3.____

4.____

5.____

Thank you for your honesty.

You must remove negative reference points and comparisons from your life to quell your psychological pain and suffering.

What reference points and comparisons do you need to work on or remove?

1.____

2.____

3.____

4.____

5.____

The Law of Transmutation

The Law of Transmutation also means transformation. When you think about the Law of Transmutation, think of the transfer of energy. Energy can't be created or destroyed—it just transforms or transfers. Energy can transfer to the good proton state, and energy can also transfer to the bad electron state. Energy takes all different forms from across the stars and planets.

The sun transfers electromagnetic waves or radiation. We receive the UV rays, which then give us vitamin D. The energy of the sun influences our planet. It drives our weather, ocean currents, seasons, and climate, making plant life possible through photosynthesis. Without the energy of the sun's heat and light, life on Earth simply would not exist.

The energy of the moon exerts a strong gravitational pull that causes the changing of our tides, oceans, and seas. Each quarter of the moon affects all mammals' moods, emotions, and behaviors.

When we kiss, touch, and make love, we are transferring energy. When we pray, meditate, and affirm, we are transferring energy. When we think, write, and even stare at something, we are transferring energy. The energy of our thoughts can cause millions of deaths and suffering, like the great energy thoughts of Adolf Hitler and Joseph Stalin before they took action.

Water is a great example of the Law of Transmutation at work. Water can transition into many things, such as ice cubes, clouds, rain, snow, fog, and steam. Water never disappears—it always exists in one form or another. Energy also never disappears—it always exists in one form or another.

Money, which we also call currency, cash, or credit, is energy. Money isn't designed to be stagnant; hence the name *currency*. People lose all their money when they try to stagnate it. The current of money needs to keep moving, flowing, investing, and reinvesting. Currency needs to keep serving as many people as possible for our society to function.

However, too much flow of the energy of cash and credit in society will cause inflation, and too little flow of that cash and credit energy will cause deflation. Too much happiness or fear will also cause inflation, or deflation, so governments bring in specialists to manage the moods and emotions of the people.

Bad news emits electron energy, and good news emits proton energy. Too much good or bad news harms the mind, emotions, and body. Too much bad news puts you in a dark, pessimistic place. Too much good news places you in a dangerous, unrealistic bubble that most dictators and people who demand "yes men" end up in. We all need a healthy balance of good and bad energy. One puts you in a happy, joyful place; the other makes you aware of all forms of plights, and dangers.

Smiling is energy. To smile internally or even externally causes a ripple effect of moods and emotions to all it encounters. This is the same for frowning, glaring, and sadness. When we try to contain energy, the energy will find a way to escape via outbursts, diseases, and traumas. Energy is way too powerful for any human being to try to contain. It will eventually cause either mental illness, self-harm, or death.

Stagnation and procrastination go against the Law of Transmutation. What starts in motion must stay in motion. Energy needs motion for it to serve the mind and the body.

Let's now use the Law of Transmutation to serve you.

Let's start with your mastermind groups.

The more positive minds that come together, the more powerful your energies will transmit.

I now want you to name five positive people that you can gather to help you to mastermind your goals.

1.____

2.____

3.____

4.____

5.____

Let's boost your mood and energy.

Exercises and positive activities boost moods and energy. Exercising and doing positive activities will increase your endorphin levels, improve your heart health, boost your cardiovascular health, improve your sleep, sharpen your focus, and improve your mental health.

Commit to these exercises and activities by circling [Yes, I will start], then set a date dd/mm/yyyy. On which you will start your journey toward boosting your mood and energy.

1. Aerobic exercise classes [Yes, I will start]
   Start date__________/___________/_____________

2. Bicycle riding [Yes, I will start]
   Start date__________/___________/_____________

3. Dancing [Yes, I will start]
   Start date___________/___________/_____________

4. Doing household chores [Yes, I will start]
   Start date___________/___________/_____________

5. Gardening [Yes, I will start]
   Start date___________/____________/____________

6. Jogging and running [Yes, I will start]
   Start date__________/____________/_____________

7. Pilates [Yes, I will start]
   Start date___________/___________/_____________

8. Resistance strength training [Yes, I will start]
   Start date___________/___________/_____________

9. Swimming [Yes, I will start]
   Start date___________/___________/_____________

10. Tai chi [Yes, I will start]
    Start date___________/____________/____________

11. Taking the stairs instead of the elevator [Yes, I will start] Start date________/___________/____________

12. Walking [Yes, I will start]

    Start date__________/__________/__________

13. Water aerobics [Yes, I will start]

    Start date__________/__________/__________

14. Yoga [Yes, I will start]

    Start date__________/__________/__________

I want you to start energizing yourself by setting your goals and dreams. Start small and build. The more successes you have—no matter how small—the more energy and momentum you accumulate. To use the Law of Transmutation, you must set end goals, dream about them, talk about them, write them down, and pray over them. Focus on your end goals and go out and work hard for them to manifest. Please set these on your KBenaire Life Board and KBenaire App.

Good luck.

The Law of Compensation

No matter how great or tiny our deeds are, we will always get what we are due in accordance with the Law of Compensation. The Law of Compensation states that a person's efforts and contributions will always be rewarded. The universal laws will all conspire together for you to reap the benefits of their generosity, no matter how small they may be. Just like with the energy of Karma, what you reap will visit you when you least expect it. The Law of Compensation will present itself when laws align and decide it's your time to be blessed.

However, there are some exceptions to the rules. Closed mouths don't get fed. If your chakras are blocked, and you fall into an electron zone for some reason, your blessings will come to visit, but you won't be in any place to receive your delivery.

I must also state that when giving, you give with an open, loving heart. Never give with a heavy heart. Giving with the energy of spite, hate, resentment, or anger can be counterproductive for all parties involved.

Serve others with love and respect, and you will be served accordingly. By going the extra mile for others; the extra mile will be eventually served back to you in some form in the future.

Please, please, please help others succeed and make money, and your wealth will grow beyond your imagination. It's not an accident that Google serves billions of people and the CEOs are now billionaires themselves. It's not an accident that Facebook, Twitter, LinkedIn, Uber, Airbnb, Amazon, Alibaba, NTT, and other companies that focus on servitude are as successful as they are, and the CEOs are rewarded way beyond their wildest dreams.

If you want to serve but not from a business-focused perspective, that's OK. We have community leaders and activists globally who are not just serving their local communities, but they are also indirectly serving the world. As you read this book, their rewards and blessings have been delivered with no return address.

Question: Do you have plans to serve others? [Yes] [No]

If not, please move on to the next law.

If yes, how would you like to serve others?

____

____

____

____

____

Thank you.

The Law of Cause and Effect

The cause: effectively training in the gym. The effect: a toned, healthy body.

The cause: throwing a stone into a pond. The effect: the rippling and waves in the water.

The cause: tyrannical rule, suppression, and oppression over others. The effect: uprisings, rebellions, and resistance.

The cause: feeling angry, feeling depressed, feeling suicidal. The effect: aggression, passive-aggressiveness, not wanting to get out of bed, attempting suicide, infections in the mind and body.

The Law of Cause and Effect doesn't care for white or black, male, or female, masculine, or feminine, fat, or thin, religious, or atheist. If any of those people jump from a high-rise building, they will fall to their death. The Law of Cause and Effect is natural and impartial to all.

You have two main types of cause and effect. You have the physical, and you have the metaphysical. The difference between the two is space and time.

There is physical instantaneous cause and effect. This is when the cause is instantaneous, in real-time, followed by the effect. For example, a person jumping from a building and landing on the ground or the motion of a ball bouncing up from the cause of the ball thrown to the ground.

Then you have metaphysical cause and effect. This is when the effect after the cause is happening but delayed in timing from the universe. Use the assistance of prayer, meditation, angels, and planets in your desired outcome. If done correctly, all will be manifested at the opportune time.

Nothing escapes The Law of Effect. All effects come from The Law of Cause. Success is not an accident. Neither is failure. Our mental health, suicide, being fired from a job, or abuse in a relationship are effects that derived from somewhere. The effects of everything come from the cause of something—either physical or metaphysical.

I want you to discover the causes and effects of the pains and pleasures in your life.

For example,

The cause: I smoke 20 cigarettes per day.

The effect: I now suffer from breathing problems and have had a stroke.

Then I want you to write a solution to your effects.

For example,

The solution: Stop smoking from today.

Let's get started:

Cause 1: ______________________________

Effect 1: ______________________________

Solution 1: ______________________________

Cause 2: ______________________________

Effect 2: ______________________________

Solution 2: ______________________________

Cause 3: ______________________________

Effect 3: ______________________________

Solution 3: ______________________________

Cause 4: ______________________________________

Effect 4: ______________________________________

Solution 4: ____________________________________

Cause 5: ______________________________________

Effect 5: ______________________________________

Solution 5: ____________________________________

Cause 6: ______________________________________

Effect 6 ______________________________________

Solution 6: ____________________________________

Cause 7: ______________________________________

Effect 7: ______________________________________

Solution 7: ____________________________________

Cause 8: ______________________________________

Effect 8: ______________________________________

Solution 8: ____________________________________

Cause 9: ______________________________________

Effect 9: ______________________________________

Solution 9: ____________________________________

Cause 10: _____________________________________

Effect 10: _____________________________________

Solution 10: ___________________________________

Now I want you to look at your successes. What caused each one, and what are the effects of that success?

Then I want you to write about how to build on the successful effects.

Cause 1: ______________________________________

Effect 1: ______________________________________

How I can improve 1: ____________________________

Cause 2: ______________________________________

Effect 2: ______________________________________

How I can improve 2: ____________________________

Cause 3: ______________________________________

Effect 3: ______________________________

How I can improve 3: ______________________

Cause 4: ______________________________

Effect 4: ______________________________

How I can improve 4: ______________________

Cause 5: ______________________________

Effect 5: ______________________________

How I can improve 5: ______________________

Cause 6: ______________________________

Effect 6 ______________________________

How I can improve 6: ______________________

Cause 7: ______________________________

Effect 7: ______________________________

How I can improve 7: ______________________

Cause 8: ______________________________

Effect 8: ______________________________

How I can improve 8: ______________________________

Cause 9: ______________________________

Effect 9: ______________________________

How I can improve 9: ______________________________

Cause 10: ______________________________

Effect 10: ______________________________

How I can improve 10: ______________________________

I now want you to look at how other people that you may admire became successful. I want you to investigate and discover what worked for them and how you can make it work for you.

Let's start with the name of a person or company you want to investigate.

What sector is this person or company in?

How does this person think? How do they look at the world, and how do they fit in the world?

What positive words does this person use when they talk?

How does this person act and behave?

What actions does this person take to be successful?

What results have this person been getting from their thinking, mindset, and actions?

Thank you.

The Law of Correspondence

What happens within us manifests all around us.

The Law of Correspondence states that what happens to us daily, monthly, and yearly directly reflects on what is happening within us—through our beliefs, self-conversations, attitudes, emotions, and feelings. Our external reality is a direct reflection of our internal 'reality'.

Your surroundings, relationships, and life experiences result from your inner world.

Your inner and outer worlds are always modified to match and mirror each other. What happens to us on our inside becomes our mirror on our outside.

Where you are right now in your life is a direct mirror of how you think and feel about yourself. Your external world always modifies itself to mirror and match your internal world. Your relationships, connection to others, and successes start as an internal journey.

What is looking out is looking in, what is above is also below, and what is on Earth is also in Heaven. If you're living in hell on the inside, you will live in hell on the outside.

Some of the poorest people in some of the poorest places on the planet live extremely happy and rich lives, while some of the richest people in some of the most affluent places live sad, painful, and pitiful poor lives.

To be wealthy externally is first to build that abundance internally.

Many surgeons, physicians, lawyers, and bankers are well-paid externally but suffer internally.

It doesn't matter how well paid you are externally if you are impoverished internally.

Suicide happens when the internal decides there is a hopeless future, regardless of how bright and abundant the external future of that person may seem to be.

However, we can turn this all around.

When you are feeling low, help someone else who is feeling low.

When you are feeling doubtful, help others who are feeling doubtful.

When you are not making the money you need or desire, help others to make the money they need or desire. Nothing in your outside world will work until you feel good and abundant about all that is happening in your inside world. You should always do unto others what you want to be done unto you. To serve others is to serve you. We match what we mirror, and we mirror what we match.

We can only control something externally once we can control how we think, act, and behave internally. Our external successes and failures are all results of the relationships we have with success and failures internally. The build-up of traumatic energy doesn't allow us to feel good, abundant, and happy. If you don't feel happiness and abundance on the inside, how can you be happy with abundance on the outside? Negative energy within will always cause negative energy to radiate to the outside.

What are some solutions?

To take control of our lives, we must first take responsibility for everything—and yes, I mean *everything*.

Were you mugged on the street? Take responsibility for it.

Did your partner cheat on you? Take responsibility for it.

Were you fired from your job through no fault of your own? Take responsibility for it.

Were you attacked on the street for no human reason? Take responsibility for it.

What has happened on your outer comes from your inner energy.

Remember and never forget, to take your power back and to take control you must first take responsibility.

Write down 10 things that you will now take responsibility for. Even if those things are not of any fault of your own, however, taking responsivity allows you to change negative narratives, to positive narratives.

Let's get started.

1.____

2.____

3.____

4.____

5.____

6.____

7.____

8.____

9.____

10._______________________________________

Now you have taken responsibility. I want you to now take control by releasing that negative energy through self-forgiveness and forgiveness of others. Forgiving others does not expunge them from their crimes against you. The universe will deal with them. This is to help you release the pain and weight you are carrying around.

Starting with self-forgiveness, what do you forgive yourself for, then what do you forgive others for?

Let's get started.

What do you forgive yourself for?

1.____

2.____

3.____

4.____

5.____

6.____

7.____

8.____

9.____

10.____

What do you forgive others for?

1.____

2.____

3.____

4.____

5.____

6.____

7.____

8.____

9.____

10._______________________________________

Professional Life

What do you need to change internally to be more successful externally?

Thinking poor, thinking you are not good enough, and thinking you are not worthy are extremely unhealthy in pursuing external wealth and success.

What negative words and statements do you need to replace with positive ones?

First, start with the negative words and statements on the first line, then the positive replacements words and statements on the second line.

1.____

1.____

2.____

2.____

3.____

3.____

4.____

4.____

5.____

5.____

6.____

6.____

7.____

7.____

8.____

8.____

9.____

9.____

10.____

Connections

To connect with others externally, you must first connect with yourself internally. I want you to self-love, self-connect, and self-comfort by tapping and massaging each part of your body while making powerful affirmations and incantations.

For example, tap and massage your left arm first and say, "This is my left arm. My left arm here is a blessing to me. My left arm serves me, and serves others. I thank my creator. My creator has blessed me with my left arm."

Then,

"This is my right arm. My right arm here is a blessing to me. My right arm serves me, and serves others. I thank my creator. My creator has blessed me with my right arm."

Next,

"This is my left eye. My left eye here is a blessing to me. My left eye serves me, and serves others. I thank my creator. My creator has blessed me with my left eye."

Next,

"This is my right eye. My right eye here is a blessing to me. My right eye serves me, and serves others. I thank my creator. My creator has blessed me with my right eye."

Next,

"This is my forehead. My forehead here is a blessing to me. My forehead serves me, and serves others. I thank my creator. My creator has blessed me with my forehead."

I want you to continue this process with every part of your body, first thing in the morning, before you go to bed at night and, when you are in the shower. Tap, Massage, and connect with every part of your body and repeat your affirmations and incantations.

Health

You are what you consume!

If you ingest positive foods and drinks from the outer world, you will feel good within your inner world. If you ingest negative foods and drinks from the outer world, you will feel negative within your inner world.

If you are watching and listening to negativity, you will feel anger, sadness, and even depression within. These feelings within will then express themselves outwardly toward yourself and others. Your internal health will match your external health and vice versa. Your health is your wealth!

Question: List all the things (foods, drinks, etc.) you ingest that make you feel negative once consumed?

Let's get started.

1.____

2.____

3.____

4.____

5.____

6.____

7.____

8.____

9.____

10.____

What can you replace the negative foods, drinks, and other intakes with that will make you feel more positive?

1.____

2.____

3.____

4.____

5.____

6.____

7.____

8.____

9.____

10.____

Visualize the Person You Want to Be

I want you now to visualize the person you want to become.

I want you to be very clear and sure about the person you want to be. I want you to feel the wealth of who you want to be. I want you to taste the richness of who you want to be. I want you to see it, feel it, hear it, and even smell it. In your mind today, be the person that you want to be in your life tomorrow.

To have absolute clarity, I want you to write down who you will be.

For example,

"I will be a loving wife. I will love my husband and love my three amazing children. I will be loving, caring, and supportive to not only my family, but to others as well."

"My body will be toned. I will be fit and healthy."

Who will you be? Write it down now.

1.____

2.____

3.____

4.____

5.____

6.____

7.____

8.____

9.____

10.____

Now, I want you to visualize what you want in the world.

For example, your ideal car. What will it look like?

What will the leather interior smell like?

How will the speed of the car feel when you're driving it?

How about your ideal home?

What will your ideal home look like?

What will the furniture look like?

What will the garden, the rooms, and the yards look like?

Imagine the smell of the beautiful new carpet.

Before you start to visualize the things you desire in the world, write them down. Then start to visualize them.

1.____

2.____

3.____

4.____

5.____

6.____

7.____

8.____

9.____

10.____

Good luck on your journey.

The Law of Divine Oneness

The Law of Divine Oneness emphasizes the interdependence of all things and is the earliest and most fundamental law of the cosmos. It means that everything we think, feel, and do is interconnected on some level, even if we can't see it.

Everything is one—so what affects you will affect me by default. For instance, if you love yourself, your self-love will cause an outward loving energy effect on others. But for those who are hurting, traumatized, and angry, it will tend to cause massive pain and hurt to others. We've seen this example of projected pain and hurt manifest itself in the 2022 Russia and Ukraine conflict. The Russia and Ukraine pain also affected the world and will continue to do so for decades to come.

By understanding the Law of Divine Oneness, we can become more aware of our current and future energy states and build a better world by loving ourselves first. When you self-love, you protect that love by creating loving, harmonious relationships with others. We must be proton-aware, neutron-aware, and electron aware to know what we radiate inwardly and outwardly. We cannot take positive action until our energy is in a proton-positive vibrational state.

We are all affected by each other's vibrational frequencies. The energy you put into the universe will come back to visit you and others. Drug dealers and gangsters never escape the crimes they have committed against the 12 universal laws. The 12 universal laws, including the Law of Divine Oneness, measures the energy that the perpetrators have put out into the ether. This energy negatively affects not only the perpetrators but also their friends and family members. Drug dealers tend to end up with loved ones who are drug users. Gangsters tend to lose loved ones to crime and violence.

If you focus on emitting positive energy, you will get positive results as permitted by your actions, network, and environment. But if you linger on the negative, you will get negative back, and that low-vibrational frequency will affect others both near and far. Once again, you will see this example repeatedly play itself out with physicians who are suffering from their traumas and depression as a result of dealing with those of patients. That is the reason why antidepressants don't fix people. They just suppress their feelings while their negative energy finds a new way to live and express itself.

I want to help you use the Law of Divine Oneness to make your life happier, more prosperous, and more spiritually abundant. Let me set some tasks for you towards your grail of Oneness.

Daily Meditations

The process and preparation before meditation are just as important as the meditation itself. If you have an over-occupied mind or you are chronically stressed or worried, it can take a lot longer and be more difficult to get into the deep Zen of your meditation. Here are some suggestions to try before your meditation.

1. Exercise, or do a hobby to help your mind and body release all the energy and tension it's been holding.

2. Do not use social media for at least two hours before meditation; social media can plant unsavory thoughts in your conscious and subconscious mind.

3. Complete your daily to-do list before meditation. When your mind discovers that you are about to have a spiritual moment, it will fight for supremacy by trying to remind you about all the household chores, what to buy, and what to collect. Shut down the possibility of its attempts to distract you beforehand.

4. Have your meditative moment in a friendly, clean, and uncluttered space. You need the positive space that gives you feng shui.

5. Wear loose, light clothing. To meditate, you need to feel free and unrestricted.

6. Try meditation music to help settle your mind and energy. Meditation is a very personal relationship with self. We all have our way of getting into that place of meditative Zen. Here are some suggestions that have worked for me:

1. Shake out your arms and legs.

2. Sit comfortably in a position where you won't get any cramps or shooting sensations.

3. Take several deep breaths.

4. Focus on your breathing to cancel out external thoughts and background noise.

5. Allow your body to breathe naturally. If your breathing is shallow, that's okay; let it be shallow. If your breathing is deep, let it be deep. Just be.

Now let's get you started:

a. Once you have loosened up, focus on your breathing. Be aware.

b. Notice when your mind tries to distract you and wander elsewhere. Don't allow it to. Be kind, but be firm. Just bond with your inner self.

c. Allow yourself to travel deep into yourself. Travel so far back that you can only observe outwardly. The purest form of self goes back to the place where eyes can't see themselves, a scale can't weigh itself, a knife can't cut itself, and you can't judge yourself.

d. Open yourself to Oneness. Open yourself to an experience that *transcends the mind.* Open yourself up to feeling a connection with everything on *every* level. *Feel* 'at one' with all things and '*be* at one' with all things.

e. You will know when you are in a place of Oneness when you feel your atoms connected to the rest of the universe.

f. Once you have connected and evolved from feeling to knowing you are the divine Oneness, you have arrived.

It may take time to get to that place of knowing. But keep going. Keep meditating, and you will get there by the grace of God.

g. Once you are in that place of knowledge, it will be a good time for outdoor meditation and group meditations with positive people.

h. You can improve your relationship with the Law of Divine Oneness through your thoughts, feelings, and behavior.

Here's a list for you to try or at least consider:

a. Positive affirmations
b. Yoga
c. Mindfulness techniques
d. Breathing techniques
e. Chanting
f. Walking in nature
g. Alexander techniques
h. Awareness techniques
i. Mantra meditation
j. Relaxation
k. Tai chi/qigong
l. Zazen meditation

The Law of Attraction

The Law of Attraction states that positive thoughts bring positive results into one's personal life, whilst negative thoughts yield negative outcomes.

My understanding and relationship with the Law of Attraction is that *'where your focus goes, your energy will flow'*. Where your energy flows, that energy will attract all that you've been focusing on into your life.

The Law of Attraction is a controversial hypothesis to many. To others, it's a certainty. I believe in the Law of Attraction, but I also believe how it's been explained has left the door open for much ridicule. Yes, no matter how positive your thoughts are, if you're standing in the desert, dying of dehydration, and needing immediate help and water, with no one around to help, you will likely die unless there is divine intervention. However, I would challenge, what energy was that person vibrating at when they got into that situation in the first place?

Also, the Law of Attraction is generally looked at in isolation. This law works in conjunction with other laws to assist it, such as The Law of Energy, The Law of Cause and Effect, The Law of Divine Oneness, The Law of Rhythm, The Law of Polarity, The Law of Relativity, The Law of Transmutation, The Law of Correspondence, The Law of Gender, The Law of Compensation, and The Law of Inspired Action.

All the universal laws work and conspire together in neutrality. We change the neutrality to positive or negative based on our focus, thoughts, feelings, and emotions. All is neutral until we change the frequencies with what we say, do, and be. All the universal laws constitute protons, neutrons, electrons, and other subatomic particles of which will serve us according to who we are.

Like attracts like—so what you put out into the world, you get back. Similarly, light attracts everything to it. When you are a bright proton light in the midst of electron darkness, all energies curiously investigate the light, you. Moths, bears, lions, spiders, snakes, alongside the good intent, the bad intent and the impartial, will all come to visit the light. The light is the goal and achievement for all energies to either conquer the light, join the light, or be the light. The electron devils and demons will try their best to persuade you to hand over your light and join the darkness with them. They can't take it from you, but they will try to influence you to extinguish the light or hand it over to them.

Your thoughts must remain pure to keep vengeance out of your heart. Be aware of the darkness, but don't entertain it. Stay within the boundaries of your light and don't hand it over or dim it for anyone. The devils and demons will visit you with smiles, gifts, sexiness, great propositions, and opportunities. By putting God first, you will brighten your light. Campaigns of slander, lies, false accusations, and ridicule will be put in place to move you away from God and your light. Do not move away from God and your light to entertain their darkness.

Connect your proton thoughts and emotions as one, then turn them into a dominating proton feeling, attitude, and behavior. With this same feeling, attitude, and behavior, The Law of Attraction will serve you positively and effectively.

Firstly, ask for what you want—not just with words, but with your feelings and emotions.

Secondly, believe what you are asking for with complete sincerity. Believe it as though you already have what you want.

Finally, receive it and be grateful that you are blessed and gifted. Practice abundance and gratitude daily. Remember, every day is the gift of life, and your previous prayers for deliverance have manifested in your every waking moment.

From today, I want you to change your mental attitude to an *as-if* attitude. I want you to walk with the certainty that God is within you, greatness is within you, and abundance is within you.

I want you to live *as if*.

Ask *as if*

Talk *as if*

Speak *as if*

Pray *as if*

Invest *as if*

Meditate *as if*

Walk *as if*

Present yourself *as if* you are here to be a leader, provider, and server to others, from the God that is within you.

When you are thinking and talking to yourself, change your vocabulary. Affirm who you are and what you are! Be sure of who you are and what you are!

Here are some affirmations I want you to use from now on:

- I am successful.
- I am confident.
- I am powerful.
- I am strong.
- I am getting better and better each day I live.
- I am a blessing from God, and I will bless others.
- I wake up motivated, and I go to bed motivated.
- I can't stop. I won't stop. I am a force of nature.
- I am a living, breathing example of greatness.

- I am full of abundance.
- I am a positive inspiration when I talk to others.
- I inspire people through my work and behavior.
- Today is a good day.
- I am filled with positive energy and focus.
- I am not my problems. I am my dreams and desires.
- I am grateful for all the blessings I have in my life.
- I am not defined by my past; I am being prepared for my successes in the future.
- Today will be a productive day.
- I am becoming healthier each day.
- I am constantly growing and evolving into a better, happier me.
- I am not my doubts and fears.
- I am going to forgive myself and free myself. I deserve to forgive and to be forgiven.
- I am healing and strengthening myself every day.
- I've made it through the hard times and tough times. I now know I can make it through anything.
- My past was ugly. My future is beautiful.
- I have made mistakes, but I am not my mistakes.
- My soul radiates from the inside and warms the souls of others.
- The only person I compare myself to is the person I was yesterday. No one else.
- I am proud of myself.
- I choose to be happy.

CHAPTER 11

CONCLUSION

It costs companies and governments billions in sick pay, mental healthcare, and well-being awareness campaigns because of occupational stress, depression, trauma, and suicidal ideations.

'Who Helps The Helpline, When The Helpline Needs Help?' is a compelling question. It is a question I have asked myself thousands of times over many years, going back to my childhood. I have seen and experienced the most amazing people tirelessly help others whilst they suffer in silence. As you have experienced in the reading of this book, all that glitters is not gold. The letters and titles before and after people's names can be more of a trauma than a success.

The people that we tend to believe are happy and successful due to their lofty perch in society, for the most part, are unhappy.

For hundreds, even thousands of years, people have been worshipping other people as idols because of their high-ranking titles and positions. The worship was once focused and connected to how close to God or the devil one was, such as a pharaoh, emperor, oracle, king, or queen. Today, people worship others on social media with a 'God-like' status because of the likes and views they get. Today's deities are celebrities and people with high-paying jobs, ranks, and careers. Women with big bums and big breasts, men with nice cars, fancy homes, and luxurious lifestyles are worshipped to the point where people are self-mutilating their bodies and getting into serious debt to be like them.

Cheslie Kryst (former Miss USA) was worshipped by millions of girls but suffered to the point where she committed suicide. Millions of people wanted to be like Robin Williams and marveled at his success, but he committed suicide. There have been thousands of what we deem as successful people, including doctors, lawyers, bankers, judges, artists, and entertainers in recent years who we **think** we know, so we marvel at their 'success' and wish we could be like them, but many of them are chronically stressed, depressed, and suffering emotionally, teetering to the edge of suicide.

All that we excessively value can result in massive pain and problems if we, as a people, do not change the course of what we worship and revere. If we over-value culture, lifestyle, career status, job security, and people's looks, we will fall into an abyss.

Pain and suffering of the mind will result in unrealistic wants and desires. Humans will want to change their body parts with animal parts. The saying 'hung like a horse' may end as an actual surgery between man and horse.

Self-harming parties and suicide parties could be standard practice in the future. You may think what I am saying is ridiculous hogwash. However, currently, there are parties worldwide in which hundreds of willing participants randomly select one secret person infected with HIV to have unprotected sex with a Russian-roulette-type of mindset and behavior.

Bestiality is slowly becoming standard practice for people to freely view online, including children. These awful behaviors will strip our children of their purity. What was once abnormal is now slowly becoming a norm.

All these behaviors come from traumatized bodies and troubled minds. If we don't help now because of what we think is none of our business or concern, our children will eventually be the recipients of our neglect in the future.

Every day, we see large companies and governments dripping with immoral behavior and greed, introducing emotionless robots and AI (artificial intelligence) systems to replace our workers. This will change the balance of this planet and born AI tyranny.

A man who cannot work for a living and make money due to the takeover of AI will eventually fight for his survival. As Malcolm X once said, 'By any means necessary.'

The world is rapidly moving towards a police state and a Total Recall, Implanted, The Matrix, and Minority Report reality.

We are all in this experience called life together; we are interconnected whether we like it are not. Another person's mental illness today could lead to a shooting at your workplace, or your children's school tomorrow; however, we can change the direction of where we are heading with the power of prayer, the spiritual consciousness of LOVE, The Universal Laws of Oneness and Action—helping the helpline when the helpline needs our help.

Please care, please self-love, and share the message and stories in this book, and more importantly, always ask the question, "Who Helps The Helpline, When The Helpline Needs Help?".

Thank you.

Love you loads, Kevin Bennett

Take pictures with your book and share your adventure with our community

#Whohelpsthehelpline

Scan me

ABOUT THE AUTHOR

Kevin Bennett is a mental and emotional strategist. Kevin has helped and empowered over 1.2 million people globally since 2010 via seminars, workshops, universities, secondary schools, TV, podcasts, radio, and online appearances. He also works with companies and governments worldwide. For more information, please email Whohelpsthehelpline@gmail.com

Kevin Bennett's services include the following:

- **Private and Group Coaching**
  - Helping people who suffer with depression, doubt, worry, pessimism, and anxiety.
  - Helping people who are suffering from mental and emotional trauma.
  - Helping people who find it hard to achieve success in their personal and professional lives.
  - Helping people to strategically discover their purpose and happiness in their personal and professional lives.

- **Business Coaching**
    - Understanding customer mindsets and behaviors.
    - Building company culture.
    - Building product and service campaigns.
- **Other services, workshops, and courses include:**
    - The 5 stages of success and failure
    - The 7 emotional brain systems that psychologically govern you
    - How to combat the 8 types of depression
    - How to assess your feelings
    - The 12 branches of your life that you must have in place (your KBenaire Life Board and App)
    - Understanding your emotions and feelings
    - Understanding the positive and negative frequencies of your jewelry and other items in your home
    - Understanding and practical use of the 12 universal laws to benefit you
    - Your yin (feminine) and yang (masculine) energies
    - How to discover your core values, legacy, spirituality, message to the world, lifestyle, investments, education, Wealth 100, mentors, mastermind group, and circle of confidence

If you would like to book Kevin Bennett for talks or workshops, please contact:

Email: Whohelpsthehelpline@gmail.com

Website: https//www.whohelpsthehelpline.com

Testimonials

LSBU—South Bank Innovation Department

Kevin Bennett has been a valuable facilitator providing workshops on 'Understanding Customer Mindset and Behaviors' to business owners enrolled in our DeK Growth London and Enterprise Steps programs.

Kevin's expertise, professionalism, and passion for going the extra mile have led to clients and stakeholders requesting more workshops and one-to-one support. I am extremely grateful for the support Kevin has provided via our ERDF programs at LSBU—South Bank Innovation Department.

My time working with Kevin has been excellent, and I look forward to working with him in the near future.

Croydon Children's Social Care

Staff morale was at an all-time low in Croydon's Children's Social Care after receiving an inadequate judgment from Ofsted, when Kevin Bennett came to provide staff with one-to-ones to not only assist them with their day-to-day work, but to inspire and reignite the light that made them choose a profession within social care. The sessions were oversubscribed, and staff requested more time due to how impactful and life-changing the sessions had been, which then led to Kevin hosting a half-day conference for a service of over 100 people. To date, staff still talk about and use Kevin to facilitate numerous workshops, which is a testament to his approach and passion for building others. As the morale started to shift, the atmosphere was changing, trust was being built, and the staff was able to rebuild a system that was previously broken with this new lease on life, something everyone was grateful for as he was given a mammoth task, of which he rose to and conquered with a smile, even when it was tough. We look forward to continuing to work with Kevin in the future.

Peckham BMX Club

Kevin Bennett plays a big instrumental part in helping our young people at Peckham BMX to reach their goals in times of difficulty when they are struggling with their mental focus at the British Olympic team. Kevin Bennett continues to give his time to help young people in reaching their goals and aspirations.

Regards

Michael Pusey MBE

INDEX

NOTES AND REFERENCES

Introduction

"1985: Riots in Brixton after Police Shooting." *BBC: On This Day*—1950–2005, September 28, 2019. http://news.bbc.co.uk/onthisday/hi/dates/stories/september/28/newsid_2540000/2540397.stm

"Police Blamed over 1985 Cherry Groce Brixton Shooting." *BBC News*, July 10, 2014. https://www.bbc.co.uk/news/uk-england-london-28248588

"New Wayne Douglas Inquest Ruled Out." *BBC News*, July 30, 1998. http://news.bbc.co.uk/1/hi/uk/142385.stm

Chapter 1: Who Helps the Physician When the Physician Needs Help?

Newsy, "Unspoken: Doctor Depression and Suicide," YouTube video, 18:04, August 9, 2018, https://www.youtube.com/watch?v=-YJQxLIg60g

"What Is an Anaesthetist?" NHS: Oxford University Hospitals, www.ouh.nhs.uk. https://www.ouh.nhs.uk/services/departments/anaesthetics/anaesthetist.aspx

"How to Become an Anesthesiologist," CareerExplorer, September 20, 2017, https://www.careerexplorer.com/careers/anesthesiologist/how-to-become/

"Anaesthetist," National Careers Service, https://nationalcareers.service.gov.uk/job-profiles/anaesthetist

Dejania Oliver, "Influencer Dies Seeking Treatment for Underarm Sweating," WebMD Health News, Accessed July 1, 2022, https://www.webmd.com/heart-disease/news/20210729/influencer-dies-seeking-treatment-underarm-sweating

Tom Bourne, Laure Wynants, Mike Peters, Chantal Van Audenhove, Dirk Timmerman, Ben Van Calster, and Maria Jalmbrant, "The Impact of Complaints Procedures on the Welfare, Health and Clinical Practice of 7926 Doctors in the UK: A Cross-Sectional Survey," *BMJ Open*, 2015;5(1):e006687-e006687,DoOI10.1136/bmjopen-2014-006687, https://bmjopen.bmj.com/content/5/1/e006687.

Chris Hemmings, "Doctors' Mental Health at Tipping Point," *BBC News*, September 3, 2018, https://www.bbc.co.uk/news/health-45356349

The Doctors, "Doctor Suicide Rates Are on the Rise," YouTube video, 4:54, May 23, 2018, https://www.youtube.com/watch?v=9dUhMPf_E60

Dignity Memorial, Obituary: Mitchell Dale Hardison, Accessed July 1, 2022, https://www.dignitymemorial.com/obituaries/raleigh-nc/mitchell-hardison-6591929

Patrick Terpstra, "Does Fear of Reporting Their Own Mental Illness Put Doctors at Risk of Suicide?" *PBS NewsHour*, October 24, 2018, https://www.pbs.org/newshour/show/does-fear-of-reporting-their-own-mental-illness-put-doctors-at-risk-of-suicide

Vanessa Van Edwards, "The 10 Happiest Jobs on the Planet You Can Work at Today," Science of People, March 9, 2021, https://www.scienceofpeople.com/happiest-jobs/

Chapter 2: Firefighters On Fire

BBC Newsnight, "Grenfell Tower: The Failings No Firefighter Could Overcome - Full BBC Newsnight Report," YouTube, July 7, 2017, https://www.youtube.com/watch?v=TrzcjUhf61w

"Grenfell Tower: What Happened," *BBC News*, October 29, 2019, https://www.bbc.co.uk/news/uk-40301289.

Mayor of London, "My Full Statement on the Grenfell Tower Report," Greater London Authority, October 30, 2019, https://www.london.gov.uk/city-hall-blog/my-full-statement-grenfell-tower-report

Dr. Anne Scoging, "How London Fire Brigade Grew Its Counselling Service after Grenfell and Coronavirus," *Emergency Services Times*, September 28, 2020, https://emergencyservicestimes.com/how-london-fire-brigade-grew-its-counselling-service-after-grenfell-and-coronavirus/

Tristan Kirk, "999 Crews Sue in £1m Claim over Grenfell Tower Trauma," *Evening Standard*, June 25, 2020, https://www.standard.co.uk/news/uk/999-crews-sue-in-ps1m-claim-over-grenfell-trauma-a4479721.html

Ricky Nuttall LFB, UK Emergency Services Giving, accessed June 30, 2022, https://ukesg.uk/news/ricky-nuttall-lfb

Chapter 3: The Helplines That Need Help?

Olivier1985, "Nicole Sirotek," YouTube video, 23:58, May 4,2020,https://www.youtube.com/watch?v=CvhTQV5FNUE&t=557s

Pauline Anderson, "Doctors' Suicide Rate Highest of Any Profession," WebMD, May 8, 2018, https://www.webmd.com/mental-health/news/20180508/doctors-suicide-rate-highest-of-any-profession

Dr. Sharon Stevelink, Prof. Neil Greenberg, Prof. Nicola Fear, Prof. Sir Simon Wessely, "Depression Is 2.5 Times More Common Than Post-Traumatic Stress Disorder in UK Police Officers," King's Centre for Military Health Research, November 19, 2020, https://kcmhr.org/depression-is-2-5-times-more-common-than-post-traumatic-stress-disorder-in-uk-police-officers/

Deborah L. Spence, and Jessica Drake, *Law Enforcement Officer Suicide: 2020 Report to Congress*, Washington, DC: US Department of Justice, 2021.

"The Numbers," First H.E.L.P., https://datastudio.google.com/u/0/reporting/45630efa-3ee8-4c8f-ab44-ccbe743f0b53/page/Kh2dC

Maggie Fox, "Suicide Rates Are up 30 Percent Since 1999, CDC Says." *NBC News*, June 9, 2018, https://www.nbcnews.com/health/health-news/suicide-rates-are-30-percent-1999-cdc-says-n880926

Rajit Sengupta, "Every Day, 28 People Dependent on Farming Die by Suicide in India," DownToEarth, September 3, 2020, https://www.downtoearth.org.in/news/agriculture/every-day-28-people-dependent-on-farming-die-by-suicide-in-india-73194

Yasmina Hatem, Lisa Desai, and Mark Abadi, "India Has a Farmer Suicide Epidemic — and Farmers Are Protesting New Laws They Fear Will Make Things Worse," *Business Insider*, January 7, 2021, https://www.businessinsider.com/india-farmers-protest-law-suicide-epidemic-2021-1?r=US&IR=T

Ofsted, "Summary and Recommendations: Teacher Wellbeing Research Report," GOV.UK, https://www.gov.uk/government/publications/teacher-well-being-at-work-in-schools-and-further-education-providers/summary-and-recommendations-teacher-well-being-research-report

Joanna Zambas, "The 30 Most Stressful Jobs(and How Much They Pay)," CareerAddict, July 22, 2022, https://www.careeraddict.com/stressful-jobs

"The 10 Most Stressful Jobs," Salary.com, April 17, 2018, https://www.salary.com/articles/the-top-10-most-stressful-jobs/

"Depression Among Demographics and Professions," MentalHelp.net, 2014, https://www.mentalhelp.net/depression-among-demographics-and-professions/

Lawson Wulsin, Toni Alterman, P Timothy Bushnell, Jia Li, and Rui Shen, "Prevalence Rates for Depression by Industry: A Claims Database Analysis," *Social Psychiatry and Psychiatric Epidemiology*, June 8, 2014; 49(*11*):1805-1821, DOI:10.1007/s00127-014-0891-3.

Dr. Ben Windsor-Shellard, "Suicide by Occupation, England: 2011 to 2015," Office for National Statistics, March 17, 2017, https://www.ons.gov.uk/peoplepopulationandcommunity/birthsdeathsandmarriages/deaths/articles/suicidebyoccupation/england2011to2015

"The Connection Between Jobs and Mental Health," Joblist, November 22, 2019, www.joblist.com. https://www.joblist.com/guides/jobs-and-mental-health

Amanda Bucceri Androus, RN, BSN, “Suicide Rates by Profession,” RegisteredNursing.org, August 30, 2022, https://www.registerednursing.org/articles/suicide-rates-profession/

Jamie N., “10 Jobs with the Highest Suicide Rates,” BlackDoctor.org, March 25, 2022, https://blackdoctor.org/10-jobs-with-the-highest-suicide-rates/2/

Cora Peterson, Aaron Sussell, Jia Li, Pamela K Schumacher, Kristin Yeoman, and Deborah M Stone, “Suicide Rates by Industry and Occupation – National Violent Death Reporting System, 32 States, 2016,” *Morbidity and Mortality Weekly Report*,69 (Jan 24, 2020), 57-62, DOI:10.15585/mmwr.mm6903a1.

Kalpana Srivastava, Suprakash Chaudhury, P S Bhat, And Jyoti Prakash, “Occupation-Related Suicide,” *Industrial Psychiatry Journal*, 28 (Dec 11, 2019), 1-3, DOI:10.4103/Ipj.ipj_77_19.

Chapter 4: The 7 Brain Systems - Understanding Mind and Emotions

Brendan M Walker, “Jaak Panksepp: Pioneer of Affective Neuroscience,” *Neuropsychopharmacology*. 42 (Nov 2017;), 2470, DOI:10.1038/npp.2017.168.

TEDx Talks, “The Science of Emotions: Jaak Panksepp at TEDxRainier,” YouTube video, 17:39, January 13, 2014, https://www.youtube.com/watch?v=65e2qScV_K8

"The Nobel Prize in Physiology or Medicine 1949," The Nobel Prize, https://www.nobelprize.org/prizes/medicine/1949/summary/

The Evolved Nest, "Jaak Panksepp – Notre Dame Symposium on Human Nature and Early Experience," YouTube video, 1:03:01, October 10, 2020, https://www.youtube.com/watch?v=hTzoeIJhKGE

Spektrum der Wissenschaft, "Why Do Rats Laugh? Interview with Jaak Panksepp - Präsentiert von Braincast," YouTube video, 1:00:54, June 19, 2012, https://www.youtube.com/watch?v=u4ICY6-7hJo

Jaak Panksepp, *Affective Neuroscience : The Foundations of Human and Animal Emotions* (Oxford: Oxford University Press,2004).

Chapter 5: Beauty, Pain, and Trauma

"Cheslie Kryst: Former Miss USA Dies Aged 30 after Falling from Apartment Building in New York," *Sky News*, January 31, 2022, https://news.sky.com/story/cheslie-kryst-former-miss-usa-dies-aged-30-after-falling-from-apartment-building-in-new-york-12529386

Ashley Joy Parker, "Cause of Death Officially Confirmed for Miss USA 2019 Cheslie Kryst," *E!News*, February 1, 2022, https://www.eonline.com/news/1318333/cause-of-death-officially-confirmed-for-miss-usa-2019-cheslie-kryst

Timothy J. Legg, PhD, PsyD, and Steph Coelho, "What Is High-Functioning Depression?" June 9, 2020, https://www.medicalnewstoday.com/articles/high-functioning-depression

Cheslie Kryst, "A Pageant Queen Reflects on Turning 30," *Allure*, March 4, 2021, https://www.allure.com/story/cheslie-kryst-miss-usa-on-turning-30

Felix Torres M.D., MBA, DFAPA, "What Is Depression?" American Psychiatric Association, October 2020, https://psychiatry.org/patients-families/depression/what-is-depression

"Symptoms - Clinical Depression," NHS, December 10, 2019, https://www.nhs.uk/mental-health/conditions/clinical-depression/symptoms/

"Overview - Postnatal Depression," NHS, August 4, 2022, https://www.nhs.uk/mental-health/conditions/post-natal-depression/overview/

"Depression Among Women," Centers for Disease Control and Prevention, May 23, 2022, https://www.cdc.gov/reproductivehealth/depression/index.htm

"Psychotic Depression," NHS, December 10, 2019, https://www.nhs.uk/mental-health/conditions/psychotic-depression/

"Bipolar Disorder," National Institute of Mental Health, September 2022, https://www.nimh.nih.gov/health/topics/bipolar-disorder

"Table 11, DSM-IV to DSM-5 Manic Episode Criteria Comparison," Substance Abuse and Mental Health Services Administration, June 2016, https://www.ncbi.nlm.nih.gov/books/NBK519712/table/ch3.t7/

"Symptoms - Bipolar Disorder," NHS, March 14, 2022, https://www.nhs.uk/mental-health/conditions/bipolar-disorder/symptoms/

Dr Tracey Marks, "Bipolar 1 Disorder or Bipolar 2 Disorder - Which is Worse?" YouTube video, 6:02, May 30, 2018, https://www.youtube.com/watch?v=ydLWlAqCpLA

Dr. Todd Grande, "What Is the Difference Between Bipolar I Disorder and Bipolar II Disorder?" YouTube video, 3:46, October 8, 2017,https://www.youtube.com/watch?v=S1HghWfxCz0

ChristianaCare, "What Is Seasonal Affective Disorder?" January 3, 2022, https://www.youtube.com/watch?v=n3UP8QjDhuo

Holland Hospital, "Seasonal Affective Disorder: More Than Just the Winter Blues," YouTube video, 1:02:02, January 22, 2014, https://www.youtube.com/watch?v=PRLATrNcftc

Dr. Tracey Marks, "Can a Depressed Person Have Good Days? - Atypical Depression," YouTube video, June 17,

2020, https://www.youtube.com/watch?v=4bH8E3Wf-WA

Tanvir Singh and Kristi Williams, “Atypical Depression,” *Psychiatry (Edgmont)*,3 (Apr 2006), 33-39, https://www.ncbi.nlm.nih.gov/pmc/articles/PMC2990566/

“Depression (Major Depressive Disorder),” Mayo Clinic, accessed July 4, 2022, https://www.mayoclinic.org/diseases-conditions/atypical-depression/symptoms-causes/syc-20369747?p=1

Dr. Tracey Marks, “Is Dysthymia a High Functioning Depression?” YouTube video, 7:54, September 26, 2018,https://www.youtube.com/watch?v=2xOdlA1aDPo

Raj K Patel and Gregory M. Rose, “Persistent Depressive Disorder,” StatPearls, June 27, 2022, https://www.ncbi.nlm.nih.gov/books/NBK541052/

Rudolf Uher, Jennifer L Payne, Barbara Pavlova, and Roy H Perlis, “Major Depressive Disorder in DSM-5: Implications for Clinical Practice and Research of Changes from DSM-IV,” *Depression and Anxiety*, 31 (Jun 2014), 459-471, doi:10.1002/da.22217.

Chapter 7: The Five Stages of Success and Failure

Leander Kahney, “John Sculley On Steve Jobs, The Full Interview Transcript,” Cult of Mac, October 14, 2010, https://www.cultofmac.com/63295/john-sculley-on-steve-jobs-the-full-interview-transcript/

TradingCoachUK. "Warren Buffett – The World's Greatest Money Maker," YouTube video, 59:02, November 1, 2014, https://www.youtube.com/watch?v=w-eX4sZi-Zs

Chapter 8: Why Do Most People Fail While Others Succeed?

PBS Newshour, "WATCH: Greta Thunberg's Full Speech to World Leaders at UN Climate Action Summit," YouTube video, 5:19, September 23, 2019, https://www.youtube.com/watch?v=KAJsdgTPJpU

WWF International, "Sir David Attenborough | A Message to World Leaders," YouTube video, 3:19, September 24, 2019, https://www.youtube.com/watch?v=fyYpExl8AJU

Chapter 9: Where Your Focus Goes, Your Energy Flows

History, "Ancient Aliens: Pyramid Power Plants (Season 12, Episode 7)," YouTube video, 4:01, September 6, 2018, https://www.youtube.com/watch?v=oeACqqOX5TU

Bảo Tín Minh Châu, "Gold Documentary: How Was Earth Made America's Gold," YouTube video, 44:01, March 16, 2015, https://www.youtube.com/watch?v=x3O-olu5iFc

TEDEd, "Where Does Gold Come From? - David Lunney," YouTube video, 4:34, October 8, 2015, https://www.youtube.com/watch?v=jf_4z4AKwJg

"Questions and Answers - How Many Protons, Electrons and Neutrons Are in an Atom of Krypton, Carbon, Oxygen, Neon, Silver, Gold, etc...?" JLab Science

Education, 2019, https://education.jlab.org/qa/pen_number.html

SEA, "Supernovae: The Most Extreme Explosions!" YouTube video, 30:03, https://www.youtube.com/watch?v=lAgwMGRvJrM

Printed in Great Britain
by Amazon

36189333R00280